High Impact

IELTS

ACADEMIC MODULE

Patrick Bourne

PEARSON
Longman

Acknowledgements

I would like to thank those responsible for their help in completing this book – particularly my wife Deborah, for her contributions and her patience; Bill W. Addell, for his late-night suggestions and for sharing his extensive experience; Stephen Phillips, for trialling the material and the suggestions throughout the book's development; and all the teaching staff at John Gang's school. I would also like to thank Margaret Love and John Gang Lee for their support and goodwill throughout.

The author and publishers would also like to thank the following for permission to use their photographs: Alexander Turnbull Library, Wellington, p. 101 (left) (DA-06803; F, War History Collection) and p. 168 (1/1-004173; G); Birthcare, p. 101 (right); Maui, p. 198.

We would also like to thank the following for the illustrations and diagrams:
Esther Chua (pp. 36, 91 (top), 92, 108, 111, 139, 205, 207)
Wayne Logue (p. 217)
Richard Rendle (all other diagrams)

www.pearsoned.co.nz

Your comments on this book are welcome at
feedback@pearsoned.co.nz

Pearson Education New Zealand
a division of Pearson New Zealand Ltd
67 Apollo Drive, Rosedale, North Shore 0632, New Zealand

Associated companies throughout the world

© Pearson Education New Zealand 2004
First published 2004
Reprinted 2005 (twice), 2006, 2007 (twice), 2008

ISBN 978-0-582-54514-4

Produced by Pearson Education New Zealand
Printed in Malaysia (CTP-VVP)
Typeset in 10.5/12 Palatino

We use **paper from sustainable forestry**

Preface	iv
Unit 1 Social issues	1
Unit 2 Life and leisure	27
Unit 3 The world around us	52
Unit 4 Cultural concerns	75
Unit 5 Health matters	96
Unit 6 Back to school	120
Unit 7 In the papers	144
Unit 8 On the road	165
Unit 9 Looking ahead	191

Reading and Listening	Writing	Speaking
1.1 Skimming and scanning (reading)	1.2 Linking words (Task I & II)	1.3 Your family
1.4 Personal information (listening)	1.5 Brainstorming	1.6 Getting ideas
1.7 Headings (reading)	1.8 Reading graphs	1.9 Beginning Part Three
1.10 Short-answer questions (listening)	1.11 Academic writing	1.12 Topic Card: Social issues
2.1 Unknown vocabulary (reading)	2.2 Preparing a plan for Task I	2.3 Hobbies and interests
2.4 Predicting/anticipating (listening)	2.5 Topic and task words	2.6 Preparing notes
2.7 Text completion (reading)	2.8 Writing an introduction to Task I	2.9 Giving and justifying opinions
2.10 Multiple choice (listening)	2.11 Building a paragraph	2.12 Topic Card: Leisure interests
3.1 Parallel expressions (reading)	3.2 Describing approximate data	3.3 Your hometown
3.4 Numbers, dates and letters (listening)	3.5 Preparing a plan for Task II	3.6 Describing places
3.7 Short-answer questions (reading)	3.8 Comparing and contrasting data	3.9 Misunderstandings
3.10 Table completion (listening)	3.11 Giving and justifying opinions	3.12 Topic Card: The world around us
4.1 Qualifying words (reading)	4.2 Describing data with prepositions	4.3 Festivals
4.4 Listening for details	4.5 Comparison and contrast	4.6 Comparing and contrasting
4.7 TRUE/FALSE/NOT GIVEN-style questions	4.8 Line graphs	4.9 Expanding your topic
4.10 Diagrams and objects (listening)	4.11 Writing an introduction to Task II	4.12 Topic Card: Culture
5.1 Reading for meaning	5.2 Describing illustrations	5.3 Food
5.4 Note taking (listening)	5.5 Improving paragraphs	5.6 Giving instructions
5.7 Labelling diagrams (reading)	5.8 Tables	5.9 Unexpected questions
5.10 Text completion (listening)	5.11 Staying on topic	5.12 Topic Card: Health
6.1 Referencing (reading)	6.2 Correlating data	6.3 Likes, dislikes and preferences
6.4 Discourse markers (listening)	6.5 Cause and effect	6.6 School life
6.7 Matching (reading)	6.8 Bar charts and pie charts	6.9 Talking about changes
6.10 Matching (listening)	6.11 Writing a conclusion for Task II	6.12 Topic Card: Education
7.1 Facts and opinions (reading)	7.2 Passives	7.3 Film and TV
7.4 Recognising speakers (listening)	7.5 Predictions	7.6 Explaining effects
7.7 Multiple choice (reading)	7.8 Processes and diagrams	7.9 Looking at both sides
7.10 Gap filling (listening)	7.11 Solutions	7.12 Topic Card: The media
8.1 Timing (reading)	8.2 Error correction	8.3 Travel
8.4 Meaning and intonation (listening)	8.5 Commonly confused words	8.6 Recounting an experience
8.7 Classifying (reading)	8.8 Appropriate language	8.9 Speculating
8.10 Labelling maps and plans (listening)	8.11 Editing	8.12 Topic Card: Transport
9.1 Review of reading skills	9.2 Review of Task I skills	9.3 Plans and ambitions
9.4 Review of listening skills	9.5 Review of Task II skills	9.6 Review of speaking skills
9.7 Test	9.8 Test	9.9 Test
9.10 On your marks...	9.11 Get set...	9.12 ....Go!

Appendix A   Unit 5.4, Exercise 4 questions   219
Appendix B   Vocabulary sheet   220

Preface

High Impact IELTS: Academic Module will take you from the basic skills needed for IELTS right through to the preparation the night before the test.
    The book is divided into nine units, each with a specific IELTS theme. Each unit is divided into 12 sections presenting specific IELTS skills.

Reading and Listening

The first and third sections of the units focus on reading skills; the second and fourth units focus on listening. In addition, the first and second sections of each unit introduce and practise essential IELTS skills, and the third and fourth units apply these skills to specific IELTS questions.

Writing

Each unit in the writing also follows the same pattern as the reading and listening, with the first and third sections focusing on Task I writing skills, and the second and fourth focusing on Task II.

Speaking

In the speaking course, the first three sections of each unit give you practice at the three different stages of the exam. The fourth unit combines what you have learned into a test format.

UNIT

1

Social issues

Unit 1.1	Skimming and scanning (reading)

EXERCISE 1 You have one hour to read three IELTS passages and answer 40 questions. What is the first thing you should do?

POINT OF IMPACT Before you start answering questions quickly skim the whole text, getting some idea of what it is talking about. You should use the title to help you. You should take one to two minutes to do this.

EXERCISE 2 Look at the headings below and suggest what these articles would be about. *Remember that the theme of this unit is social issues.*

Psychological impact of unemployment	**Car park stinginess a driver's torment**	Champions of colour blind justice
Heart defect gene found	Surfing the web	**DONORS SAVE LIVES**
Harsher penalties for truant children	Native spiders creep back	Internet advertising

Dying to eat	Children and the Net	Auckland on the right tracks
Global marketing success	The billionaire and the pauper	New Global Culture

EXERCISE 3   Which of the following strategies do you think are useful when skimming a reading text?

	Good idea	Bad idea
Reading the title		
Reading every word		
Reading the first sentence of each paragraph		
Underlining names (people, places, etc.)		
Concentrating on difficult vocabulary		
Looking at illustrations		

EXERCISE 4   Using the good strategies above, quickly skim the following article and write a short sentence describing what it is about.

Champions of colour blind justice

READING PASSAGE 1

During the past century, as the United States of America has wrestled with the problem of inequality between blacks and whites, two names remain paramount in the struggle – Martin Luther King and Malcolm X.

Although there were some surface similarities – both started their own movements, organised rallies and gave many speeches both in America and abroad – their approaches and beliefs were radically different. King believed in peace, encouraging only a 'passive resistance' with the eventual aim of black and white people integrating and living together peacefully. While King tried to unite the races through peace, Malcolm X, on the other hand, adopted a more direct, aggressive approach. Unlike King, he did not support the idea of integration but separatism, encouraging his listeners to recognise the suffering whites had caused blacks and to live apart in their own communities.

These men were different not only in their approaches to the problem, but also in the religious convictions that motivated them. Martin Luther King's philosophy of peace and positive reasoning was influenced by Christianity. He was active in the Church and was the leader of the Christian Leadership Conference. Malcolm X started many Muslim groups which practised a violent form of defence against any white oppression, real or imagined.

Despite their very different perspectives, there is one more similarity between these two men – both were assassinated. Malcolm X was shot in 1965 at a rally in Harlem, victim of former supporters who had taken his doctrine of violence to heart. On 4 April 1968 King was shot as he was organising a demonstration in Memphis, but little is known of his assassin.

In the current racial climate of America, it could be said that both men succeeded, at least to a degree. There are still racial tensions, but not to the same degree. Whether Malcolm X would have approved or King would be satisfied today is another question.

EXERCISE 5   Skim the following text and add one of the titles from the first page.

READING PASSAGE 2

As adults, how do we encourage our children to explore the rich resources of the Internet without exposing them to a steady stream of marketing messages, such as junk e-mail or sexually explicit material? This is a question that many people, especially parents, are struggling to answer. Although a solution has not yet been found, one possibility is to filter or block this objectionable material from children without interfering with the rights of adults to view and visit any website they like. When the US Supreme Court rejected the Communications Decency Act in June of 1997, industry and government officials alike looked to computer technology companies to create screening and filtering products to fill the gap left by this court decision.

Started in 1998, the Erasmus study set forth a plan for a family-friendly Internet that would include as a key element filtering, blocking and rating tools for parents, educators and other concerned adults. Much of the debate about appropriate content has focused on the spread of sexually explicit materials online, but there are other, equally insidious aspects. Now banned from an increasing number of traditional advertising markets, cigarette and alcohol companies have turned to cyberspace to reach their future market.

Virtually every major alcoholic beverage manufacturing company has an Internet website which developers claim targets adults of legal drinking age. Many alcohol companies 'card' visitors by requiring them to provide their date of birth before entering the site. Most sites also include a disclaimer on the opening screen indicating that visitors must be of legal drinking age. Many children, however, easily bypass these simple precautions by providing falsified birth date information to access these sites. Once inside, it is clear that these companies are creating an environment full of activities that can and do appeal to children and teens. On some sites, visitors are encouraged to play games, download screensavers, and enter draws to win a free T-shirt.

Social, legal and political pressures have denied tobacco companies web-based marketing, but there is no shortage of sites devoted to the consumption and glorification of smoking cigarettes and cigars. Pictures of women smoking cigarettes appear on sites which feature cool ways to smoke and offer lessons in smoking 'tricks'.

Although no one seems to know exactly the relationship between online marketing and alcohol and tobacco consumption, studies have shown advertising to be extremely effective in increasing youngsters' awareness of, and emotional responses to, products, their recognition of certain brands, and their desire to use these advertised products. This trend becomes even more alarming when the relationships are created between children and spokespersons for alcohol and tobacco products. Alcohol and tobacco advertising and marketing practices are also a cause for concern, with many focusing on the industries' successful efforts to target youth.

There is no easy solution to the problem, except to monitor online alcohol and tobacco promotions and develop any additional safeguards needed to protect youth that are already at risk. We are quickly moving into a digital age that will profoundly affect how children and youth grow and learn, what they value, and, ultimately, who they become. Helping our children and teens navigate in this digital culture presents both a challenge and an opportunity.

POINT OF IMPACT   With only 20 minutes for each reading passage, it is very important to be able to find answers quickly. One way of answering specific information questions is to scan: run your finger or pen quickly across the text until you find the answer.

EXERCISE 6   Quickly scan the text 'Champions of colour blind justice' and find the following.

a Another word for one hundred years	
b A verb with a silent 'w'	
c A noun beginning with 'o'	
d A place in America	
e A month	
f A word with 's-o-n' in it	
g A word with four syllables	
h The number of times a colour is mentioned	

EXERCISE 7   Scan the text for the answer to the following question.

When was the Erasmus study launched?

What word(s) helped you find the answer quickly? _____

POINT OF IMPACT   When scanning for specific information, you often find matching words/phrases or parallel expressions. In *Exercise 7*, 'started' in the text has become 'launched' in the question.

EXERCISE 8   Now answer the following questions as quickly as possible.

1   When did the US Supreme Court overturn the Communications Decency Act?
2   Name one way companies encourage viewers to surf their sites.
3   What three pressures have prevented tobacco being marketed on the Internet?
4   Is the relationship between online marketing and the sale of alcohol clearly understood?

Unit 1.2   Linking words (Task I & II)

EXERCISE 1   Complete the sentences below with *so, yet* or *because*.

Unemployment is increasing		the government is not reacting.
		social welfare costs are rising.
		of the depressed economy.

POINT OF IMPACT   *So, yet* and *because* are three basic examples of linking words – words which allow you to put together ideas either through contrast, comparison, example, cause, effect or sequence. Good use of linking words makes your writing flow better and sound more academic.

EXERCISE 2   Underline the linking words or phrases in each of the sentences below.

a   Illegal immigrants continue to arrive in the country in spite of stricter government measures.
b   In addition to having a lot of money, he is very good-looking.
c   The level of English continues to be a problem amongst migrant workers. As a result, many companies have begun insisting on an IELTS result of at least 6.0.
d   Building a road here will destroy an area of great natural beauty. Furthermore, nobody is really in support of it.
e   Not only is the tourist situation deteriorating, it is also spreading to other industries.

EXERCISE 3   The linking words and phrases below are grouped in different categories. Put the words below in the correct rows. *The first one has been done for you.*

~~Time~~
Contrast (talking about differences)   Comparison (talking about similarities)   Cause and effect
Addition (giving more information)   Concession (admitting another point of view)   Examples
                                             Sequence (describing the order of something)

Time	in the meantime / meanwhile / while
	likewise / in the same way / equally
	whereas / in contrast / on the other hand / nevertheless
	for example / for instance / to illustrate
	consequently / hence / thus / as a result
	although it may be true / granted / admittedly
	following which / subsequently / afterwards
	moreover / furthermore / in addition / not only ... (but) also

---

POINT OF IMPACT   Linking words are very important in academic writing, but only if you apply them appropriately. Some linking words connect ideas in two sentences, while others connect ideas within one sentence. You also need to be aware of where linking words can be placed within a sentence.

EXERCISE 4   Use a linking word or phrase from the box below to complete the sentences. Use each word or phrases only once.

moreover	so	hence	yet	in spite of	whereas
even though	nevertheless	consequently	even so	while	in contrast

a Cigarettes are expensive. _____, they are detrimental to your health.
b Governments spend a considerable amount of money on defence, _____ neglecting areas such as healthcare.
c An increasing number of businesses are going bankrupt, _____ the rising level of unemployment.
d _____ politicians should be accountable for their actions, corruption can still be rife.
e Whales are an endangered species. Some groups believe we should still hunt them _____.
f AIDS education was slow to begin with in some countries. _____ epidemics are common in undeveloped countries.
g Gun-related homicides are widespread in the US. _____, gun control seems as far off as ever.
h _____ tougher sentences, crime is still increasing.
i France is predominantly Catholic, _____ Britain is mainly Protestant.
j The distance between Spain and Africa is less than ten kilometres, _____ Spain has a problem controlling the influx of illegal immigrants.
k Some people work hard all their lives _____ never own their own houses.
l Reports suggest academic performance in the west is in decline. _____, results in Asia have been improving.

EXERCISE 5   Use the linking words to improve the sentences. Rewrite each of the following sentences twice using the linking words in parentheses.

Example. Developing nations have a surplus of food. People from poorer countries often starve. (while – in spite of)

Developing nations have a surplus of food, while people from poorer countries often starve.

In spite of developing nations having a surplus of food, people from poorer countries often starve.

a Children from low-income families often do not pursue further education. Children from higher-income families often stay in education to university level or beyond. (whereas – in contrast)
b An increasing number of marriages are ending in divorce. Many people are choosing not to get married. (consequently – so)
c The situation may be beyond repair. The government should try to resolve it. (even though – even so)
d Many people still sunbathe for long periods of time. They know the dangers. (while – in spite of)
e There is a global agreement to reduce the number of nuclear weapons. Governments still stockpile them. (nevertheless – yet)
f English is easy. It is useful. Lots of people learn it. (moreover – hence)

EXERCISE 6   *Example 1.* (A) is <u>good</u>. On the other hand, (A) is <u>expensive</u>.
    Example 2. (A) is <u>good</u>. In contrast, (B) is <u>bad</u>.

a Which of the underlined words are positive? Which are negative?
b Is the subject the same in both sentences for *Example 1*?
c Is the subject the same in both sentences for *Example 2*?

POINT OF IMPACT Many students make mistakes when using 'On the other hand' and 'In contrast'. If you are contrasting ideas about the same general subject, use 'On the other hand'. If you are contrasting the subjects and the idea (the object), use 'In contrast'. This is a simple guide to using these two linking phrases correctly. You may find exceptions to this rule, but if in doubt it is a useful rule to follow.

EXERCISE 7   Complete the following pairs of sentences using either 'On the other hand' or 'In contrast'.

A 1 English is a difficult language to master. _____, it is really useful to know.
   2 English is a difficult language to master. _____, Spanish is relatively easy.
B 1 England is a small country. _____, there is plenty to see.
   2 England is a small country. _____, the USA is huge.
C 1 Britain has a cold climate. _____, Spain has a warm climate.
   2 Britain has a cold climate. _____, it is very green.

EXERCISE 8   Sometimes it is difficult to identify whether longer paragraphs actually share the same subject. Complete the paragraphs below with either 'On the other hand' or 'In contrast'.

Education is good not only for the individual, but also for society. A society without scientists, researchers and intellectuals has little ability to further itself in a number of fields, specifically medicine, literature and technology. **(a)** _____, the cost to the taxpayer has to be considered, as most countries offer either free or heavily subsidised schemes for further education.

Education should be made available to all. State-funded education systems offer a solid level of schooling with dedicated and qualified teachers. **(b)** _____, private schools are advantageous only to those that can afford to pay to go to them, and this runs the risk of encouraging teachers only interested in the better wages and conditions offered in such establishments.

EXERCISE 9   Complete the paragraphs using a suitable linking word or phrase.

Over recent years, there has been a dramatic increase in international migration, often **(a)** _____ political and economic pressures at home. As with many social issues, this has had both positive and negative effects, as can be seen in an analysis of both Sydney and Auckland.

In Sydney, there are many areas which have been shaped by the cultures of other nationalities and ethnic groups making Australia their new home. There is an area steeped in the culture and tradition of the Chinese (**(b)** _____ the name Chinatown), an area which has become so famous it even has its own website!

With one quarter of the population being foreign immigrants, Auckland has **(c)** _____ become very cosmopolitan, with representatives of over 35 nations living and working in or around New Zealand's largest city.

For both cities, this migration has had many advantageous effects. **(d)** _____, dazzling arrays of different cuisines are available, from Indian curries to Turkish kebabs. **(e)** _____ to food, such a multicultural mix exposes us to much more of a variety of different traditions, outlooks and languages. **(f)** _____, we gain a much wider understanding of international cultures.

(g)_____, with so many different perspectives in relatively close confinement, there are bound to be problems. Cultural communities develop, sometimes isolating themselves and importing their own sense of tradition and belief at the expense of the traditions of their new country. (h)_____, racial suspicions can grow, often developing into tense situations.

To conclude, (i)_____ the inevitable pressures inherent in such a variety of cultures, both Sydney and Auckland (j)_____ remain good examples of cross-cultural toleration and understanding.

EXERCISE 10 Now practise using linking words in an essay form.

ESSAY TASK

Visa regulations should be relaxed for overseas students.

Do you agree or disagree?

Unit 1.3　**Your family**

EXERCISE 1 What is the difference between the following two instructions?

A 'Tell me about your parents.'　　　　B 'Tell me about your family.'

POINT OF IMPACT Throughout the course, you will practise many of the questions you may be asked in Part One of the speaking test. Be careful to answer the question the examiner asks, not what you imagine she or he might ask.

EXERCISE 2 Different cultures do not always think of 'family' in the same way. What does family mean to you?

EXERCISE 3 Listen to the paragraph your teacher will read, and write the names of the people you hear in the three columns below.

Mary's immediate family	Mary's extended family	Other

How are they related to Mary?

EXERCISE 4   Think of three important people in your life: one from your immediate family, one from your extended family and one other. Prepare to talk briefly about them to the class. Use *Exercise 3* as a model.

EXERCISE 5   When talking about your family, you will almost certainly need adjectives describing personality. Are the following adjectives positive, neutral or negative?

indecisive	open-minded	impatient	careful	trustworthy	selfish	optimistic
sociable	attentive	cheerful	ambitious	spontaneous	sensitive	hardworking
reserved	aggressive	impolite	moody	lazy	generous	caring

Positive	Neutral	Negative

POINT OF IMPACT   In Part Two of the speaking test, you may be asked to talk about a member of your family. You will probably just use positive or neutral adjectives, but remember that you need to use a variety of structures. The following two sentences have the same meaning.

My father is a very generous man. He always buys presents for everyone in the family.

My father is not a mean man at all. Every year he buys presents for everyone in the family.

EXERCISE 6   In pairs, use a range of adjectives to describe a member of your family (you could use the same person you used in *Exercise 4*). Justify the adjectives you use with some examples.

Unit 1.4   Personal information (listening)

EXERCISE 1 What is *personal* information? In what situations do you think you will need to listen for personal information in the IELTS test?

EXERCISE 2 In the listening test, you might find that you need to complete a table with personal information. Copy and complete this form with your personal information.

Surname:	Other names:	Telephone number:
Sex:		Current occupation:
Marital status:		Educational qualifications:
D.O.B:		
Nationality:		
Current address:		

POINT OF IMPACT If you have to complete a form or anything with personal information, you often have to write down names and addresses which are difficult to spell. Practise spelling words with a partner whenever you can.

EXERCISE 3 Listen and write down the names and places you hear.

	Name	Place
a		
b		
c		
d		
e		
f		
g		
h		

EXERCISE 4 All the people in *Exercise 3* are famous in New Zealand. Do you know what they are famous for?

Copy the table on the right and write their names in the last column (guess if you do not know).

	Famous for being ...	Who?
A	the inventor of the disposable syringe	
B	the first man to climb Everest	
C	a revolutionary motorcycle designer	
D	a nineteenth-century writer and poet	
E	the leader of the women's suffrage movement	
F	a brilliant mathematician	
G	a Maori doctor, politician and anthropologist	
H	the first man to split the atom	

POINT OF IMPACT When completing a table, some of the questions will be about personal information, but there will nearly always be *extension questions* – questions asking for more information. Looking at the heading of the table will help you predict what other questions you may find.

EXERCISE 5 The following exercise asks you to complete a course application form for Quickstart Technical College. What are the extension questions?

EXERCISE 6 Now listen and complete the form using *NO MORE THAN THREE WORDS OR A NUMBER*.

Quickstart Tech

Course Application Form

Name: (1)_____

D.O.B: 04/08/82____

Nationality: (2)_____

Current address: 32 (3)_____, Auckland

Home telephone: None

Mobile: (4)_____

Current occupation: (5)_____

Educational qualifications: (6)_____ 'A' levels

First choice of study: BA in (7)_____

How will tuition be funded?: (8)_____

How did student hear of us?: (9)_____

Student to be contacted by: (10)_____

POINT OF IMPACT The kind of extension questions and personal information depends on the kind of table you are completing. In *Exercise 6* the heading of the form told you that the extra information is probably study related.

EXERCISE 7 Look at the headings in the following table and write notes about the kind of information you would expect to hear. *Some examples have been given.*

Paid Leave Application	Video Supreme Rentals	Bevis Rent-a-Car
How long?	Membership fee	Driving license

EXERCISE 8   Now practise. Listen and complete the following 10 questions. You would not have so many questions on one form in the IELTS test.

Towers Car Insurance Ltd

Form to be completed for every telephone quotation.

Name: **(1)**_____

D.O.B: **(2)**_____

Address: **(3)**_____, *Chester*.

Other drivers?: **(4)**_____

Vehicle to be insured (year, make and model): *1998* **(5)**_____

Value: **(6)**_____

Previous convictions/disqualifications: **(7)**_____

No claims bonus (years): **(8)**_____

Previous insurer (name): **(9)**_____

Quotation (per year): **(10)**_____

Unit 1.5   Brainstorming

POINT OF IMPACT   The most common failing in Task II is a lack of ideas. Before you can begin writing, you must have something to say, so it is worth spending a few minutes preparing some ideas. One way to get ideas is to first think of anything related to the subject.

EXERCISE 1   Look at a simple example. The question may be:

The poor only have themselves to blame. Do you agree or disagree?

Here are some ideas. Can you think of any more?

depends on education

economy causes rich/poor gap

those unable to work/earn   they socialise too much

difficult to break out of a generational cycle of poverty

rich people earned their money   harsh government policies

some people do not have the ability to save   shopaholics

location of country can lead to limited development opportunities

inheritance   welfare payments in some countries

government should distribute wealth equally

people sometimes lose a lot of money gambling

because they are unmotivated

POINT OF IMPACT It can sometimes help when brainstorming to think of question words that you could apply to the question or topic. For example, if the topic was:

Everyone should be made to learn English.

You could consider aspects such as:
- **why** should everyone have to learn?
- **what** would happen to non-English peoples' native language?
- **where** would people study?
- **how** would this be controlled/regulated?
- **who** should pay for it?
- **when** would many people find a use for English?

EXERCISE 2 Now practise by brainstorming the following essay topics.

1 People should not be allowed to become too rich. Do you agree or disagree?
2 The rise in the number of elderly people is a cause for concern. Discuss.
3 Traditional cultures are being lost as migrants settle in foreign countries. To what extent do you agree?

EXERCISE 3 Look back at the ideas brainstormed in *Exercise 1*. Now reject those points that you feel do not truly apply to the question or do not fit the approach you are going to take.

EXERCISE 4 These ideas can now be divided. For the essay title in *Exercise 1*, they can be classified under the two categories of 'their fault' and 'not their fault'. Add points in each of the categories.

Their fault

Not their fault

POINT OF IMPACT To help you form paragraphs for your essay and also to keep a logical flow throughout, you should also consider classifying the points further. You can group them together under almost any classification you feel is suitable – political, economic, environmental, personal, etc.

| EXERCISE | 5 | What further classifications could you make to the points you divided in *Exercise 4?* |

| EXERCISE | 6 | Using one of the topics in *Exercise 2,* follow the steps in *Exercises 3, 4* and *5.* |

Write the title here

Divided ideas			Divided ideas		
Any further classifications	Any further classifications	Any further classifications	Any further classifications	Any further classifications	Any further classifications

| EXERCISE | 7 | Now write the essay you planned in *Exercise 6.* |

Unit 1.6   Getting ideas

POINT OF IMPACT   With only one minute to look at the topic card, you have to be able to get your ideas together quickly. You should apply the same skills here as you do to brainstorming ideas for the writing topic. Remember that you will be given three or four prompts telling you what you should say during your talk.

| EXERCISE | 1 | Add some ideas to the following Part Two topics. |

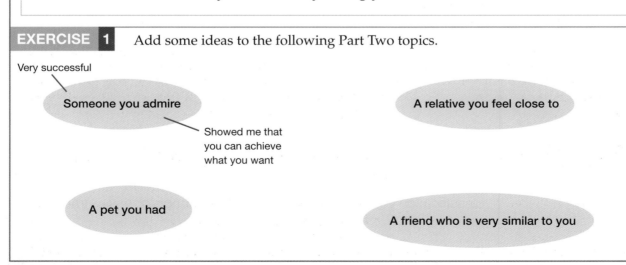

Very successful

Someone you admire

Showed me that you can achieve what you want

A relative you feel close to

A pet you had

A friend who is very similar to you

POINT OF IMPACT In most answers, you will automatically use the present and past simple tense. However, you need to consider how to use other tenses. When preparing your answer on the topic card, think of sentences that require more complex tenses.

EXERCISE 2 How would you extend the notes you have made in order to talk for up to two minutes?

Unit 1.7 Headings (reading)

POINT OF IMPACT In Unit 1.1 you looked at skimming text and practised by giving a reading section a title. These skills can be applied to paragraph headings, a common IELTS reading question type.

EXERCISE 1 How much do you know about 'headings' questions? Complete the table.

		True	False
A	There are always more headings than paragraphs.		
B	There are never more than five paragraphs.		
C	Some of the headings are similar.		
D	At least one word from the heading can always be matched in the text.		
E	The same heading is used more than once.		
F	If you are given an example, it will always be the first paragraph.		

EXERCISE 2 Read the paragraph below. Which heading do you think fits best? Why?

a Disappointment in GM foods.
b GM foods could be the answer.
c The history of GM foods.

When the idea was first put forward, the concept of genetically modified (GM) food seemed to be the answer to so many problems. The ability to harvest foods that could grow in specific climates and were resistant to disease would end famine in many countries, saving millions, even making fortunes for farmers. The truth, however, is a little different. Lower yields, expensive research and general public distrust of 'tampered' food have not made genetic modification the solution it promised to be.

EXERCISE 3 Think of a suitable heading for the following paragraph. It continues the topic from the previous exercise.

In fact, many countries are putting laws and regulations into place specifically limiting or even banning GM food as the general public shows discomfort with the idea of genetic farming. The discovery of quantities of modified grain in harvests presumed to be 'natural' has further fuelled fears, showing that genetic mutations are actually more mobile and widespread than first believed.

READING & LISTENING   READING & LISTENING   READING & LISTENING   READING & LISTENING

POINT OF IMPACT   Here are some useful points to help you match headings to paragraphs.

1 Read the first and last part of the paragraph carefully.
2 Underline key words, phrases or sentences.
3 Pick more than one heading for each passage if you are not sure. When you have completed this for all paragraphs, you can see if any have been used twice.
4 Make sure the whole heading matches, not just single words.
5 Look for what is *different* between each paragraph, not what is the same.
6 If an example is given, cross it off the list of headings.

EXERCISE 4   Use points 1 and 2 from the Point of Impact above for Reading Passage 1 below.

READING PASSAGE 1

The GM controversy – is it worth it?

A Four genetically modified foods are currently being tested in the UK in the hope that they will be resistant to the most common herbicides. The aim is to create a crop which can be sprayed to kill everything around it, allowing more room and an easier harvest. Yet the project has been under heavy pressure, as it promotes the use of broad spectrum herbicides which have already been linked with the decline in farmland wildlife, a result of its highly efficient removal of weeds and a consequent decrease in food supplies for invertebrates and birds.

B In order to pacify the environmentalists, the experiment into herbicidal side effects will be run on four fields, all divided into two – one half growing the GM crop and the other half growing a non-GM variety – with numbers of insects, wild flowers and birds being compared in each half of the field. However, the GM crop will be grown for only one year and each trial field will be monitored for only a further two years. Farmland ecology is poorly understood and the wildlife in these fields will never have been studied before. Soil type is an important factor in determining what lives in the field, yet it may vary from one part of the field to another. Modern fields are often two or three older fields joined together, each of which may have a different history, soil structure and wildlife. Insect numbers vary naturally from one year to the next, so effects would have to be large, otherwise they would not be detected. Earthworms, fungi and bacteria are vital to the health of the soil, yet their numbers are not being monitored.

C Naturally, those who are opposed to the experiment claim that the effects of GM crops and their herbicides are likely to be subtle. It took many years for the devastating effects of DDT on birds to be realised and over 50 years for scientists to discover the damage caused to the ozone layer by CFCs, previously thought to be inert. Three years of limited studies is simply not long enough to say that GM crops are 'safe'. DNA from GM crops may spread into the wider environment through the transfer of genetic material to soil microbes. DNA from GM sugar beet persists for up to two years in the soil. In laboratory experiments DNA from GM plants was taken up by both fungi and bacteria. Agricultural soils are often very mobile, so it is likely that soil contaminated by GM crops will spread to other fields. In addition, sugar beet seeds can remain in the ground, dormant but fertile, for at least 10 years, giving rise to GM sugar beet plants long after monitoring of the fields has stopped.

D GM contamination will affect livelihoods of other farmers, especially organic farmers, who will be unable to sell contaminated crops. Honey contaminated with GM pollen from last year's crop trials has already been found. Beekeepers provide a vital service to fruit growers but will be forced to move their hives from areas near GM crop trials if they wish to avoid GM contamination, and this will affect land values.

E But perhaps the most persuasive reason to abandon GM food is that nature is already evolving beyond our advances in the field. GM insect-resistant crops are starting to become less effective, as the insect pests they were designed to resist rapidly develop tolerance. Similarly, weeds will develop herbicide tolerance as they are exposed to more of the same few herbicides, and as nature adapts to the new environment, another weakness of GM foods is exposed – it cannot change. By being manipulated and modified, GM crops have lost their ability to adapt as natural crops would, and are unable to cope with the environmental changes the planet is experiencing.

EXERCISE 5   Now use points 3, 4 and 5 from the Point of Impact on page 16 and match the headings below with a paragraph from *Exercise 4*.

List of headings		
i	Looking at the long term	Paragraph A
ii	Weaknesses of the test	Paragraph B
iii	Benefits to farming	Paragraph C
iv	Subsidiary effects	Paragraph D
v	Controversial experiments	Paragraph E
vi	GM food adaptability	
vii	The flexibility of nature	
viii	The science of genetic modification	

Unit 1.8 Reading graphs

EXERCISE 1 Look at the graph below and the sentences that follow. Only one sentence is correct. Which one? What is wrong with the other sentences?

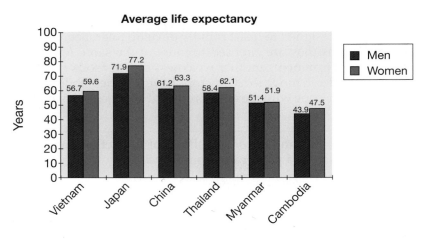

a In China, slightly more than 61% of men live longer than women.
b According to the graph, all women live longer than men.
c There are more men in Thailand than in Myanmar. ✓
d The graph shows that in these six countries, women generally live longer than men. ✓

POINT OF IMPACT Before you can begin Task I, you have to look carefully at what is being represented. *Do not assume that every graph is talking about percentages!*

EXERCISE 2 Look at the graph below and answer the three questions.

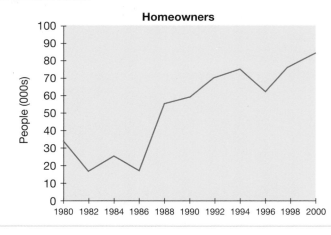

a Is the graph about people or houses?
b What do the numbers along the horizontal axis represent?
c What do the numbers along the vertical axis represent?

POINT OF IMPACT Once you have a clear understanding of the axes, you need to be able to describe the trends you see.

EXERCISE	3	Decide whether the phrases below mean an *upward, downward* or *even* trend.

a fall	to increase	to remain steady	to decline	a drop
to decrease	a rise	to climb	to deteriorate	a plateau
to level off	to plummet	to plunge	to recover	to improve

1	2	3

EXERCISE	4	The adjectives and adverbs below describe amount or degree of change. Put the words in the correct column. *Some can go in more than one column.*

rapidly	moderately	sharp	significant
gradual	rapid	marginal	gradually
sharply	marked	significantly	dramatic
marginally	moderate	dramatically	abrupt
slightly	abruptly	slight	markedly

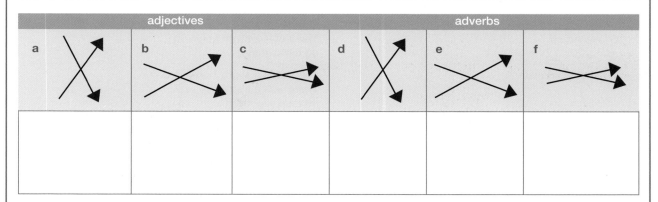

adjectives			adverbs		
a	b	c	d	e	f

EXERCISE	5	Complete the table by matching a set of definitions with a graph.

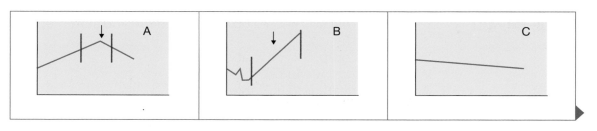

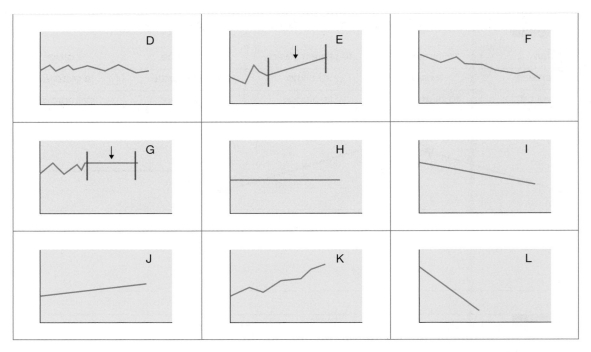

The description	The graph	The description	The graph
(X) fluctuated There were fluctuations in (X) (X) was erratic		(X) fell dramatically There was a dramatic fall in (X) (X) plunged	
(X) reached a peak (X) peaked		(X) recovered dramatically There was an abrupt rise in (X) (X) soared	
(X) reached a plateau (X) levelled off		There was a slight decrease in (X) There was a slight fall in (X) (X) fell slightly in...	
(X) remained constant		There was a slight increase in (X) There was a slight rise in (X) (X) rose slightly in...	
There was an upward trend in (X) Overall, (X) increased		There was a steady decline in (X) (X) declined steadily There was a moderate decline in (X)	
There was a downward trend in (X) Overall, (X) decreased		There was a steady recovery in (X) (X) recovered steadily There was a moderate increase in (X)	

POINT OF IMPACT   Here is a checklist you should go through before you start preparing an answer for Task 1.

1   What is the graph or table about?
2   What is being measured?
3   Are there any general/notable trends?

EXERCISE 6   Now write a Task I essay using the following graph.

ESSAY TASK

The graph below shows four areas of accommodation status in a major European city from 1970 to 2000.

Write a report for a university lecturer describing the information shown below.

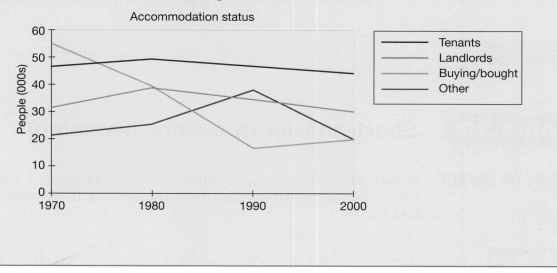

Accommodation status

Legend:
- Tenants
- Landlords
- Buying/bought
- Other

y-axis: People (000s) — 0, 10, 20, 30, 40, 50, 60
x-axis: 1970, 1980, 1990, 2000

Unit 1.9   Beginning Part Three

POINT OF IMPACT   In Part Three the questions the examiner will ask will be related to the topic card.

EXERCISE 1   Prepare some questions based on the following topic card.

Describe something you own that has a special significance for you.
You should say:
- what it is
- where you got it
- how you got it.
You should also say why it has special significance for you.

POINT OF IMPACT When answering Part Three questions, it may help to consider the question in terms of the following three steps.

1 What do I know about the interviewer's question?
2 What's my opinion?
3 Do I have any examples to support what I am going to say?

EXERCISE 2 Using the extension questions you prepared in *Exercise 1*, apply the three steps from the Point of Impact above.

Unit 1.10   Short-answer questions (listening)

POINT OF IMPACT As with all IELTS questions, make sure you read the instructions closely. Do not write more than the number of words the questions asks you for.

EXERCISE 1 Listen to the recording and answer the following questions using *NO MORE THAN THREE WORDS OR A NUMBER.*

a What festival can he see?   _____
b When does it start?   _____
c How many people go?   _____

POINT OF IMPACT Looking for key words in the question will help you identify the answer more easily. Short-answer questions often look for specific information, so make sure you have some idea what to expect. The question words themselves are often very useful.

EXERCISE 2 Make a note of the key words in the questions in *Exercise 1*.

EXERCISE 3 What kind of answer would you look for if the following question words were used (e.g. a person/place, a number)?

a Who
b When
c Where
d Why
e What
f Which
g How
h How many
i How often

EXERCISE 4 Read the short-answer questions below and make a note of the key words. Now listen to the recording.

a What specific problem is the talk about? _____
b Where is the speaker talking about? _____
c How many people live there? _____
d Why is the problem getting worse? _____
e Who should be finding a solution to the problem? _____

REVIEW **Personal information (Unit 1.4)**

Listen to the recording and answer Questions 1–10.

Questions 1–5 Complete the form below with the applicant's personal details using *NO MORE THAN THREE WORDS OR A NUMBER.*

Name: **(1)**_____
D.O.B.: **(2)**_____ 1981
Address: **(3)** _____Simon Place, Brighton
Contact number: **(4)** (01903)_____
Mobile: **(5)**_____

REVIEW **Short-answer questions (Unit 1.10)**

Questions 6–10 Answer the following questions using *NO MORE THAN THREE WORDS.*

6 What is the applicant's current job?
7 What university course has she already completed?
8 Why might the student not get on the MBA course?
9 What is her second choice?
10 Which department will contact the applicant?

Unit 1.11 Academic writing

EXERCISE 1 The text below talks about the IELTS test, but each paragraph is inappropriate for IELTS. What is wrong with each one?

A The International English Language Testing System IELTS is really good because it is recognised all over the world. They developed the first test in the early 1960s. You can do two types of test – academic, if you want to study in English, and general training for people who want to live in a country that speaks English as its first language.

B The IELTS is a very popular exam. Three features of IELTS contribute to its success. These can be summarised under three headings. It is a genuinely international test. It assesses the communicative use of English. It provides convenient and informative reports on candidates for test users and receiving institutions.

C Higher education institutions in britain australia ireland new zealand and south africa use IELTS for assessment, and a growing number of institutions in the united states and canada are following suit. Immigration authorities adopted the IELTS exam in 1996 which almost doubled the number of candidates taking the test.

POINT OF IMPACT Register (the level of formality), complex sentences and punctuation are all essential in academic writing.

EXERCISE 2 Match the five texts with one of the following descriptions.

Description	Written in a formal style, presenting both facts and opinions	Written in a formal style, presenting facts	Written in an informal style, presenting opinions	Written in a neutral style, presenting facts	Written in a neutral style, presenting opinions
Text					

A Hi there,
Haven't really got much to say, as we've all been really busy since I spoke to you. I've been studying hard as my test is coming soon. I don't think I'm going to do very well – I haven't done any homework for weeks. By the way, I heard you got a 7.0 for speaking! Congrats! Anyway, keep in touch.

B Nearly 100 kilometres south of Auckland, Hamilton Gardens is a popular day trip. There are six small gardens, each representing a different country and allowing an insight into their respective cultures and traditions. From the fantasy-inspired Chinese landscaping to the stark American modernist garden, there is a lot to see, and there are plans for additional gardens in the future.

C Dear Sir,
I wish to complain in the strongest possible terms. Despite having made reservations at your hotel over three weeks ago, I was appalled to discover that due to an error on your part, my wife and I were left with no accommodation for the first two nights of our holiday. I am therefore requesting an immediate and full refund for those nights. In addition, I would like to point out that your catering was not of the standard claimed in your brochure.

D Further to your e-mail, I am forwarding information regarding upcoming IELTS test dates. The next test is three weeks from today. Should you wish to book a place on this test, please do so as soon as possible, as places are limited. Should you have any other questions, please let me know.

E Of all the new restaurants that have opened recently in the city, 'The Loaded Dog' on King St came out on top. Although their menu has little that is unique, I found the meals tasty and the service good, all at a reasonable price, making this a good choice for the family.

EXERCISE 3   Where do you think each text may have come from?

EXERCISE 4   Compare the sentences below. Which one is better?

a   The International English Language Testing System is a globally recognised exam. It was first developed in the early 1960s.
b   The International English Language Testing System, which was first developed in the early 1960s, is a globally recognised exam.

POINT OF IMPACT   Relative clauses allow you to link ideas or add extra information in more complex sentences, an essential part of academic IELTS writing.

There are two types of relative clauses.

A Defining. Defining relative clauses identify which person or thing we are referring to; the information is essential to the grammar of the sentence and cannot be omitted.
B Non-defining. Non-defining relative clauses give additional information about a person or thing, and the information can be omitted.

EXERCISE 5   Which type of relative clause are the following (defining or non-defining)?

a   The IELTS interviewer that I had for my speaking test was very friendly.
b   The Academic IELTS test, which is used for university entrance, is more difficult than the General Training modules.
c   The teaching methods that some schools favour require students to learn new vocabulary every week.
d   Any listening test which has four sections is bound to be difficult.
e   My friend, who is Scottish, is an IELTS examiner.

EXERCISE 6   All of the following sentences are incorrect. Identify the mistake and correct it.

a   America which is one of the world's most developed countries gives millions of dollars in aid to developing nations every year.
b   Students communicate with their classmates in English often become considerably more fluent and confident.
c   We should, of course, punish those which break the law.
d   The population is increasing, that is putting strain on both the environment and our supply of natural resources.

POINT OF IMPACT   Relative clauses are very important in academic writing. There are hundreds of Internet websites with practice exercises – simply type 'relative clauses exercises' in most search engines.

Punctuation is also very important.
A Defining. Defining relative clauses do not take commas.
B Non-defining. Non-defining relative clauses take commas.

ESSAY TASK

Individuals should not be allowed to carry guns.

Do you agree or disagree?

EXERCISE 7   The paragraph that follows is part of an answer to the Task II question above, but there are a number of mistakes. Rewrite the paragraph considering the register, complex sentences and punctuation.

> A big reason why I don't think the government should let people have guns is because of accidents. In america you can shoot people, that come into your house to rob things, But it is possible that mistakes can be made. Don't forget crimes where people get upset about something and act without thinking like shooting their husband or wife. More importantly, guns are supposed to be for defence. Guns are often used aggressively

Unit 1.12   Topic Card: Social issues

POINT OF IMPACT   It is important to show your examiner a wide range of vocabulary throughout the test. You should practise a number of different skills to avoid repeating yourself.

EXERCISE 1   What vocabulary could you use to talk about the topic below?

> Describe a friend who is very important to you.
> You should say:
> • who they are
> • how you met
> • what they are like.
> You should also say why they are special to you.

EXERCISE 2   Think of some extension questions you could be asked about the topic card in *Exercise 1*.

EXERCISE 3   Now work with a partner and practise the interview. One of you should act as the candidate and the other should be the interviewer. The interviewer should make some notes considering the following areas.

a   Can you understand the speaker?
b   Did they use suitable vocabulary?
c   Did they answer your extension questions accurately?
d   Did they sound natural?

UNIT
2
Life and leisure

Unit 2.1   Unknown vocabulary (reading)

EXERCISE 1   Read the following passage. What do you do if you meet this kind of problem in your IELTS test?

The increasing popularity of quasing is not difficult to explain. Considering all the factors that circumstitialised the prenudery, we should perhaps be more gerstined that the sprindle has not overglouted many years earlier.*

POINT OF IMPACT   When you meet new vocabulary, don't panic! Throughout the course, avoid jumping straight to your dictionary. There are five pointers that can help you.

* Exercise 1 is only an example. Many of these words are made up!

EXERCISE 2

1   **Context.** Read the passage below. Write down what you think the word in *italics* means.

In every country you visit, you will find a sport that captures the passions of the nation. New Zealand has its rugby supporters, England has its legions of football fans, the Japanese have taken baseball to their hearts and Scotland still proudly supports its *curling* heroes.

2   **Contrast.** Read the passage below. Write down what you think the word in *italics* means.

It should come as no surprise that younger people spend much of their leisure time on their feet, engaged in energetic activities, whereas older people opt for more *sedentary* pursuits like going to the theatre or watching television.

3 **Explanation.** Read the passage below. Write down what you think the word in *italics* means.

There are many examples of the cooperation between people and dogs. Guide dogs, for example, give essential assistance to the blind, while *beagles*, small dogs with short legs, are often used by hunters.

4 **Word groups.** Read the passage below. Write down what you think the word in *italics* means.

In my opinion, boxing is an *abhorrent* sport. Modern society should be opposed to such violent contact sports.

5 **Logic.** Read the passage below. Write down what you think the word in *italics* means.

Although technology has made mountain climbing both safer and easier, it is not a sport without risks. Bad weather can come quickly and last for long periods and the effects of severely cold weather can lead to *hypothermia* and, if untreated, death.

Explanations:
1 You know the subject of the paragraph is national sports. You can also see the pattern of country or nationality followed by sport. Therefore, it is logical that *curling* is a sport.
2 The first clause talks about young people, energetic activities and being 'on their feet'. The word 'whereas' tells you that the second clause is a contrast, so *sedentary* must have the opposite meaning – not active or energetic, not 'on their feet'.
3 It is always a good idea to look closely at the sentence before and after vocabulary that is unfamiliar, as you often find that the word has been explained. From the passage, you know that *beagles* are 'small dogs with short legs'.
4 Look at the grammar. There is a subject (boxing), followed by the verb 'to be' (is), and the sentence ends with a noun (sport). So *abhorrent* must be an adjective of opinion and it follows from the second sentence that it has a negative meaning.
5 Think about it! Use your own knowledge and experience to work it out – what happens to people stuck in cold weather for long periods?

POINT OF IMPACT   During this course, you will see a lot of unfamiliar vocabulary. Before you ask your teacher or check in a dictionary, try applying the five pointers you have just studied and remember to write any new words in a vocabulary notebook.

EXERCISE 3   Now read the sentences below. Write down what you think the words in *italics* mean.

A English football supporters are often accused of being *hooligans*, although the majority are actually well-behaved fans who have no intention of causing trouble.

B Although it can be a little expensive, *thermal* clothing is essential when skiing.

C *Pilates*, a form of exercise, is becoming increasingly popular.

D Children from *impoverished* families rarely have overseas holidays or modern toys.

E When climbing Everest, Sir Edmund Hillary experienced some of the world's harshest natural dangers, such as freezing weather, sudden snowstorms, and even *avalanches*.

Which of the five pointers did you apply to which number?

POINT OF IMPACT   No matter what skills you apply, you may find a word or words that you still do not understand. If this happens, do not panic. Take a guess and move on. Do not spend too much time trying to work it out. It has been scientifically proven that the human brain is unable to process more than 20 new words at a time before it starts to forget some. The best thing to do is to write 10 new words with a definition and an example sentence in a pocket-sized notebook and have it with you at all times. Waiting for the bus, sitting in a café or just relaxing at home – these are all good opportunities to quickly take out the notebook and revise. When you are sure you are familiar with these words, write down 10 more and start again. Once a week, review all the vocabulary you have written in your notebook.

EXERCISE 4   Read the text and use the vocabulary skills on the numbered words.

Write down a definition for each of the numbered words in the text.

READING PASSAGE 1

A brief history of the Olympics

Most people have heard of the Olympics[1], a sporting event held every four years, where people from around the world congregate in one place to compete in various sporting events. But how much is known of its history?

A The Olympics first began in Ancient Greece nearly 2700 years ago as a religious occasion, very different from the *secular*[2] event we see now. It was primarily a festival celebrating the ancient Greek gods. Named after the goddess Olympia, the festival was actually in praise of the god Zeus and was held in a specially constructed stadium called *The Hippodrome*. Unlike the modern Olympics, there were very few events, the most popular being running, fighting and *javelin throwing*[3].

B For the athletes, the honour of winning was the reason for participation, not only for themselves, but also for their city, as the winner of each competition was given prizes to *bestow*[4] on the citizens of his hometown. Prizes were often food – grain and meat – but occasionally also precious metals. Naturally, this *engendered*[5] a degree of rivalry amongst competitors and cities, but one of the most notable aspects of the Olympics was that, for the duration of the festival, there was peace, at least outside the *arena*[6]. By government decree, there were no arguments or hostilities, convicted criminals were to be treated well and the death penalty was not carried out. All wars – domestic and international – had to be suspended. Nothing of importance was discussed as the games became the *paramount*[7] focus of the nation.

C Despite the prizes, the honours and the enforcement of peace, the Games were not entirely *philanthropic*[(8)] in nature. In accordance with the customs of the time, they still carried the traditional exclusion of women and slaves, who were not allowed within the stadium. Transgression of this rule resulted in severe punishment. It was not until 1900 that women were finally allowed to compete.

D Nonetheless, for nearly 700 years, the Olympics represented something noble in that it promoted, albeit for only five days, a period of peace around which the whole country could gather. It was somewhat *ironic*[(9)], then, that the original Games were abolished after the Roman invasion in AD356, and for a period of just over a *millennium*[(10)] and a half, there were no more Olympics.

E It was in 1896 that Baron Pierre de Coubertin, a Frenchman, and Dimitrios Vikelas, a Greek, revived the games. *Fittingly*[(11)], the first of the modern Olympics was held in Greece, but although the intentions of the Games were good, they no longer represented the original ideals of the Olympics. World War I caused one game to be cancelled and World War II caused the cancellation of another two – a far cry from the period of peace the games first inspired. To try and revive the spirit of peace and understanding that the original games represented, Baron de Coubertin designed an Olympic flag with five intertwining rings which symbolised the union of the five continents. This was first used at the Antwerp Olympics in 1920 together with the release of doves at the beginning of the Games as a symbol of peace. However, athletes competing to be the best in the world, financial rewards in the form of sponsorship, financial problems and allegations of drug abuse have further *tarnished*[(12)] what was once the embodiment of a desire to bring people together harmoniously.

F However, there is still much to admire in the Olympics of today. It has become an opportunity for people of nearly 200 nationalities to come together in the spirit of friendly competition, much as they did nearly 3000 years ago. Now the rewards come in the form of medals and the knowledge that the athlete is one of the best in the world. The importance of the games has been reinforced with the introduction of the Winter Olympics and the Paralympics Games, the latter of which is specifically for people with physical disabilities. It can now be said that the Olympic Games is truly a competition for all people.

REVIEW   **Headings (Unit 1.7)**

Using Reading Passage 1, answer the following questions.

Questions 1–6   From the list of headings choose the most suitable for each paragraph.

List of headings

i	Re-emergence of the Games
ii	Traditional discrimination
iii	The way to peace
iv	Origins
v	The contemporary Olympiad
vi	Worldwide recognition
vii	Dissolution through conquest
viii	A feeling of animosity
ix	Harmony through competition

1 Paragraph A

2 Paragraph B

3 Paragraph C

4 Paragraph D

5 Paragraph E

6 Paragraph F

REVIEW   **Skimming and scanning (Unit 1.1)**

Using **NO MORE THAN THREE WORDS,** answer the following questions.

7 How many times has war cancelled the modern Olympics?
8 Why were there no Olympics between 356 and 1896?
9 To whom were the original Olympics dedicated?
10 Were the original Olympics entirely a time of goodwill?
11 Before AD356, how long was each Olympics?
12 How many countries are represented in the modern Olympics?

Unit 2.2   Preparing a plan for Task I

EXERCISE **1**   What is the first thing you would do if you were writing an essay on the graph below? Refer to Unit 1.8 for some advice.

ESSAY TASK

The graph shows the percentage of people in Sydney who watch television at various times on a typical weekday.

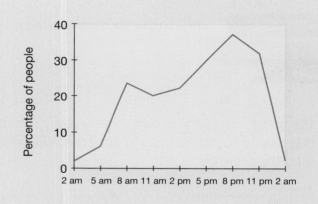

EXERCISE **2**   Now look at the graph below. How is it different from the graph in *Exercise 1*?

ESSAY TASK

The graph shows the difference between men and women in Sydney who watched television at various times on a typical weekday in 1999.

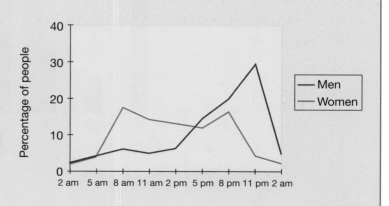

POINT OF IMPACT In Unit 1.8, you saw a three-point checklist you should apply before writing your essay.
- What is the graph or table about?
- What is being measured?
- Are there any general / notable trends?

You can now extend this into a fuller plan by adding two more points
- What tense should I use?
- What are the topic words?

This can now be re-organised into a short checklist that will help you plan your essays.
1 Topic words?
2 Tense?
3 Axes?
4 About?
5 Trends?

EXERCISE 3 Write a plan for the following graph.

ESSAY TASK

The graph shows the results of a survey in which 100 boys and 100 girls were asked whether they liked a number of leisure activities. The information recorded is from boys and girls who liked the activities.

Write a report for a university lecturer describing the information shown below.

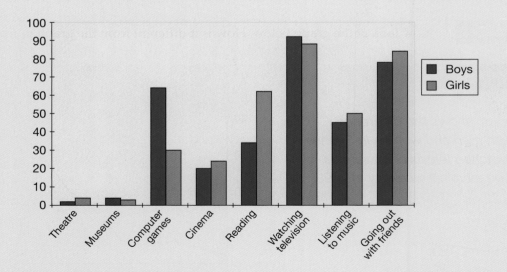

POINT OF IMPACT   From what you have learned in this unit and Unit 1.8, you can prepare a five-point plan like this.

1 Topic words?	leisure activities/children/interested in
2 Tense?	past tense
3 Axes?	number (boys/girls)/types of activity
4 About?	number of boys and girls interested in various leisure activities
5 Trends?	going out with friends and watching television are the highest. Boys are considerably more interested in computer games than girls are. Girls are more interested in reading.

EXERCISE 4   Study the graph below and complete a plan like the example for *Exercise 3* above.

ESSAY TASK

The graph shows the most popular sports watched by different age groups in an average European city.

Write a report for a university lecturer describing the information shown below.

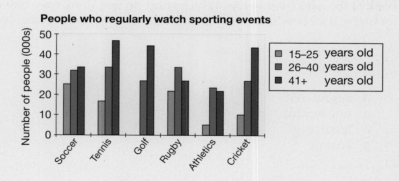

EXERCISE 5   Now write the essay. *Remember to use the plan you have made!*

SPEAKING   SPEAKING   SPEAKING   SPEAKING   SPEAKING   SPEAKING   SPEAKING

Unit 2.3   Hobbies and interests

EXERCISE 1   Write down some ways the interviewer could ask you about sport.

e.g. What sports do you like?

EXERCISE 2   **a**   What is wrong with this dialogue?

> Question: What sports do you like?
> Answer: Football.

b   In order to extend your answer, you could begin by *describing* how you feel about the sport. Which adjective completes the sentence below?

I think football is exciting/excited.

EXERCISE 3   Match the adjectives below with the sport they best describe.

Rugby
Skydiving
Bowls

relaxing
exhilarating
energetic

EXERCISE 4   Look at the adjectives below. Which sport do you think they best describe? Write **R** for rugby, **B** for bowls, **S** for skydiving. *You can write more than one sport for each adjective.*

    a   breathtaking
    b   physical
    c   slow
    d   aggressive
    e   uneventful
    f   terrifying
    g   boring

POINT OF IMPACT   You should be able to build a dialogue like this:

Question: What sports do you like?
Answer: Well, I'm quite fit so I like rugby. It's a very energetic game and good exercise.
            I'm not very keen on sports like bowls. I find them very boring.

EXERCISE 5   Now think of a sport you like and prepare an answer similar to the one in the Point of Impact above.

EXERCISE 6   **Student A:** Use one of the phrases you brainstormed in *Exercise 1* to ask your partner about sport.
Student B: Answer the interviewer with as much detail as you can.

Unit 2.4   Predicting/anticipating (listening)

POINT OF IMPACT   As the listening begins, you hear a voice on the recording telling you what section you are about to complete, as well as the question numbers. Then you are given a short amount of time to read the questions. You have a choice of what to do with this time.

1 Plan what you will have for dinner tonight.

2 Read the questions, thinking about some of the language you might hear.

Although it is easy to see which answer is better, it is surprising how many students lose concentration and do not use this time to their best advantage.

EXERCISE 1   Look at a typical Section 1-style question below. Try to predict as much as you can about what is missing (e.g. **(1)** surname).

MANUKAU SPORT AND FITNESS CLUB

APPLICATION FORM

NAME: Mary _____**(a)**

ADDRESS: _____,**(b)** Lansdale Street, _____**(c)**

TELEPHONE NUMBER: _____**(d)**

REQUIRED MEMBERSHIP TIME: _____**(e)**

MEMBERSHIP TYPE Circle as appropriate: FULL / GYM AND SWIMMING / GYM ONLY **(f)**

HOW DID YOU HEAR ABOUT US? _____**(g)**

POINT OF IMPACT   Although it is essential to use the time you are given to predict or anticipate some of the answers, it is very important that you listen closely for the unexpected. For example, it is possible that for TELEPHONE NUMBER, the person may not have a telephone.

EXERCISE 2   Look at the following form and predict as much as you can. Remember that you will have a limit on the number of words, so think of possible answers that do not go beyond the limit.

Complete the following using *NO MORE THAN THREE WORDS OR A NUMBER.*

Evening Classes for Adults

a   Courses will run for _____.

b   Maximum of _____ students per class.

c   Cost will depend on _____.

d   Those interested should contact _____ on 263-8147.

e   Evening courses will be held at the _____.

EXERCISE **3**   Now listen to the recording and fill in the missing information.

POINT OF IMPACT   Predicting and anticipating in the listening is also useful when you have to select a picture or diagram in a multiple-choice question.

EXERCISE **4**   Look at the pictures below. They have the same context but there are obvious differences. Quickly write notes by each illustration, describing the differences between them.

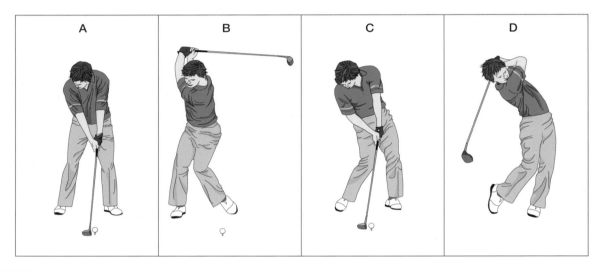

REVIEW   **Short-answer questions (Unit 1.10)**

The following questions are based on a report about leisure time and modern conveniences. Before you listen to the recording, try to predict as much as you can.

Questions 1–8   Answer the questions using *NO MORE THAN THREE WORDS*.

1 What specific recent lifestyle changes is the speaker talking about?
2 Which two examples of goods have now become thought of as necessities?
3 What have these goods given us more time for?
4 What do richer societies become?
5 What does the 'race of acquisition' encourage us to buy?
6 Who is mostly responsible for creating the demand for new products?
7 Why should we be concerned with the increasing number of unnecessary appliances?
8 What does the speaker recommend for the future?

Unit 2.5 Topic and task words

ESSAY TASK

Advances in technology and automation have reduced the need for manual labour. Therefore working hours should be reduced.

To what extent do you agree?

EXERCISE 1   If you were writing an answer to the task above, what would be the main focus of your essay?

POINT OF IMPACT   Task II writing questions can often be divided into different parts. Commonly, these are:

1   a situation which is generally accepted as being true
2   an opinion, speculation or suggestion about the situation
3   words telling you what you should do.

Point 1 introduces the general topic.
Point 2 focuses on the specific topic you should write about.
Point 3 refers to the task words – the words which tell you how you should respond to the topic.

EXERCISE 2   Look at the question in *Exercise 1* and the Point of Impact above. Divide the question into three parts.

EXERCISE 3   Now complete the table on the next page for the essay titles. *The first one has been done for you.*

WRITING

Essay title	Point 1	Point 2	Point 3
A wide variety of vegetarian food is now available. However, although an increasing number of people are adopting a vegetarian diet, it is not healthy. Do you agree?	Wide variety of vegetarian food available	Vegetarianism is not healthy	Do you agree?
1 High-salary jobs often include free health insurance as part of an employment contract. However, such private medical insurance is unfair, as it offers preferential treatment to the wealthy. Do you agree?			
2 The number of elderly people in the world is increasing. This will lead to a number of social and medical problems. To what extent do you agree?			
3 Computer games have become the primary source of entertainment for most young children. As a result, children are not forming traditional social skills. What do you think could be done to reverse this trend?			

EXERCISE 4   The most common task words are:

Do you agree or disagree? and *To what extent do you agree?*

What is the difference?

POINT OF IMPACT   Not all Task II essays have three clear parts. Nonetheless, you still need to identify the topic and task words. When particularly difficult or technical vocabulary is used in the question, it will sometimes be explained.

EXERCISE 5   Underline the topic in each of the Task II titles below.

a   Some people need medical treatment due to an addiction such as to smoking or drugs. Should they be treated regardless of the cause?
b   Euthanasia* is a moral right. What is your opinion?
c   The government fails to provide sufficient medical care for the elderly. To what extent do you agree?
d   We are becoming obsessed with diet and health. Suggest possible reasons why.

*the act of killing someone painlessly (especially someone suffering from an incurable illness)

EXERCISE 6   What are the task words?

POINT OF IMPACT   Now you have identified both the topic words and the task words, it often helps to rewrite the question in a more logical order.

A wide variety of vegetarian food is now available. However, although an increasing number of people are adopting a vegetarian diet, it is not healthy. Do you agree?	Is a vegetarian diet healthy?

| **EXERCISE** | **7** | Rewrite the three questions in *Exercise 3*. |

| **REVIEW** | **Brainstorming (Unit 1.5)** |

Now select one of the questions from *Exercise 7* and brainstorm ideas.

Unit 2.6   Preparing notes

| **EXERCISE** | **1** | Which words do you think are important? Underline them. |

Describe your favourite leisure activity. You should say:
* what it is
* how often you do it
* when you first started doing it.
You should also say why it is important to you.

| **EXERCISE** | **2** | When you are preparing notes, do you think it is better to write full sentences or just main points? |

POINT OF IMPACT   It is very important you do not spend the whole time staring at the notes on your card when you are speaking. This is why your notes should be clear but brief. Do not try to write full sentences!

| **EXERCISE** | **3** | Make short notes about the topic card in *Exercise 1*. |

POINT OF IMPACT   Remember that the IELTS test is a communication test – it is not a memory test. If there is a fact you cannot remember, then tell the interviewer. You can show your English ability just as well by explaining that you do not know something. For example:
'I'm not really sure when I began doing this, but I'm sure I was very young'
is just as good an answer as giving a date.

| **EXERCISE** | **4** | Prepare a topic card of your own. Make notes about it, but do not tell anyone what your subject is. When you have finished, show your notes to your partner. They should be able to recreate the topic card. |

| **EXERCISE** | **5** | Now speak about what you have prepared making sure that you only glance at your notes. |

POINT OF IMPACT   Do not worry if you decide to change a little of what you have planned. It is much better to keep the conversation natural than stick rigidly to something that you are not so comfortable with.

Unit 2.7   Text completion (reading)

POINT OF IMPACT   There are three different types of instruction for text-completion questions.
- Use words from the text (*Exercise 1, question a*).
- Use words from a box (*Exercise 1, question b*).
- Use your own words (*Exercise 1, question c*).

EXERCISE 1   Read the short paragraph below and then complete the three questions that follow.

The importance that used to be attached to 'working in the city' is slowly becoming less significant. Apart from a few remaining areas like Wall Street in New York, the actual place where most of the work is completed has little or no impact on whether the work is successful. On occasions when appearance is important, many business people often prefer to meet clients in a more neutral environment such as a restaurant or conference room.

Complete the sentence below with words taken from the passage. Use ***NO MORE THAN THREE WORDS.***

a   Having an office in the city is _____.

Complete the sentence below. Choose your answer from the box to the right.

Wall Street
The city
New York

b   _____ is one of the exceptions to this trend.

Complete the sentence below. Use ***NO MORE THAN ONE WORD.***

c   Successful business rarely depends on _____ .

POINT OF IMPACT   These three types are almost always in the form of a paraphrased summary of the text. In the exam, it helps to think about other ways of expressing parts of the text as you are often only looking for general, not specific, information.

EXERCISE 2   Read the following three paragraphs and summarise them.

A For John Taylor, an Auckland businessman, the day starts like any other. He gets up at 7.00 a.m., showers, shaves and has a light breakfast before heading to work – and it is here that Mr Taylor is a little unusual. Like an increasing number of business professionals, Mr Taylor has found that, armed with a notebook computer and an Internet connection, he can be just as productive at home as he could in the city.

B The benefits of working from home are largely time related. Whether stuck in a traffic jam or a crowded train, commuting to and from work can be time consuming and irritating. Working at home, you can start work immediately and with much more flexibility. Many people can tailor their working day around their most productive hours: a perfect solution for those whose mornings are spent in a daze or for those who wind down in the early afternoon. The flexibility of working hours also allows busy professionals to work around other commitments, especially family ones.

C Strangely enough, it is this very flexibility that can cause stress. Working at home, the pressure is constant. Physically, the office is never left, and therefore many people also find that they cannot mentally detach themselves from their work. Working alone allows a certain degree of independence but the lack of social interaction means that working at home can be a lonely experience.

EXERCISE 3   What are the key words in the following text-completion questions?

Questions 1–4   Complete the sentences below. Use *NO MORE THAN THREE WORDS*.

1 Without office technology we couldn't _____.
2 With fewer requirements for space, businesses _____.
3 Despite political pressure, public transport is still _____.
4 The social aspects of working in an office must not be _____

Now use the text on page 42 to complete *Exercises 3, 4* and *5*.

EXERCISE 4

Questions 5–9   Complete the summary by using words from the box below.

Technology has allowed us to **(5)** ____ at home instead of the office. For the company, there are **(6)** _____ incentives and for the employee there is more **(7)** _____. There are even **(8)** _____ for the environment. However, there is a **(9)** _____ factor to be considered.

benefits   psychological   workplace   friendships   conduct business   financial   flexibility   release

REVIEW   **Headings (Unit 1.7)**

Questions 10–15   Choose the appropriate heading for each paragraph of the following text from the list below.

List of headings

i   Time for a change?
ii   Social impact
iii   Management decisions
iv   Flexibility of technology
v   Wasted time on the road
vi   Technology keeping us at home
vii   Benefits for all
viii   Business in the workplace
ix   Keeping it clean
x   The best of both worlds

10 Paragraph A
11 Paragraph B
12 Paragraph C
13 Paragraph D
14 Paragraph E
15 Paragraph F

Working from home

A Can you feel your anxiety and stress levels increasing every time you get caught in a traffic jam? Do you find it difficult to control your tongue when your boss points out your shortcomings yet again? Do you just not have the right kind of office attire, hate spending hours shopping for it and, frankly, would feel much better if you only had more independence, more freedom, more flexible hours and fewer people on your back? Do you yearn for state-of-the-art technology in your home, that ... wait for it ... you haven't had to pay for? If you are shouting an enthusiastic 'Yes!' in answer to these questions, then it could be time to make a career and life change that may not even require you to quit your job. Just suggest to your boss that you wish to become one of the new breed of executives whose office is based at home.

B Working from home is a relatively new phenomenon, but is becoming an increasingly popular option with both businesses and employees. The technology available to us now means that we no longer need to be in the same office building as our colleagues to communicate effectively with each other. E-mail, video conferencing, mobile telephones and more, mean that we can do business just as efficiently, regardless of our location.

C Companies may choose to employ a proportion of their staff as home-based workers, as, of course, a workforce set up in such a way requires far less office space and fewer parking facilities. The fixed costs of a business can be dramatically reduced. Employees can enjoy the added benefits of freedom to schedule the day as they choose and freedom to spend more time at home with their families. Working from home can be a particularly valid option for young mothers who wish to pursue their careers but find it impossible to be out of the house for nine or ten hours per day.

D We can even go so far as to say that the working-from-home phenomenon could be one of the answers to the pollution problems which the modern world has inflicted upon itself. Fewer people travelling to work every day equals fewer cars. Fewer cars, of course, equates to lower CO_2 levels in the atmosphere. Governments have been trying for years to persuade us to forsake our private car journey to work each day for the hideous experience of a crowded bus or train. Most of us have been resistant, even when parking fees in city areas have been on the rise and unpredictable traffic patterns mean we have to leave our house 30 minutes earlier than necessary anyway. But working from home gives us no excuse whatsoever to emit CO_2 into the atmosphere twice a day in our working week.

E But what are the drawbacks to working from home? There must be some or everybody would be doing it. For many of us, work is a means of escaping our nearest and dearest and making our own mark on the world. The relationships we have with our colleagues, be they good or bad, are a significant part of our life – after all, full-time workers spend a third of their day in their workplace. After-hours pursuits of a game of squash or a pint in the pub become part of our daily routine. We cement sound friendships at work and an astounding percentage of us meet our life partner at our place of work. The people there have similar ambitions and business interests and we are, after all, social animals. The majority of us become depressed and withdrawn if we do not have enough interaction with others. Some people who work from home feel that, because they do spend a large proportion of the day at home alone with few distractions, they are actually much more productive and can get tasks done in a much shorter time than in an office environment. Others, however, may be demotivated by the isolation and find it difficult to get down to tasks which have a more intangible deadline.

F As with most aspects of life, a balance is probably the best solution for the majority of workers – a job based at home which requires regular contact with colleagues at regular meetings. Management surveys show that successful business is easier if we operate as a team: brainstorming and sharing ideas and offering support and motivation to each other. After all, we are only human and we need others to complain to if we have a bad day at work!

Unit 2.8   Writing an introduction to Task I

EXERCISE 1   Look at the graph below and the paragraph to the right. Where do you think the paragraph would fit in the essay? Why?

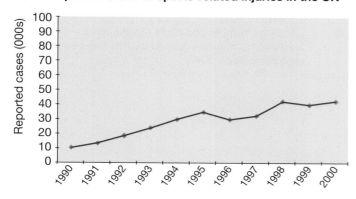

Reported cases of sports-related injuries in the UK

> According to the graph, I can see a rising trend in the number of injuries connected to sport. It's really interesting. It can be divided into three distinct periods as I will now explain.

EXERCISE 2   The introduction is not very good. What do you think the main weaknesses are?

EXERCISE 3   Look at the table below. Decide if the points on the left are good or bad when writing an introduction.

		Good idea	Bad idea
a	Vocabulary like *really interesting*		
b	Rephrasing the words from the graph (... *injuries connected to sport* ...)		
c	Giving a general overview of the graph (... *three distinct periods* ...)		
d	Using the construction *I can see*		
e	Giving the reader an indication of the essay's structure (... *as I will now explain* ...)		

POINT OF IMPACT   The first paragraph of your Task I essay (the introduction) should summarise what is in the graph, but be careful not to copy the title of the graph directly. Instead, use parallel expressions.

EXERCISE 4   Look at the three introductory sentences below and work out some rules for using the words in italics. *There is no graph for this exercise.*

The graph shows the population of America.
The graph shows *that* the population of America *increased*.
As can be seen from the graph, the population of America *increased*.

EXERCISE **5**   Match the introductory phrases below with an appropriate ending. Sometimes more than one answer is possible.

a	The graph shows...
b	It is clear from the graph ...
c	It can be seen from the graph ...
d	As is shown by the graph,...
e	As is illustrated by the graph,...
f	From the graph it is clear...
g	As the graph shows, ...

1	...the rising degree of reported cases of sports-related injuries in the UK.
2	...there has been a rising trend in sports-related injuries in the UK since 1990.
3	...that the number of people registered as suffering from sports-related injuries has been increasing since 1990.

REVIEW   **Preparing a plan for Task I (Unit 2.1)**

Write a plan for the graph below using the five points.

1 Topic words?
2 Tense?
3 Axes?
4 About?
5 Trends?

ESSAY TASK

The chart below shows days taken off work due to stress-related illnesses by job for men and women.

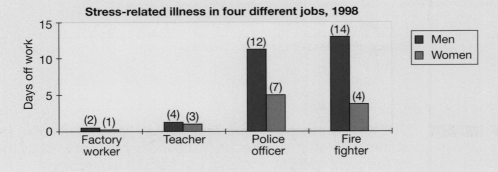

Stress-related illness in four different jobs, 1998

EXERCISE **6**   Now write an introduction for this report.

Unit 2.9   Giving and justifying opinions

EXERCISE 1   What's wrong with the following?

I don't like museums or theatres. They are boring and have no value. People should realise that and stop going, and the government should definitely stop funding and supporting the arts. The money would be better spent on more popular forms of entertainment.

POINT OF IMPACT   When you are asked for your opinion on a subject, you can avoid sounding too dogmatic* by using suitable language to present what you have to say.

The sentence '*The arts are boring and have no value*' would sound better phrased as:

I think *the arts are boring, and* **to me** *they have no value.*

*Being sure that your beliefs are right without need of proof or evidence.

EXERCISE 2   What other words or phrases of opinion do you know? Write them down.

EXERCISE 3   Look at some of the extreme opinions below. How could you make them less dogmatic?

1 Students only fail the IELTS exam because they don't listen to the teacher.
2 Foreigners should not be allowed to buy houses in other countries.
3 Passports should be abolished.
4 Single-sex classes make learning easier.
5 Nobody should eat meat.

POINT OF IMPACT   The IELTS speaking test is like most conversations. If you give an opinion, you should *justify it* and, if possible, offer a **reason, solution or speculation**.

'I don't think people should automatically be entitled to three weeks' holiday a year, *because companies may need their labour.* **As I see it, two weeks' holiday a year is acceptable, with any additional days off acting as an incentive for overtime.**'

Whenever you state an opinion, either in the speaking or the writing test, ask yourself *why*. This will often lead you to think of how to justify what you have said.

EXERCISE 4　Respond to the statements below. *Justify* the opinion you give.

a　Everybody should be entitled to at least three weeks' holiday a year.
b　There is no need to settle into a career until the age of 30.
c　Women should not put a career before family.
d　Visa regulations should be relaxed for foreign students.
e　Men are worse drivers than women are.

Unit 2.10　Multiple choice (listening)

Multiple-choice questions in the listening section have two basic styles. There are normally three or four possible answers.

1　Answering a short question.	What did the student say about the lecture? **A** It was boring. **B** He couldn't understand. **C** He had heard it before. **D** He disagreed with the lecturer.
2　Completing a sentence, where the 'question' is the first half of the sentence, and the answer is the second half.	One of the most notable changes in our leisure time is that **A** we have longer holidays **B** we get paid more for our holidays **C** people are increasingly going abroad.

EXERCISE 1　What could you do to prepare for the following question?

The pohutukawa tree has
A yellow flowers
B dark orange flowers
C red flowers.

POINT OF IMPACT　Multiple choice in the IELTS test can be difficult because very often there is no grammatical or logical reason to reject any of the answers. When the answers have similarities and differences, the first thing you can do is highlight the **differences** between the options. In *Exercise 1* listening only for the word *flower* is obviously not good enough, as all the options include the word. Instead, concentrate on the colours. Remember that in most questions, parallel expressions may be used to express the same information.

EXERCISE 2　Highlight the differences between these multiple-choice answers.

The student
A is joining a gym
B wants to become a member of the library
C is asking about video club membership.

POINT OF IMPACT In some multiple-choice questions, however, there are no real similarities. In this case, the second thing you can do is think of other ways the information may be expressed. Look at the example below.

What does Professor Roberts say about sports injuries?	Could be expressed as
A Apply an ice pack to the injured area.	Put/press / something cold/frozen / painful/hurt
B Bandage the area firmly and rest.	Wrap/bind tightly/hard / relax/sit down
C Call for medical help only in serious cases.	Contact the doctor/ an ambulance / not trivial/light

EXERCISE 3 Look at the following multiple-choice questions. Find some parallel words and phrases for them.

1 Emiliano is hoping to rent a house for
  A 8 months
  B 6 months
  C 7 months
  D 12 months.

2 As proof of identity, Emiliano gives his
  A passport and student card
  B passport and bank card
  C student card and bank card
  D student card and driving licence.

3 Emiliano can be contacted
  A on his mobile
  B by leaving a message at his homestay
  C by telephoning his school
  D by e-mail.

4 Emiliano is looking for a house which is less than
  A half an hour away by bus
  B one hour away by bus
  C one hour away by bus or train
  D half an hour away by bus or train.

5 He can find the weekly cost of the house by
  A asking the estate agent
  B looking at the house list
  C looking at the sign outside the house
  D asking the owner of the house.

6 When he moves out, Emiliano will get back
  A his deposit and agent fee
  B the equivalent of one week's rent
  C his deposit
  D the equivalent of one week's rent and his deposit.

EXERCISE 4 Now listen to the recording and answer the questions in *Exercise 3*.

POINT OF IMPACT Although only one answer is correct, you will often hear some or all of the choices mentioned in the listening. Be careful to think about what is being said, what is being contradicted (directly or indirectly) and what is not exactly being said.

EXERCISE 5 Make a few notes on the multiple-choice question below. Look for similarities and differences as well as alternative ways of expressing the information.

According to the speaker, why do more people rent rather than buy their houses?
A Most people do not have the money to put down as a deposit.
B There are fewer worries about maintenance and repairs.
C Job mobility means people do not want to make long-term commitments.
D There is a risk of buying a house and losing money.

EXERCISE **6**   Now listen to the recording and put a letter (A–D) in each of the columns below.

The correct answer	Directly contradicted	Indirectly contradicted	Not exact

EXERCISE **7**   Look at the multiple-choice question below. What is wrong with the notes on the right?

Sports psychologist Dr Johnson argues that today's top athletes
A win because of a positive mental attitude   They feel positive.
B occasionally use performance-enhancing drugs   They take drugs.
C are under considerable pressure from the media.   They talk to people from newspapers, etc.

POINT OF IMPACT   When answering multiple-choice questions it is also very important to consider the whole statement, especially if you are making notes before the listening begins. Focusing on single words is not an accurate skill as the speaker(s) may not phrase the answer in the manner you are expecting.

EXERCISE **8**   Make notes on the following multiple-choice questions, using all the skills you have learned.

1 Who is the speaker addressing?
   A property agents
   B people selling houses
   C people in the countryside
   D people buying second homes

2 Rental property in the city
   A is very easy to find
   B is becoming more difficult to find
   C is an investment opportunity
   D is often the only option.

3 Lisa Brown believes
   A most people will own their own home at some time
   B there is a psychological factor involved in owning your own home
   C most young people need a deposit before they can buy a house.

4 Property in the countryside is becoming more popular because
   A people want to get away from the city
   B some parts of the city are becoming overcrowded
   C the concept of the home office means that some people don't need to go into work
   D public transport is beginning to serve outlying areas.

5 What kind of properties does the speaker specialise in?
   A commercial
   B investment
   C first homes
   D rural

EXERCISE 9	Now listen to the recording and answer Questions 1–10. The first five questions are in *Exercise 8*.

REVIEW   **Short-answer questions (Unit 1.10)**

Answer the following questions using **NO MORE THAN THREE WORDS**.

6 What end of the market are the properties?
7 What does the speaker compare buying houses with?
8 What is the danger in buying a property when the market is high?
9 How does she describe careful but successful property investment?
10 How can you ask the speaker a question?

Unit 2.11   Building a paragraph

EXERCISE 1	Below is the first sentence of a paragraph. What do you think this paragraph is going to be about?

Nothing has had more of a negative impact on modern lifestyles than stress.

POINT OF IMPACT   A good paragraph often begins with a sentence explaining what the paragraph is about. Learning how to write a topic sentence can help you organise your essay into a cohesive format and it will also help you with your reading.

EXERCISE 2	Which of the sentences below is the most appropriate 'topic' sentence for the paragraph that follows? Why?

a   It is important to remember that there are positive and negative aspects to stress.
b   It is important to analyse why stress has become so common.
c   The problems of stress are not particularly widespread; they mostly concern people in the workplace.

On the one hand, it is commonly linked with medical problems such as headaches and heart problems. It causes sufferers to become both less productive in the workplace and less sociable in their private lives. On the other hand, stress is a natural warning sign, telling us that we are in danger of overtaxing ourselves and giving us the opportunity to slow down. The combination of overwork, lack of relaxation and poor diet are all contributory factors.

EXERCISE 3	Read the following paragraphs and write suitable topic sentences.

A It provides an important release from the tensions of the workplace, allowing us an outlet for our energies in an increasingly hectic world. There is also the social aspect, as people often use their leisure time to interact with others in a society that is becoming arguably less sociable.

B Traditional foods with better nutritional values are often overlooked as being time consuming and laborious and are often rejected in favour of more convenient options. Another reason that could account for this is the financial factor: the cost of a McDonald's meal can often be considerably cheaper than a balanced and well-prepared meal cooked at home.

C The clearest indication of this is the brevity of most e-mails. In a letter, we would never consider communicating with a single word or phrase, yet it is perfectly acceptable to do so using a computer. There is also the personal aspect: reliance on e-mail communication is undeniably distancing us from more direct contact, even the telephone. However, we cannot underestimate the convenience of e-mail, especially in situations which involve long-distance communication.

POINT OF IMPACT   In essays, paragraphs usually have a standard format.
- The first or second sentence introduces the topic.
- The next few sentences should support and develop the theme of the topic sentence.

The last sentence in each paragraph can do one of three things. It can:
- lead into the next paragraph
- summarise the paragraph you are finishing
- paraphrase the topic sentence.

EXERCISE 4   Read the following sentences and arrange them into a short paragraph.

a   There are also options for those who do not want to spend too much.
b   Equipment, from rowing machines to workout videos, is readily available for those wishing to create their own 'home gym'.
c   Even so, there are still some people who have difficulty finding the time and discipline to exercise regularly.
d   Reasonable membership costs for local gyms and clubs provide ample opportunity for the amateur interested in a little exercise.
e   These days, there are many ways to keep fit.

POINT OF IMPACT   A good paragraph may also contain a qualifying statement or concession. By giving an opposite or contrasting point of view you can give a sense of balance to your essay as well as add a few extra words to your total.

EXERCISE 5   Now complete a paragraph based on the following topic sentence:

People are turning to more extreme sports as a result of increasingly uneventful lives.

Make a few notes before you start writing.

Unit 2.12   Topic Card: Leisure interests

POINT OF IMPACT   In the speaking test, remember to use a variety of accurate sentence structures, including the use of tenses. That means not only using the present and past simple!

EXERCISE 1   What tenses could you use to talk about the topic below?

> Describe something you enjoyed doing as a child.
> You should say:
> • what you did
> • when you did it
> • if you still do it.
> You should also say why you enjoyed it so much.

EXERCISE 2   Write one sentence for each grammar form below based on the topic card in *Exercise 1*.

a 'used to'
b past simple
c present perfect
d past perfect

EXERCISE 3   Now work with a partner and practise the interview. One of you should act as the candidate and the other should be the interviewer. The interviewer should make notes using the following headings.

• Is there a variety of tenses?
• Are they used accurately?
• Does the speaker sound confident?

UNIT 3

The world around us

Unit 3.1 Parallel expressions (reading)

EXERCISE 1 Read the short text below and answer the questions that follow. Use words from the text.

There is a dark corporate conspiracy at work in the petroleum industry. On television and in the media we are constantly bombarded with images of green trees and bright blue skies, promised a fuel that is '97% cleaner than ever before' and told we are heading towards 'a healthier future'. Yet the reality is nowhere near as appealing. Our cities are becoming increasingly polluted as the number of cars continues to rise and petrol emissions show no sign of easing. Much like car manufacturers who market their products under the image of freedom and independence, we are being sold a fantasy which simply does not hold true.

A Who is responsible for the shadowy scheme of selling dreams, not the truth? _____

B What images are we constantly bombarded with? _____

C Who sells their product as a symbol of independence? _____

> **POINT OF IMPACT** In the IELTS reading test, you can find answers by:
> 1 matching exact phrases in the text
> 2 scanning for matching words
> 3 looking for parallel expressions.

EXERCISE 2 Which of the questions in *Exercise 1* match the description in the Point of Impact above?

Question	Point of Impact number
A	
B	
C	

POINT OF IMPACT   Locating parallel expressions is an essential IELTS skill. It involves *transforming* vocabulary into words or phrases which have the same or similar meaning as the original.

This can be done by different word families.
Our cities are becoming increasingly polluted.   *Pollution is increasing in our cities.*

Or with different vocabulary.
Yet the reality is nowhere near as appealing.   *The truth, however, is far less attractive.*

EXERCISE 3   Practise by completing the chart below.

Noun	Person	Verb	Passive	Adjective	Adverb	Alternative vocabulary
pollution pollutant	–	to pollute	be polluted	polluted	–	SYNONYM contaminant, impurity, toxin, effluence ANTONYM clean
	ecologist					SYNONYM ANTONYM
					naturally	SYNONYM ANTONYM
			be endangered			SYNONYM ANTONYM
industry						SYNONYM ANTONYM
		to conserve				SYNONYM ANTONYM
				destructive		SYNONYM ANTONYM

EXERCISE 4   Rewrite the sentences so they have the same meaning but use as much different vocabulary as possible.

A The environmental impact of the increasing number of cars on the road is devastating.

B Without a convenient and economical public transport system, people will continue to use their cars for most journeys.

C The situation is intensified by the rising number of two-car families.

D Car-sharing schemes, where people travel together in one vehicle, have not been particularly successful.

E Although contaminants in petrol have been reduced, they still pose a significant threat.

F The lack of government legislation to control exhaust fumes, especially from older cars, has exacerbated the problem.

G In addition to environmental damage, increased air pollution has direct health consequences.

H Respiratory diseases have increased, especially within inner-city areas.

I Benzene, a by-product of the combustion of petrol, has been linked to birth defects.

J Yet while the car retains its image of freedom and individuality, it is unlikely that people will opt to take the bus.

EXERCISE 5 Practise your predicting skills by completing these questions with a possible answer or type of answer.

1 A deterioration in lakes and forests in northern Europe was first noticed in _____
2 Pollution in rain is a result of _____
3 Nearly half of manmade sources of acid rain are due to _____
4 Some animals have declined in number by over 50% because of scarcer _____
5 Land used for farming is becoming _____
6 Urban household water supplies are contaminated by _____
7 Air pollution is travelling further as it is disgorged through _____
8 Legislation passed in the 1980s and the 1990s was a response to _____

EXERCISE 6 Now rewrite the sentences using parallel expressions.

Example

In (probably a time), people in Europe observed a decline in the quality of its lakes and forests.

EXERCISE 7 Questions 1–8 from *Exercise 5* are based on the reading passage below. Complete the sentences using words from the text. You should write **NO MORE THAN THREE WORDS**.

READING PASSAGE 1

Poison rain

A In the late 1970s, people in northern Europe were observing a change in the lakes and forests around them. Areas once famous for the quality and quantity of their fish began to decline, and areas of once-green forest were dying. The phenomenon they witnessed was acid rain – pollutants in rain, snow, hail and fog caused by sulphuric and nitric acids.

B The principal chemicals that cause these acids are sulphur dioxide and oxides of nitrogen, both by-products of burning fossil fuels (coal, oil and gas). A percentage of acid rain is natural, from volcanoes, forest fires and biological decay, but the majority is unsurprisingly manmade. Of this, transportation sources account for 40%; power plants 30%; industrial sources 25%; and commercial institutions and residues 5%. What makes these figures particularly disturbing is that since the 1970s, nitrogen oxide emissions have tripled. Each year the global atmosphere is polluted with 20 billion tons of carbon dioxide, 130 million tons of sulphur dioxide, more than three million tons of toxic metals, and a wealth of synthetic organic compounds, many of which are proven causes of cancer, genetic mutations and birth defects.

C For natural causes of acid rain, nature has provided a filter. Naturally occurring substances such as limestone or other antacids can neutralise this acid rain before it enters the water cycle, thereby protecting it. However, areas with a predominantly quartzite- or granite-based geology and little top soil have no such effect, and the basic environment shifts from an alkaline to an acidic one. Recycled and intensified through the water table, acid rain has reached such a degree in some parts of the world that rainfall is now 40 times more acidic than normal – the same acidic classification as vinegar.

D Environmentally, the impact is devastating. Lakes and the life they support are dying, unable to withstand such a battering. This has a direct effect on the animals that rely on fish as a food source. Certain species of American otter have had their numbers reduced by over half in the last 20 years, for example. Yet this is not the only effect. Nitrogen oxides, the principal reagent in acid rain, react with other pollutants to produce ozone, a major air pollutant responsible for destroying the productivity of farmland. With scientists working on producing ever bigger and longer lasting genetically modified foods, some farmers are reporting abnormally low yields. Tomatoes grow to only half their full weight and the leaves, stalks and roots of other crops never reach full maturity.

E Naturally it rains on cities too, eating away stone monuments and concrete structures, and corroding the pipes which channel the water away to the lakes where the cycle is repeated. Paint exposed to rain is not lasting as long due to the pollution in the atmosphere speeding up the corrosion process. In some communities the drinking water is laced with toxic metals freed from metal pipes by the acidity. After any period of non-use, we are encouraged to run taps for at least 60 seconds to flush any excess debris, as increased concentrations of metals in plumbing such as lead, copper and zinc result in adverse health effects. As if urban skies were not already grey enough, typical visibility has declined from ten to four miles, in many American cities, as acid rain turns into smog. Also, now there are indicators that the components of acid rain are a health risk, linked to human respiratory disease.

F Acid rain itself is not an entirely new phenomenon. In the nineteenth century, acid rain fell both in towns and cities. What is new, and of great concern, is that it can be transported thousands of kilometres due to the introduction of tall chimneys dispersing pollutants high into the atmosphere, allowing strong wind currents to blow the acid rain hundreds of miles from its source. Thus the areas where acid rain falls are not necessarily the areas where the pollution comes from. Pollution from industrial areas of England are damaging forests in Scotland and Scandinavia. Acids from the Midwest United States are blown into northwest Canada. More and more regions are beginning to be affected, and given that 13 of the world's most polluted cities are in neighbouring Asia, countries like Australia and New Zealand are increasingly under threat.

G Transboundary pollution, the spread of acid rain across political and international borders, has prompted a number of international responses. International legislation during the 1980s and 1990s has led to reductions in sulphur dioxide emissions in many countries but reductions in emissions of nitrogen oxides have been much less, leading to the conclusion that without a cooperative global effort, the problem of acid rain will not simply blow away.

REVIEW   **Headings (Unit 1.7)**

Answer the following questions.

The text in *Exercise 7* has seven sections A–G. Choose the most suitable heading for the paragraphs from the list below.

List of headings	
i	How it affects us
ii	A global problem
iii	Recent changes in Europe
iv	Artificial causes of acid rain
v	Metals in acid rain
vi	International reactions
vii	The indirect dangers
viii	First signs
ix	Acid rain in Asia
x	Effects of the natural environment

9 Paragraph A

10 Paragraph B

11 Paragraph C

12 Paragraph D

13 Paragraph E

14 Paragraph F

15 Paragraph G

Unit 3.2 — Describing approximate data

EXERCISE 1   What is wrong with this description of the pie chart?

In most municipal landfills, 22% is paper. Garden refuse accounts for a further 22%. Kitchen refuse is 11% and plastic is 1% more at 12%. Wood accounted for 10%. Textile and rubber, metal and glass is 5%, 5% and 2% respectively, and 11% was composed of all remaining sources of waste.

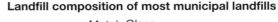
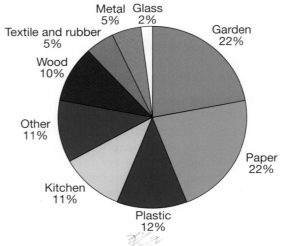

Landfill composition of most municipal landfills

- Metal 5%
- Glass 2%
- Textile and rubber 5%
- Garden 22%
- Wood 10%
- Other 11%
- Paper 22%
- Kitchen 11%
- Plastic 12%

POINT OF IMPACT

Remember that in the IELTS exam you should use a variety of sentences and structures. When dealing with data, you should use as many different descriptions as possible to avoid repetition or simply listing numbers.

EXERCISE 2   Write down any alternative ways of expressing the information shown in *Exercise 1*.

EXERCISE 3   Use an alternative below to express the percentages that follow.

a tenth	a third	slightly more than a fifth	slightly less than a third	three quarters	nearly half
half	a quarter	just over three quarters	a fifth	the vast majority/ almost all	over half

a 10%   b 20%   c 25%   d 22%   e 31%   f 33%
g 48%   h 50%   i 57%   j 75%   k 77%   l 95%

POINT OF IMPACT

In Task I, you often have to describe quantities, not only as percentages but also in other forms. Again, be careful to use a wide range of structures.

EXERCISE 4   Put these expressions of quantity in order of size: the vast majority / a few / a considerable number / a minority / almost none / the majority / all / many / very few

Biggest ◄─────────────────────────────────────► Smallest

1 _____	2 _____	3 _____	4 _____ 5 _____	6 _____ 7 _____	8 _____ 9 _____

EXERCISE	5	Write a sentence for each of the quantity expressions from *Exercise 4*. Your sentences should be about recycling, a topic related to the theme of 'The world around us'. Example: <u>All</u> *governments should encourage their citizens to recycle to the utmost practical degree.*

EXERCISE	6	Here are some more useful phrases for giving more information about data. Match a graph with a sentence below.

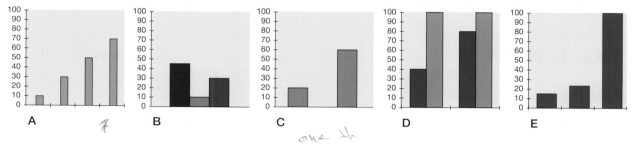

A   B   C   D   E

1   X was the largest producer, with 45% of the total production.
2   There were three times as many users as in the previous year.
3   Exports doubled, to reach 80% of imports.
4   Pollution levels rose at a rate of one-fifth per annum.
5   The number of users increased five-fold.

EXERCISE	7	Now practise using as many different expressions as possible in the essay task below.

ESSAY TASK

The table below shows the attitudes to recycling of people in different age groups.

Write a report for a university lecturer describing the information shown below.

Opinion \ Age group	5–14	15–25	26–40	41–55	56–70	71+
Actively recycle	8	59	48	47	39	8
Recycle when they remember	21	20	34	26	16	34
Don't know anything about recycling	52	8	4	7	28	42
Preferred not to comment	19	13	14	20	17	16

*All data are percentages

WRITING   WRITING   WRITING   WRITING   WRITING   WRITING   WRITING   WRITING   WRITING

Unit 3.3   Your hometown

Interviewer: Tell me about your hometown.
Candidate: I'm from Bahrain. It has a population of over 600 000. It is quite cool in winter but very hot in summer. The main industries are banking and pearl diving. Oil is not so important.

EXERCISE 1   How could the dialogue above be improved?

POINT OF IMPACT   To get the best result, give some detail to your answers and think of some aspects particular to your hometown.

EXERCISE 2   Add phrases from the box below into the dialogue.

> which is quite small in comparison with some of our Middle Eastern neighbours.
>
> in the Arabian Gulf.
>
> although tourism is becoming increasingly important.
>
> I much prefer the cooler weather.
>
> yet many people think it is our main source of revenue.

EXERCISE 3   Copy the diagram below. Write the name of your hometown in the box, and write about some things which are only found in your hometown.

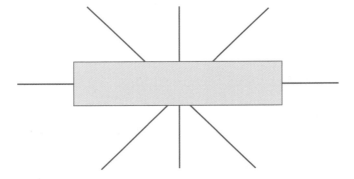

EXERCISE 4   Now write a paragraph about your hometown.

POINT OF IMPACT   Too much practice does not always make perfect! Reciting a speech you have prepared about your hometown will sound rehearsed and your intonation will suffer.

EXERCISE 5	Student A: Tell your partner about your hometown. Student B: Take notes about your partner's hometown.

When you have finished, change roles.

Unit 3.4   Numbers, dates and letters (listening)

EXERCISE 1   Match the numbers below with a word from the box.

a clock time	b distance	c fraction	d address	e telephone number
f date	g decimal	h money	i per cent	j Roman numeral

1 $^3/_4$
2 5.74
3 $56.95
4 26/02/71
5 9.30

6 60%
7 III
8 021 4573458
9 900 km
10 16A

EXERCISE 2   In the listening test, some answers may be in *number* form. What kind of situations may involve numbers? *Use Exercise 1 to help you.*

POINT OF IMPACT	Some instructions will ask you to use **NO MORE THAN THREE WORDS OR A NUMBER**. Obviously this is a good indication that you may be asked to write a number! Make sure you write the correct figure. One thousand = 1000 Half a million = 500 000 One million = 1 000 000 One billion = 1 000 000 000

EXERCISE 3   Complete the table below. The first one has been done for you.

a Twelve thousand six hundred and eighteen	=	12 618
b Seventeen thousand and two	=	
c	=	74 272
d Eight million four hundred thousand	=	
e One million, four hundred and twenty-two thousand six hundred and nineteen	=	
f	=	7 818 614 993

EXERCISE 4   Listen to the recording and note down all the numbers you hear. What do they refer to?

POINT OF IMPACT   Telephone numbers are often delivered in blocks of three or four digits at one time. For example:

266...0619   021... 466... 5688

EXERCISE 5   John Edwards's 27th birthday was one month ago today. Complete this short form with his personal details.

Name _John Edwards_
D.O.B. ____/____/_____

Now complete the gaps in the following dialogue between John and his friend.

Julie: Hi John. Happy birthday!
John: You're too late. My birthday was in _____, on the _____.

POINT OF IMPACT   A number of different constructions are used to talk about dates. For example:

The 26th of February, 1971   February the 26th, 1971
The 26th of the 2nd, 71

EXERCISE 6   Listen to the recording and write down the ten dates you hear and what they refer to. *Write the date in the construction you hear.*

POINT OF IMPACT   Practise numbers, dates and letters by listening to the radio or watching the news on television, then checking your answers either on the Internet or with your teacher.

Unit 3.5   Preparing a plan for Task II

POINT OF IMPACT   You have 40 minutes to do Task II for the academic module of the IELTS test – that is, you must write an essay, starting from now! Tick, tick, tick. What do you do? How do you do it? Tick, tick, tick. Immediately start writing anything, right? Wrong! It is very important that your essay shows some organisation and must be planned!

You have already looked at brainstorming (Unit 1.5) and topic and task words (Unit 2.5). Now you need to prepare a plan that puts these skills together.

Modern technology has made great improvements in the efficiency of the workplace. As a result, employees should only be working a four-day week.

EXERCISE 1   In Task II you are often asked to consider two sides of an argument or opinion. Rewrite the title above as a direct question.

POINT OF IMPACT   Once you have rephrased the title into a direct question, it often becomes easier to divide it into two parts. For example, in *Exercise 1* the two parts would be:

Should we work a four-day week?
1 Yes we should – more free time for workers.
2 No we shouldn't – less productive for the country.

Notice that by dividing the question, it becomes easier to prepare a plan. Also remember that you do not need to write complete sentences in your plan – short notes are good enough.

EXERCISE 2   Look at the following essay titles. Rephrase the title into a direct question and identify both sides.

a The number of vehicles on the road is having a serious environmental impact. In order to clean the air, governments should place a higher tax on private cars.
b In many countries, students can stay in further education until their mid-20s. However, any education students receive that does not prepare them for future employment is a waste. Do you agree or disagree?
c Global warming is becoming an increasing danger, yet many countries are still not addressing the problem. Do you agree or disagree?
d Celebrities from sport or the media are often paid many times the average wage. Should famous people be so well-paid when the money could go to other causes?
e Many people lead unhealthy lifestyles. It is therefore not the duty of the government to offer free healthcare. To what extent do you agree?

POINT OF IMPACT   For every Task II essay you write throughout the rest of this course, follow these steps.
1 Identify the topic and task words (rephrase the question if necessary).
2 Brainstorm for ideas.
3 Identify any opposing arguments within the question (if possible).
4 Reject weaker points.

EXERCISE 3   Use the steps in the Point of Impact to prepare a plan for this essay.

ESSAY TASK

Modern appliances in the home have become common, leaving no doubt that advances in technology have improved our lifestyle.

Do you agree or disagree?

EXERCISE 4   Add more points to the columns below.

Yes (Agree)	No (Disagree)
• labour-saving electrical goods (e.g. washing machines save hours every week on handwashing clothes)	• people are constantly competing to have the most modern devices (and are therefore at the mercy of each advertisement that offers something new)

EXERCISE 5   Once you have completed this part of the plan, you have to decide how to structure your essay. The standard format has an introduction, three to five body paragraphs and a conclusion. How would you divide the plan you made into paragraphs?

POINT OF IMPACT   As you develop your plan, it becomes easier to prepare a suitable introduction. By using the plan to write your introduction, you are making sure that the essay flows well.

Impact of innovations and inventions on our daily lives – increased dramatically – has both positive and negative aspects. Definitely some improvements – couldn't live without. However, negatives – equally definable.

You will look more at writing an introduction in Unit 4.11.

EXERCISE 6   Prepare a plan and develop your paragraphs using the Task II title at the top of the page.

Unit 3.6   Describing places

POINT OF IMPACT   In Unit 3.3 you talked about your hometown. In the speaking test, you could be asked to describe more about where you are from, for example the weather or the countryside.

EXERCISE 1   Look at the list of vocabulary below. Do they refer to weather, countryside or opinion? Write W, C or O beside each word. You can write more than one letter.

awe-inspiring	tropical	peaceful	amazing	breathtaking	humid
serene	rugged	lively	packed	mountainous	pleasant
clear	spectacular	hilly	green	sun-drenched	

EXERCISE 2   Complete the following description using words from *Exercise 1*.

Well, one place I love in New Zealand is Tongariro National Park. You can do the Tongariro circuit – you walk right around the mountains, staying in huts. It takes about three days. The views are absolutely **(a)**_____ – on a **(b)**_____ day you can see all the way to Mount Taranaki in the west. It can be extremely hot, yet as with any **(c)**_____ environment, the temperature can drop incredibly quickly, so you have to be prepared. At weekends or holidays, it can get a little crowded, and some nights the huts are **(d)**_____, but everyone is so **(e)**_____. I must have said 'Hello' a hundred times a day when I was there!

EXERCISE 3   Look at the words in italics in *Exercise 2*. What purpose do they serve?

POINT OF IMPACT   When you want to emphasise your opinion on something, use *intensifiers*.

so   such   very   incredibly   amazingly
astoundingly   absolutely   outstandingly

EXERCISE 4   Now write a short paragraph about one of your favourite places using the language presented in *Exercises 1, 2* and *3. Do not write about your hometown.*

Unit 3.7   Short-answer questions (reading)

From the beginning of civilisation, people have always been awed by the power of nature. Even now, when technology and science have combined in an attempt to harness its power and reduce its impact, nature still has the ability to demonstrate how little we are really in control.

EXERCISE 1   Read the question below. If this was an IELTS test, which answer (a or b) would be better? Why?

According to the paragraph above, how do people feel about the power of nature?

a   The writer states that people have always been awed by nature.
b   Awed.

POINT OF IMPACT   With short-answer questions, always remember that the answer must be short! The instructions for the question will give you a word limit, e.g. Answer the following questions in **NO MORE THAN THREE WORDS.**

Short-answer questions often require you to scan for parallel expressions, matching phrases, words or meanings.

EXERCISE 2   You are going to read a passage about earthquakes. Before you read the text, underline the key words.

a   Who concluded that earthquakes are the result of the movements of tectonic plates?
b   How many types of shock waves are there?
c   Which shock waves are stronger?
d   What do tectonic plates sit on?
e   What kind of earthquake is caused by subterranean experiments?
f   What is the main danger from earthquakes in urban areas?
g   What can be interpreted as a warning sign for earthquakes?
h   Where has earthquake prediction already proved successful?

EXERCISE 3   Now think of some parallel expressions for the questions above.

POINT OF IMPACT   Remember that looking at the question words gives you an idea of the kind of answer to expect. For example, in *Exercise* 2, question 1, the question word is 'Who ...?' so the answer is likely to be a name.

EXERCISE 4   Read the passage below and answer the questions from *Exercise 2*, in *NO MORE THAN THREE WORDS*.

READING PASSAGE 1

On shaky ground

The attempt to understand, measure and predict earthquakes is by no means a modern fascination. Ancient wisdom thought earthquakes were the result of underground winds, while others blamed them on fire spirits living deep underground. It was not until the mid-1800s that Robert Mallet, an Irish engineer, concluded that earthquakes were caused by the movement of plates beneath the earth's surface.

It is now scientifically accepted that earthquakes are the result of underground volcanic forces pushing just beneath the surface, building up until a sudden release of pressure causes a movement of the tectonic plates which cover the earth. These movements are known as shock waves and can be classified into two different categories: primary and secondary.

Primary waves, also called compression waves, travel upwards through the earth and through the earth's crust creating the epicentre of a volcano. They are the most powerful waves and the first to register on a seismograph. Secondary waves travel along the earth's crust moving considerably slower than compression waves as they spread the shock-wave energy from the epicentre outwards. There are three types of earthquake: tectonic, volcanic or artificial. Tectonic earthquakes are caused by movements of the earth's plates far below the surface which make up the crust of the earth. As the plates move over a bed of molten lava, the friction they cause can result in massive shock waves, and, as a result, tectonic earthquakes are the most powerful and destructive. Volcanic earthquakes are generally much smaller and less intense and often signal the creation of a volcano. Finally, there are artificial earthquakes caused by underground atomic testing or the building of new reservoirs, although these rarely cause much damage.

Contrary to what is portrayed in many movies, the main reason for injury or death from an earthquake is being struck by falling objects. With an earthquake's ability to collapse buildings, bridges and any other artificial constructions, people in heavily built-up areas such as Tokyo are particularly vulnerable; but there are other effects. Earthquakes can trigger a number of secondary natural disasters such as flooding, fires or landslides, and the effects are just as dangerous.

By recording and analysing data from foreshocks, a degree of earthquake prediction has been possible. A good example of successful prediction occurred around the Haicheng earthquake of 1975 where nearly 100 000 people were evacuated just two days before the city was completely destroyed. However, earthquake prediction is far from precise and a number of countries are funding further investigation into the subject. Water levels, changes in magnetic fields and even the behaviour of animals could hold the key to predicting when and where an earthquake will occur and how strong it is likely to be.

Questions 1–14 are based on the text below.

READING PASSAGE 2

Tapping the depths

A   It has been predicted that, at the current rate, New Zealand will increase its energy demand by 20% in the next 10 years. It has also been predicted that emissions from fossil fuels could rise by as much as 45%, a statistic that has prompted the government to announce plans to increase renewable energy supplies by nearly 50% as part of a NZ$79 million energy strategy.

B   Of the available options, the cost of establishing efficient solar power sources remains prohibitive and there is opposition to the location of wind farms near populated areas. Most of New Zealand's renewable energy currently comes from hydro schemes, but this solution alone is not sufficient. Indeed, the Energy Minister of New Zealand stated that the country has been slow to utilise its sustainable forms of energy production. However, there is one renewable source of energy that is currently proving itself a viable alternative to fossil fuels: geothermal energy, the heat contained in rocks beneath the earth's surface. Water is injected down a borehole and retrieved after being heated by the rocks.

C In aquifers (porous rocks like limestone and sandstone about 2 km beneath the earth's surface), the water temperature may reach 100 °C, and at 3 km it may exceed 200 °C. The high pressure underground prevents the water from turning to steam, but at the surface it can be allowed to expand and drive a steam turbine linked to an electricity generator. The water is then pumped from the borehole to a heat exchanger from which it can be used for a number of purposes.

D People have been using hot spring water for a very long time – most famously, the Romans 2000 years ago at Bath in England. If sufficiently hot, spring water can be used to provide heating for buildings. It is also possible to use geothermal energy to generate electricity. Of all countries experimenting with its exploitation, New Zealand is leading the field, with geothermal energy accounting for nearly 30% of its total needs as a result of its naturally volcanic environment. No other country has reached 1% as yet, although in the UK it is estimated that geothermal power could supply 10% of electricity for 125 years if it could be exploited efficiently. The world's largest geothermal power station is at Geyserville, California, which generates 1500 MW. Other nations generating electricity this way include China, Indonesia, Japan, Kenya, Mexico, New Zealand, the Philippines and Russia.

	Generating capacity (GW)	% of total
New Zealand	2.21	29.4
USA	1.74	0.25
Pacific region	0.50	0.22
Japan	0.24	0.13
Turkey	0.02	0.11

E Although it fulfils most of the requirements demanded of an alternative energy source, geothermal energy is not a perfect solution. Extracting the heat in large quantities at a particular site lowers the temperature, meaning the site must then be abandoned at least until it recovers, which could take many years. The water contains mineral salts which would eventually corrode or block the boiler systems that extract the energy from the water. In addition, although using geothermal energy does not release carbon dioxide or pollutants, there is the problem of the sulphurous smell of hot aquifers and possibility of radioactive gases such as radon rising in boreholes. Engineers would also need to consider any possible effects on the local geology in unstable regions, such as subsidence or slippage.

REVIEW   **Headings (Unit 1.7)**

Choose the most suitable headings for sections A–E from the list below. Use each heading once only.

List of headings

i	The science of geothermal energy
ii	Water heating
iii	Government planning
iv	The search for perfect solutions
v	Looking at alternatives
vi	Global use
vii	In comparison
viii	Unresolved drawbacks
ix	Problems overcome

Example	Section A	iii
1	Section B	
2	Section C	
3	Section D	
4	Section E	

REVIEW   **Text completion (Unit 2.7)**

Complete the text below using *ONE OR TWO WORDS* from the reading passage.

5 Geothermal energy is the result of extracting heat from water passed through _____.
6 This may provide us with an alternative to _____.
7 Not a new discovery, geothermal energy was first tapped by _____.
8 Only one quarter of a per cent of energy is extracted through this method in _____.
9 As well as blockages, water heated through aquifers is not used in boilers as it causes _____.
10 Potential effects to the surrounding land also have to be taken into account by _____.

REVIEW   **Short-answer questions (this unit)**

Answer the following questions in *NO MORE THAN THREE WORDS*.

11 What is the problem with solar power?
12 What is the advantage in boring deeper into the rock?
13 Why is New Zealand using geothermal energy more than any other country is?
14 What potential emissions from boreholes need further investigation?

Unit 3.8   Comparing and contrasting data

EXERCISE **1**   From the graph below, which country has the highest level of pollution? Which country has the lowest level?

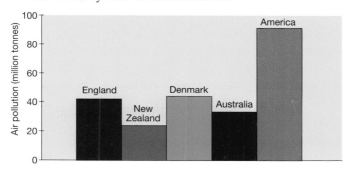

EXERCISE **2**   In *Exercise 1* above, the graphs compare and contrast *countries*. What other variables do you think you could be asked to compare or contrast in different Task I questions?

POINT OF IMPACT   Being able to compare and contrast data is an essential skill for IELTS writing, especially in Task I. Comparatives and superlatives are one of the simplest ways of doing this.

EXERCISE **3**   Complete the table below reviewing comparatives and superlatives.

	example adjective	comparative	superlative
Words with one syllable	high		
Words with three syllables or more	productive		
Words ending in -y	wealthy		
Short words ending with a consonant/vowel/consonant	hot		
Irregular	good		

EXERCISE 4   Write five comparative and five superlative sentences comparing your country with others. *Use different adjectives from those given in the table.*

POINT OF IMPACT   Comparatives and superlatives are useful when comparing and contrasting, but do not forget that you should always aim to use a wide range of structures and vocabulary.

EXERCISE 5   Underline the different types of comparison and contrast.

a   Developed countries are more reliant on alternative energy sources than more developing countries are.
b   Solar power accounts for far less of the total energy production than gas or coal does.
c   The more fossil fuels are used, the higher the level of urban pollution.
d   Hydropower is not as efficient as windpower.
e   Like Japan, South Korea does not produce any natural gas.

EXERCISE 6   Now write five sentences of your own, using each of the comparative structures you underlined in *Exercise 6*. Write about public versus private transport.

EXERCISE 7   Now write the following Task I essay, using a range of comparisons and contrasts. You should first plan the essay, develop an introduction, and use appropriate vocabulary to refer to *approximate data*.

ESSAY TASK

The table below shows the production and consumption of natural gas in different countries in 2001.

Write a report for a university lecturer describing the information shown below.

Natural gas consumption and production, 2001

Country	Consumption*	Production*
The USA	588.9	500.0
The United Kingdom	86.1	97.3
The former Soviet Union	7.1	0.4
The United Arab Emirates	30.0	35.9
Australia	19.1	28.0
Japan	68.6	-
New Zealand	4.9	5.1
South Korea	18.9	-
China	24.3	25.0

*in millions of tonnes

Unit 3.9   Misunderstandings

EXERCISE 1   The interviewer has just asked a question which you did not hear clearly. Which candidate gives the best response?

Examiner: So could you tell me a little more about the influence ***** has had on your society?
Candidate 1:   What?
Candidate 2:   I'm sorry, I didn't catch that. Could you say it again?
Candidate 3:   Oh ... um ... yes, well ... I ...

POINT OF IMPACT   Even among native speakers of a language, people sometimes do not understand everything the first time they hear it. This is natural, so do not feel that this will affect your results. Learn some techniques and phrases and practise them throughout the course, so if there is a misunderstanding during your test your response will be natural.

EXERCISE 2   Look at the five possible problems you may have in the speaking test. Match a situation to a phrase on the right.

1   The interviewer has used a word you do not know.
2   The interviewer has spoken too quickly.
3   The interviewer has just asked you about something you have never thought about.
4   You realise you have just made a mistake.
5   You are not 100% certain, but you think you know what a word means.

A   I'm sorry, could you say that again?
B   Well, that's not something I've ever really thought about, but I suppose ...
C   Sorry, I mean ...
D   If by (X), you mean ...
E   Sorry, I'm not too sure what you mean by (X).

POINT OF IMPACT   If you realise you could have said something better, **do not panic**. Stop, use a suitable phrase and say what you meant to say.

EXERCISE 3   Ask your partner questions based on environmental issues. If any of the situations from *Exercise 2* occur, then use the appropriate vocabulary to clarify.

Unit 3.10   Table completion (listening)

EXERCISE 1   What type of answer would you expect for the table-completion question below?

Complete the table below with *NO MORE THAN THREE WORDS OR A NUMBER*.

Travel Abroad Ltd – summer trips to Europe departing from the UK			
Destination	Paris	Berlin	(1)_____
Mode of transport	(2)_____	Coach	Train
Date of departure	12 May	17 May	(3)_____
Cost of trip	£712	(4)_____	£245
Travel time	Less than two hours	18 hours	2 days

POINT OF IMPACT   *Exercise 1* is a simple example and is a little easier than you can expect in your test, but it shows the basic skills that you should use. With table-completion questions, look at the other data in the table. Often you will see patterns which will indicate the type of information you should be listening for. If one column has nouns, then it is reasonable to expect you are looking for a noun. Also, be logical – use the information you have to roughly predict the information you will be listening for. For example, it is logical that a coach trip will be cheaper than a train trip.

EXERCISE 2   Look at the table below. What could you predict? What different factors is it comparing?

	Sam	John	Mary
Attitude to recycling	Doesn't have time	(1)	(2)
Availability	(3)	No local recycling areas	(4)
Ideas for the future	_____	(5)	A reward scheme for people who recycle

EXERCISE 3   Listen to the recording and complete the table in *Exercise 2. There is no word limit for this exercise.*

POINT OF IMPACT   In table-completion tasks, you are often given two axes with which you need to compare people, places, objects, etc. In the table above, you can expect to compare three peoples' attitudes towards recycling. This means that by looking closely at the columns, you can predict, to some extent, the type of answer to expect.

EXERCISE 4   Look at the table below. Complete the table with a possible type of answer. There is no recording for this exercise.

Complete the table below with *NO MORE THAN THREE WORDS.*

	indicators	frequency	response
earthquake	vibrations, tremors	common	find shelter in doorways or open ground
volcano	heat, escaping gas, rising water temperatures	rare	evacuate the area, find high ground
tsunami			
tornado			close and lock all windows, stay inside
avalanche		occasional	
forest fires	rising air temperature, unusual animal and bird activity		

POINT OF IMPACT There will be times when the two axes of the table are all you have to help you predict the information. You should still apply the skills you have studied. It is also worth remembering that the answers are always in the order of the listening in table-completion questions.

REVIEW   **Short-answer questions (Unit 1.10)**

Listen to the recording and then answer questions 1–10.

Questions 1–4   Answer the following questions using *NO MORE THAN THREE WORDS*.

1 How long is the radio show?
2 What does the programme focus on?
3 Where is Professor Ripley from?
4 According to Professor Ripley, what animals do people most associate with the African bush?

REVIEW   **Table completion (this unit)**

Questions 5–8   Complete the table below using *NO MORE THAN THREE WORDS*.

	Threats	Natural habitat	Population
African lions		bush	(5)_____
Tigers	(6) _____	forests and plains	fewer than (7) _____
Snow leopards	(8) _____	high-altitude pastures	

REVIEW   **Multiple choice (Unit 2.10)**

Circle the appropriate letter A–D.

9 Where is the WWF currently funding projects to help the snow leopard?
   A Nepal, Pakistan and Bhutan
   B Nepal and Pakistan
   C Bhutan and Nepal
   D Pakistan and Bhutan

10 Listeners should telephone
   A immediately if they want to put forward an opinion
   B during the commercial break
   C in 10 minutes if they have anything they want to ask the professor
   D if they have any information regarding pumas or jaguars.

Unit 3.11   Giving and justifying opinions

EXERCISE 1   What do you think of the following?

We should not devote time or resources to endangered species. In many respects this is irrelevant. Some animals may become extinct, but too much money is spent on this kind of nonsense.

POINT OF IMPACT   Although you are expected to present opinions in a Task II essay, you have to be careful not to be too direct. You should avoid being too dogmatic by using suitable language for opinions. Don't feel that you have to express your own opinion in the IELTS test. If you can write more fluently about an opinion that may not be your own, then do so!

The structures below will help you present ideas or opinions without being too direct or dogmatic.

> People argue that ...
> Some people think that ...
> It is understood that ...
> It is generally accepted that ...

EXERCISE 2   Add any other structures you know to the list above.

EXERCISE 3   Now write a sentence expressing an opinion using the following notes.

1 Extinction / natural process / evolution
2 Deforestation / control / international pressure
3 Animals / captivity / immoral
4 Ecotourism / support / government

POINT OF IMPACT   Having given an opinion, you should then justify it. Often this is simply a matter of considering why you believe something.

EXERCISE 4   Look back at *Exercise 3*. Justify the opinions you have made.

EXERCISE 5   In Unit 1.2 you studied a number of linking words and phrases. What is the linking phrase in the sentence below?

It could be argued that green issues have been excessively debated. While I admit that concern for the environment is very important, a more relaxed approach to problems may have better results.

POINT OF IMPACT   Another way of putting forward an argument without being too dogmatic is to make *concessions* by admitting that there are arguments that may differ from your own.
One way of presenting a concession is shown below.

Opinion	Concession	Supporting your opinion
It could be argued that green issues have been excessively debated.	While I admit that concern for the environment is very important,	a more relaxed approach to problems may have better results.

EXERCISE 6   Look at the topics below and write arguments for and against.

Topic	For	Against
a Banning cars in city centres		
b Making public transport free		
c Charging drivers a tax for using motorways		

EXERCISE 7   Now write a short paragraph on each topic from *Exercise 6* beginning with your main argument and then clarifying your view, including making a concession.

EXERCISE 8   Throughout this unit, you have looked at a number of issues related to the world around us. Write a short paragraph related to each of the following headings. Give an opinion, a concession and justification.

POLLUTION   ACID RAIN   GLOBAL WARMING   RECYCLING   NATURAL DISASTERS

EXERCISE 9   Now write the following essay. Remember to include some concessions.

ESSAY TASK

It is the responsibility of governments to ensure that environmentally friendly policies are adopted.

To what extent do you agree?

SPEAKING SPEAKING SPEAKING SPEAKING SPEAKING SPEAKING SPEAKING SPEAKING SPEAKING

Unit 3.12   Topic Card: The world around us

POINT OF IMPACT   As you studied in Unit 3.6, using a range of adjectives is a simple way of expanding what you say and showing the examiner that you have a broad vocabulary.

EXERCISE 1   What adjectives could you use to talk about the topic below?

> Describe a place you would love to visit.
> You should say:
> • where it is
> • what you can do there
> • what is special about it.
> You should also say why you would like to go there more than anywhere else.

EXERCISE 2   Make notes about the topic above.

EXERCISE 3   Now work with a partner and practise the interview. One of you should act as the candidate and the other should be the examiner. The examiner should make notes using the following headings.

• Does the speaker sound keen?
• Are they hesitating too much?
• Can you follow what they are saying?

UNIT 4

Cultural concerns

Unit 4.1	Qualifying words (reading)

EXERCISE 1   Read the short passage below and answer the questions that follow.

For most people, traditional forms of culture have little impact on their daily lives. Opera, fine art, classical literature – these are special events, not the common fare of the average household. Popular culture, on the other hand, dominates almost all of our leisure time. We are becoming a nation with very short attention spans, spending most evenings in front of the TV, with very few people making the effort of actually entertaining themselves.

Questions 1–3   Are the following statements TRUE (T) or FALSE (F)?

1   Traditional culture has no impact on our daily lives.
2   Popular culture dominates all our leisure time.
3   Nobody makes their own entertainment.

POINT OF IMPACT   Do not just look at the verbs or nouns – be careful of qualifying words or phrases such as 'all' and 'nobody'. Qualifying words can specify time, amount or degree.

EXERCISE 2   Look at the diagram below. Which letter (A–F) corresponds with which collection of qualifying words?

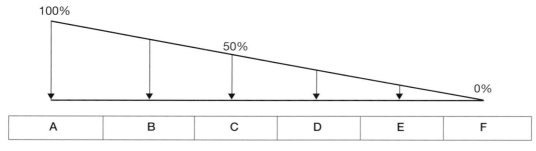

1	virtually nil, an insignificant number, negligible, rarely
2	a few, a minority, a small number, occasionally
3	always, everyone, the entirety
4	all but a few, the majority, most, little doubt
5	nil, zero, nobody, absolutely none
6	roughly half, sometimes, neither one way nor the other, no particular emphasis either way

EXERCISE 3   Read the article below. Underline the qualifying words you see. Not all of them are in *Exercise 2*.

READING PASSAGE 1

Virtual culture

A   Culture is defined as the 'socially transmitted behaviour patterns, arts, beliefs, and institutions that are the expression of a particular class, community or period' (www.dictionary.com). To most people, this is seen in terms of books, paintings, rituals and ceremonies, but recently there has been a new entrant in the field of what is considered to be 'culture' – the Internet.

B   On the Internet, science and art, media and mind combine to create a modern culture which is far more widespread than any of its predecessors. Not referring to the casual user who has no particular interest in the Internet, active supporters of the Internet as a culture have given themselves nomenclature to reflect their cultural aspirations – they are the new cyberpoets. A cyberpoet can be defined as 'one who makes frequent trips to the edge of technology, society and traditional culture and strives to be artful in their use of virtual space'.

C   Supporter or opponent of this new culture, there is little doubt that the Internet offers a lot to our traditional view of culture. In just a few minutes in front of a keyboard, we can read almost anything that has ever been written, yet no paper had to be made, no library had to stay open and thus the cost remains minimal. All of this encourages even the casual surfer to explore further than he or she otherwise would have. The same effect can be observed with works of art. Previously available to be viewed only in museums if they were not in the hands of private collectors, all but a few famous works are now replicated on the Internet.

D   Yet the Internet is not merely a mirror of traditional culture – it is also a new culture in its own right. The medium of the Net allows for wider distribution and new platforms for most forms of art. 'Kinetic art' and other such computerised art forms occur with increasing regularity, both motivated by and generating an upsurge in popular and computer-mediated art.

E   In addition, if culture is said to be 'socially transmitted', then the Internet is remarkable in its ability to share, on an almost global scale, all the factors that constitute culture. We have only to hear the influence of jargon as we visit dub-dub-dub dot sites and surf the web to see how international the Internet has become to the majority.

F   Very few people would disagree that the cyberpoets are increasingly asserting themselves into popular culture. What is not so certain is how far this will go, as the Internet continues to assimilate more and more forms of culture, reaching global audiences. It is not inconceivable that our entire perception of culture will soon become cyber-focused.

EXERCISE 4   According to the article in *Exercise 3*, are the following statements true or false?

a   The majority of people consider 'culture' to be represented by books, paintings, rituals and ceremonies.
b   Our understanding of what constitutes culture is unaffected by the Internet.
c   Through the Internet, every written word can be accessed.
d   The Internet provides a stage for all forms of art.
e   An insignificant number remain unaffected by the international nature of the Internet.
f   Only a few people believe that 'cyberpoets' are becoming part of our popular culture.

REVIEW   Headings (Unit 1.7)

The article in *Exercise 3* has six paragraphs (A–F). Write a possible heading for each paragraph.

REVIEW   Text completion (Unit 2.7)

Write a short summary of the text. Leave gaps for other students to complete the missing information.

REVIEW   Short-answer questions (Unit 3.7)

Write some short-answer questions for other students to answer.

Unit 4.2   Describing data with prepositions

EXERCISE 1   Look at the graph on the right and complete the eight sentences on the left with the correct number.

a   It started at _____
b   There was an increase of _____
c   It increased by _____
d   It peaked at _____
e   It decreased from _____ to _____
f   There was a drop of _____
g   It fluctuated at around _____
h   It finished at _____

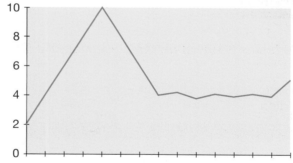

EXERCISE 2   Now look at the graph at the top of page 78 and read the report that follows. Fill in the gaps with a suitable preposition.

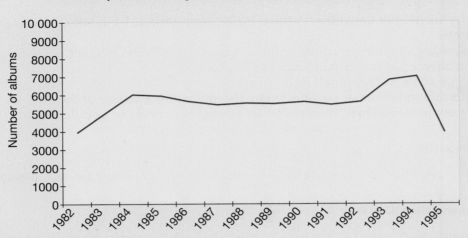

Albums produced by a small record label from 1982 to 1995

The first three years saw album production increase **(a)**_____ about four thousand albums per year **(b)**_____ approximately six thousand, an increase **(c)**_____ about two thousand albums. There was a slight decline from mid-1984, and from 1986 to mid-1992 this figure fluctuated **(d)**_____ around five-and-a-half thousand albums per year.

In mid-1992 there was a dramatic recovery, and in 1994 production rose **(e)**_____ a peak of nearly seven thousand albums before decreasing rapidly **(f)**_____ about four thousand albums **(g)**_____ just under three thousand albums per year in 1995.

ESSAY TASK

The tables below show which section of a library males and females used most in a year.

Males

AGE	Sections			
	Fiction	Non-fiction	Reference	Internet
5–15	71%	8%	4%	17%
16–25	22%	9%	15%	53%
26–65	15%	35%	15%	35%
66+	40%	34%	20%	6%

Females

AGE	Sections			
	Fiction	Non-fiction	Reference	Internet
5-15	80%	10%	7%	3%
16-25	30%	11%	15%	44%
26-65	23%	29%	20%	38%
66+	42%	37%	17%	4%

EXERCISE 3   Use the table on the previous page, to work out what the phrases refer to. *The first one has been done for you.*

a   at 3% – *refers to 5–15 year-old females using the Internet*
b   ranged between 23% and 80%
c   from 71% to 22%
d   from 9% at
e   within a 2% range
f   between the ages of 26 and 65

POINT OF IMPACT   Prepositions are important in most Task 1 questions. Some are used to describe changes in data over time and some describe static data.

EXERCISE 4   Complete the sentences below using the phrases from *Exercise 3*.

1   The biggest difference in results came from females visiting the fiction section, where the percentage _____.
2   _____, the lowest result for any category was in the females aged 5 to 15 using the Internet.
3   Between the ages of 5 to 15 and 16 to 25, use of the fiction section fell _____ for males.
4   There was a considerable increase in the number of males using the non-fiction section, _____ 16–25 to 35% for the next age range.
5   The results for males and females aged 66 and above were _____ of each other with regards to visiting the fiction section.
6   _____, only one fifth of females used the reference section.

EXERCISE 5   **Student A:** Draw a line graph and prepare to explain it to your partner. Use prepositions to support your data. Base your graph on a cultural issue, e.g. international migration. There should be two clear axes.
Student B: Listen to your partner and draw the graph he or she describes.

EXERCISE 6   Now write a paragraph describing your partner's graph.

Unit 4.3   Festivals

EXERCISE 1   What special events are the three passages below describing?

A   A special occasion that's important for me is _____. People decorate their homes and often have a tree with lights; I used to love all the colours when I was a child. It's a time when families get together and everyone exchanges gifts. Once, there were 18 of us all sitting around a small table at home. There wasn't much room but everyone had a good time. I love it because you get cards from a lot of old friends, and everyone is very friendly and cheerful.

B   A special day in my country is _____. Most people have a bonfire in their garden, and there are always lots of firework displays. People sometimes bring potatoes and cook them in the fire, but they don't cook very well.

C When I was at school, I never used to like _____. It seemed like everyone else was getting cards except me. It was much better when I was at university, as I did get a few cards and gifts. It's a good time if you have a girlfriend or boyfriend, but it can be a little awkward if you are single. Most people don't really worry about it too much as they get older.

POINT OF IMPACT   In the speaking test, you may be asked to talk about a special occasion or event that is important to you. It is very important to say why it is special *for you*.

EXERCISE 2   Make a list of other important occasions or events, and give one reason why they might be **special**. They don't have to be from your country.

Special occasion/event	Why is it special?

POINT OF IMPACT   You can show the interviewer that the event is special by giving a specific example. In *Exercise 1A*, for example, the candidate talks about a Christmas dinner when 'there were 18 of us all sitting around a table at home'.

EXERCISE 3   Choose an event or occasion that is special for you. Spend one minute making some notes.

EXERCISE 4   **Student A:** Tell your partner about your special event.
Student B: As you listen, make notes. Does the speaker sound interested in his or her topic?

Unit 4.4   Listening for details

EXERCISE 1   Listen to the recording. What do the following numbers refer to?

a 1946
b 180
c 60
d 2001

EXERCISE 2   Listen to the recording. Write the date for the following well-known days.

a Bastille Day
b Elvis's death
c Burns' Night
d Martin Luther King Day
e ANZAC Day

EXERCISE 3   Listen to the recording and answer the questions.

a   What is the speaker's name?
b   Where is he from?
c   What group of people is he referring to?
d   What language did they speak?

POINT OF IMPACT   'Listening for details' is a review of many of the skills you have already learned. You need to consider numbers, letters, dates and spelling. You will also need to consider qualifying words.

EXERCISE 4   Listen to the recording and make complete sentences using the prompts.

1   People / not / appreciate / cultural heritage.
2   Young people / see / value in / traditions.
3   Traditional cultures / will / disappear.

EXERCISE 5   Listen to the news report. Write as many details as possible.
When you have finished, compare notes with a partner.

Unit 4.5   Comparison and contrast in Task II

EXERCISE 1   If you were asked to compare and contrast the following, what aspects would you consider?

a   Rome and Tokyo
b   Classical music and pop music
c   Oil paintings and computer animation

EXERCISE 2   Read the passage below. Are the statements that follow true or false? *They are not in order.*

Although they are both highly respected institutions, there are many factors to be considered when comparing the Louvre and the Guggenheim.

The most important factor is the quality of their displays. The Guggenheim is excellently organised and offers fine examples of most forms of art, including traditional, modern and impressionist. The Louvre, on the other hand, lacks this variety of art forms, concentrating more on the traditional.

As regards location, both museums are well situated with convenient access for the public, although they are both a little expensive to visit. The Louvre, however, is a piece of architectural history in itself, whereas the Guggenheim is far more of a modern building with no real sense of history.

a   *Both* the Louvre and the Guggenheim have something to offer the art lover.
b   *Just as the Guggenheim museum displays impressionist works, so too does the Louvre.*
c   *Neither* the Louvre *nor* the Guggenheim is cheap to visit.
d   *Compared* with the Louvre, the Guggenheim concentrates more on traditional art forms.
e   The Louvre *and* the Guggenheim are *similar in that they are both* well situated.
f   The Louvre is *similar* to the Guggenheim *in that* it has good public access.
g   The Guggenheim and the Louvre are equally respected.
h   The Guggenheim is an historic building, *whereas* the Louvre is relatively modern.

POINT OF IMPACT   The words in italics in the sentences above are used to highlight comparisons and contrasts. You have looked at comparing and contrasting data in Unit 3.8. In this section you will look at comparing and contrasting for Task II.

EXERCISE 3   Look at the list of words and phrases below and decide if they compare or contrast.

while	although	in the same way
similarly	in contrast to	however
likewise	as well as	whereas
by contrast	like the Louvre ...	as opposed to
equally	as ... as ...	
in a similar way	instead	

EXERCISE 4   Make three sentences about each of the prompts below. Use words or phrases from *Exercises 2* and *3*.

Art on the Internet / art in museums
Live music concerts / CDs
Watching television / listening to the radio

EXERCISE 5   Contrast can also be shown by using specific verbs, adjectives and nouns. Copy and complete the table with the following vocabulary, changing the word family to complete all columns wherever possible.

change   compare   contrasting   different   distinction   distinct   resemble   same   similar   vary

Verbs:	Adjectives:	Nouns:
Example compare (to/with)	compared (to/with) comparing	in comparison (to/with)

POINT OF IMPACT   Be careful with compared/comparing!
Compared with that of the Guggenheim, the Louvre has a long history.
BUT
Comparing the Louvre and the Guggenheim, it can be observed that the former has a considerably longer history.

REVIEW   Using the essay task below, complete the following three steps.

a Mark the topic and task words (Unit 1.5) and rephrase the question.
b Plan the essay (Unit 2.5) (make notes using comparing and contrasting words).
c Write the introduction (Unit 3.11).

ESSAY TASK

The difference between popular culture and more traditional culture is vast.

Discuss.

Unit 4.6   Comparing and contrasting

EXERCISE 1   For a foreign student, which language do you think is more difficult to learn – English or your native language?

POINT OF IMPACT   Comparing and contrasting ideas or opinions can be a useful way to demonstrate a wide range of vocabulary and good control of the language. You have already studied this in Unit 4.5 of the Writing course. However, there are some slightly different constructions you can use when speaking. For example:

They are pretty similar in that ...
One feature they don't really share is ...

EXERCISE 2   A possible topic card related to culture may ask you to describe a traditional food from your own country. How would *comparing* and *contrasting* help you extend your answer?

EXERCISE 3   Make notes in the three columns below. *Think of a country for the third column before you begin.*

Traditional food from your country	Fast food	Food from _____

EXERCISE 4   Prepare to speak about the topic card below.

> Describe a popular food from your country.
> You should say:
> - what it is
> - how it is made
> - when it is eaten.
> You should also say why it is more popular than other dishes.

Unit 4.7   TRUE/FALSE/NOT GIVEN-style questions

EXERCISE 1   Read the passage below and the two questions that follow.

For students keen on improving their English, there are definite advantages to studying in a country where English is the first language. In Sydney, for example, language schools often offer homestay accommodation with native speakers, which, combined with a multicultural school setting, provide perfect environments for students to immerse themselves in the language.

The reality, however, is that many people will find and befriend other students of their own nationality, spending their free time speaking their native language rather than taking the opportunity to practise and improve their English. The reasons for this can be partly explained by looking at the concept of *culture shock*.

Question 1.

Does the following statement agree with the views of the writer?

Write   **YES** if the statement agrees with the writer
         NO if the statement does not agree with the writer
         DOES NOT SAY if there is no information about this in the passage.

Many students do not take full advantage of opportunities to speak English. _____

Question 2.

Look at the following statement and decide if it is TRUE or FALSE according to the information given.

Write   **TRUE** if the statement is true
         FALSE if the statement is false
         NOT GIVEN if the information is not given in the passage.

Homestay accommodation can be expensive. _____

EXERCISE 2   What is the difference between the two types of questions you answered in *Exercise 1*?

POINT OF IMPACT   With this style of question, make sure that you read the instructions carefully before you begin. Some require you to compare *information* from the text and the question, other questions require you to identify the *writer's opinions or claims*. The answers you can choose from can also be different. Sometimes you should answer TRUE or YES, FALSE or NO, NOT GIVEN or DOES NOT SAY. It is here that you must be particularly careful and read the instructions closely as marks are easily lost simply by writing FALSE when you should have written NO on your answer sheet.

EXERCISE 3   Read the YES, NO, NOT GIVEN questions below. What skills can you use when looking for an answer?

Write   **YES** if the statement agrees with the writer
    NO if the statement does not agree with the writer
    NOT GIVEN if there is no information about this in the passage.

1   People from all around the world are united by the way they think about culture.
2   Our 'values' are the most important aspect of ideology.
3   Secularism is the most widely accepted system of beliefs, values and ideals.
4   Shamans act as intermediaries between spirits and the living.
5   Agricultural societies benefited from religion.
6   All the people from the Aztec civilisation were rich.
7   In the seventeenth and eighteenth centuries, European people began turning towards science.

EXERCISE 4   Now read the text and answer the questions in *Exercise 3*.

READING PASSAGE 1

The dawn of culture

In every society, culturally unique ways of thinking about the world unite people in their behaviour. Anthropologists often refer to the body of ideas that people share as *ideology*. Ideology can be broken down into at least three specific categories: beliefs, values and ideals. People's beliefs give them an understanding of how the world works and how they should respond to the actions of others and their environments. Particular beliefs often tie in closely with the daily concerns of domestic life, such as making a living, health and sickness, happiness and sadness, interpersonal relationships, and death. People's values tell them the differences between right and wrong or good and bad. Ideals serve as models for what people hope to achieve in life.

There are two accepted systems of belief. Some rely on religion, even the supernatural (things beyond the natural world), to shape their values and ideals and to influence their behaviour. Others base their beliefs on observations of the natural world, a practice anthropologists commonly refer to as secularism.

Religion in its more extreme form allows people to know about and 'communicate' with supernatural beings, such as animal spirits, gods, and spirits of the dead. Small tribal societies believe that plants and animals, as well as people, can have souls or spirits that can take on different forms to help or harm people. Anthropologists refer to this kind of religious belief as *animism*, with believers often led by *shamans*. As religious specialists, shamans have special access to the spirit world, and are said to be able to receive stories from supernatural beings and later recite them to others or act them out in dramatic rituals.

In larger, agricultural societies, religion has long been a means of asking for bountiful harvests, a source of power for rulers, or an inspiration to go to war. In early civilised societies, religious visionaries became leaders because people believed those leaders could communicate with the supernatural to control the fate of a civilization. This became their greatest source of power, and people often regarded leaders as actual gods. For example, in the great civilisation of the Aztec, which flourished in what is now Mexico in the fifteenth and sixteenth centuries, rulers claimed privileged association with a powerful god that was said to require human blood to ensure that the sun would rise and set each day. Aztec rulers thus inspired great awe by regularly conducting human sacrifices. They also conspicuously displayed their vast power as wealth in luxury goods, such as fine jewels, clothing and palaces. Rulers obtained their wealth from the great numbers of craftspeople, traders and warriors under their control.

During the period in seventeenth- and eighteenth-century Europe known as the Age of Enlightenment, science and logic became new sources of belief for many people living in civilised societies. Scientific studies of the natural world and rational philosophies led people to believe that they could explain natural and social phenomena without believing in gods or spirits. Religion remained an influential system of belief, and together both religion and science drove the development of capitalism, the economic system of commerce-driven market exchange. Capitalism itself influences people's beliefs, values and ideals in many present-day, large, civilised societies. In these societies, such as in the United States, many people view the world and shape their behaviour based on a belief that they can understand and control their environment and that work, commerce and the accumulation of wealth serve an ultimate good. The governments of most large societies today also assert that human well-being derives from the growth of economies and the development of technology.

Rapid changes in technology in the last several decades have changed the nature of culture and cultural exchange. People around the world can make economic transactions and transmit information to each other almost instantaneously through the use of computers and satellite communications. Governments and corporations have gained vast amounts of political power through military might and economic influence. Corporations have also created a form of global culture based on worldwide commercial markets. As a result, local culture and social structure are now shaped by large and powerful commercial interests in ways that earlier anthropologists could not have imagined. Early anthropologists thought of societies and their cultures as fully independent systems, but today, many nations are multicultural societies, composed of numerous smaller sub-cultures. Cultures also cross national boundaries. For instance, people around the world now know a variety of English words and have contact with American cultural exports such as brand-name clothing and technological products, films and music, and mass-produced foods.

In addition, many people have come to believe in the fundamental nature of human rights and free will. These beliefs grew out of people's increasing ability to control the natural world through science and rationalism, and though religious beliefs continue to change to affirm or accommodate these other dominant beliefs, sometimes the two are at odds with each other. For instance, many religious people have difficulty reconciling their belief in a supreme spiritual force with the theory of natural evolution, which requires no belief in the supernatural. As a result, societies in which many people do not practice any religion, such as China, may be known as secular societies. However, no society is entirely secular.

REVIEW   **Text completion (Unit 2.1)**

Complete the summary of the reading text using words from the box.

There are two main _____(8)_____ systems which can contribute to our ideology – animism and secularism. The _____(9)_____ can be said to dominate older civilisations and tribal societies, whereas

▶

larger, more contemporary societies have gone in a more ____(10)____ and scientific direction. One reason that explains the ____(11)____ of more secular beliefs is the importance given to other factors, such as free will and capitalism. Nonetheless, ____(12)____ remains at least to some degree even in the most secular of societies.

| belief | latter | religion | faith | ascendancy | former | rational | decline | animism | shaman |

REVIEW   **Short-answer questions (Unit 3.7)**

Answer the questions below using *NO MORE THAN THREE WORDS*.
13 What are beliefs, values and ideals specific categories of?
14 What was said to be necessary for the continuation of sunrise and sunset in ancient Mexico?
15 In Europe, what title was given to the advance of science and logic?
16 What influenced the development of capitalism?
17 Before modern advances in technology, what did anthropologists consider societies to be?
18 What theory is symbolic of the tensions between religion and science?

Unit 4.8   Line graphs

ESSAY TASK

The graph shows population changes in four ethnic groups in New Zealand from 1990 to 2002.

Write a report for a university lecturer describing the information shown below.

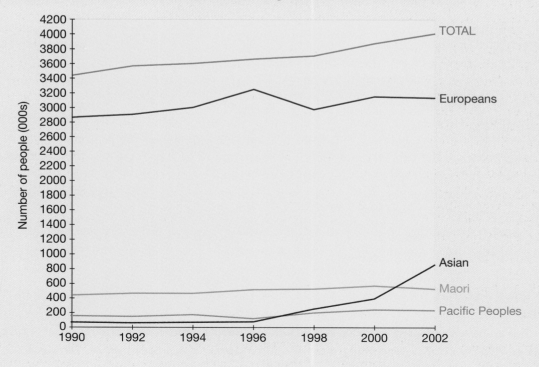

EXERCISE 1   Which of the following are relevant to the Task I question on the previous page?

Describing trends   Academic writing   Describing approximate data
Register   Preparing a plan   Comparing and contrasting data
Sequencing and linking   Topic and task words   Giving and justifying opinions
Brainstorming   Writing an introduction   Describing data with prepositions
Reading the axes   Building a paragraph

EXERCISE 2   Briefly review the language of trends by writing six different sentences about the graph.

EXERCISE 3   Now complete the plan using the graph on the previous page.

Topic words?	
Tense?	
Axes?	
About?	
Trends?	

EXERCISE 4   Now write an introduction to the Task I title given on the previous page.

EXERCISE 5   Below are two descriptions of the graph on the previous page. Match each essay with a comment.

A   This line chart shows that the number of four nationalities in New Zealand have changed from 1990 to 2002. Totally, there was a increasing trend among the four ethnic.

It is immediately apparent from the diagram that the number of Asian increased dramatically, however, the trend of European, Maori and Pacific peoples was even during 1990-2002 period.

In 1990 European was up to over 2.8 million and the number raised to a pick around 3.1 million in 1996 and decline gradually during the period 1996 to 1998 and again raised a bit in 2002.

In comparison, the population of Maori based on over 400 thousand, and there was not clear fluctuation. The lowest population was Pacific Peoples, which was nearly 200 thousand in 1990 and kept steady increasing until in 1996. Then the number increased slightly, but just had approximately 500 thousand higher than in 1990.

Overall, Asian had the lowest number but increased sharply then the others. Although the entire trend had an uneven increasing, European, Maori and Pacific Peoples were correlates.

B   The graph illustrates the number of people from four ethnic origins in New Zealand from 1990 to 2002.

There was a significant increase in the total of people from 3 400 000 to about 4 000 000 between 1990 to 2002. Interestingly, over the same period, the proportion of European was much higher than other ethnic groups. After 1996 it increased slowly, then from 2000 it was a dropping trend. In comparison, the amount of Maori people rose slightly from about 450 000 in 1990 to one tenth of the total in 2002.

However, the trend of the number of Pacific people was similar to that of Maori people, but it about 250 000 less. The change of the number of Asian is obvious. Before 1996 it remain constant at 100 000. After that, it increased magically to about 800 000 in 2002. In 1997 it was the third biggest group instead of pacific people. Furthermore, after 2001 it took over Maori people and was only less than the number of European.

To sum up, during this period, the number of all groups' people increased.

Comments

1 This is a fairly acceptable attempt at describing the chart information.

   The paragraphs are not as well balanced as they could be. The first paragraph is lifted almost verbatim from the given wording though an attempt at rewording is evident. Adding a general 'overall picture' to this paragraph would have given the introduction much more impact. The second paragraph should have been divided into several shorter ones and been supplied with supplementary details. This would have created a better 'flow' for the reader.

   The writer is clearly able to calculate the arithmetic outcomes of the figures and identify where trends lie within the graph, though there is a certain vagueness at times, which is questionable. Sentence structures are limited in variety. What appears to be carelessness (evidence of sloppy work can be seen, for example, in the misspelling of copied information from the chart itself), questions the writer's care and/or understanding of the simplest grammar forms. This is countered by some well-structured phrases. The summary, albeit flawed grammatically, is appropriate and to the point.

   So, on balance, the writing does not show any particular strengths or weaknesses.

2 This is a reasonable report conveying the chart information.

   There is a clear attempt to paraphrase the given instructions for the introduction, though not with convincing success. Some details are lacking in clarity. More precise details could have been included.

   The writer has used appropriate language to compare and contrast areas of the graph with standard linking words/phrases. It is questionable, though, if the writer is in control of how to use these phrases to maximum effect or even understands what they mean. The grammar appears to indicate pre-learned stock phrases which have been inserted into the report with dubious understanding of their proper meaning.

   This report neither lacks evidence of understanding language use or shows an especially good control of English.

SPEAKING SPEAKING SPEAKING SPEAKING SPEAKING SPEAKING SPEAKING SPEAKING

Unit 4.9   Expanding your topic

EXERCISE 1   Consider the following question. How could you expand your answer?

Do you think traditions are important?

POINT OF IMPACT   In previous units you have looked at how justifying your answer can expand what you want to talk about. In this section, you will practise further ways of expanding the topic you are talking about.

EXERCISE 2   Read the candidate's answer for the question in *Exercise 1* and answer the questions.

Yes, I do because they give us a sense of connection with the past. This is important because it can bring people together and remind us of the history we share. However, I believe traditions should also be flexible. They should reflect not only the past but also the present. Only by doing this can any tradition continue to have relevance today.

a Why does the speaker think traditions are important?
b Why is it important to have this connection?
c What qualification does the speaker make?
d Why is this qualification important?

POINT OF IMPACT   The answers for *Exercise 2* give some examples of how to expand your topic. As a short checklist, consider the following four points: Why? So? But? Then?
In *Exercise 2* this is:
* **Why?** connection with the past
* **So?** brings people together
* **But?** should be flexible
* **Then?** continue to be relevant

EXERCISE 3   Use the points in the Point of Impact above on the following question.

Does tourism have a negative effect on a country's culture?

Unit 4.10	**Diagrams and objects (listening)**

EXERCISE 1   What does the following illustration represent?

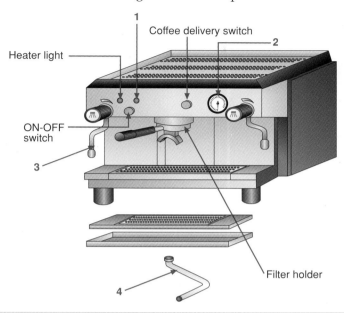

1
Coffee delivery switch
2
Heater light
ON-OFF switch
3
Filter holder
4

POINT OF IMPACT   In the listening and the reading tests, you may have to choose between or label different diagrams or illustrations. The most important skill is to look at the picture to *get a clear idea of what you are looking at*. This will help you predict some of the possible vocabulary. You should also use any headings or other labels presented with the diagram as they will help you follow the flow of the description. Remember that the questions come in the order of the listening.

EXERCISE 2   Now listen to the recording and label numbers 1–4 on the illustration in *Exercise 1*.

EXERCISE 3   Look at the diagram below. What language could you anticipate hearing? Remember that in the IELTS test you are not expected to have any specialist knowledge.

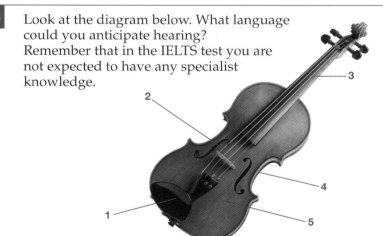

2
3
1
4
5

EXERCISE 4 Draw and label a common household appliance. You should now describe it to your partner, who should draw it from your description.

EXERCISE 5 Listen to the recording and identify the labels 1–5.

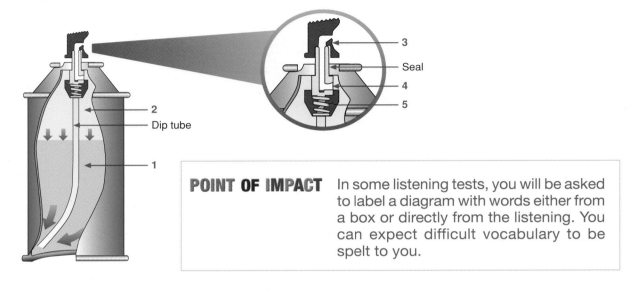

3
Seal
4
5
2
Dip tube
1

POINT OF IMPACT In some listening tests, you will be asked to label a diagram with words either from a box or directly from the listening. You can expect difficult vocabulary to be spelt to you.

Unit 4.11   Writing an introduction to Task II

EXERCISE 1 Brainstorm some ideas on the following topic and prepare a basic plan.

ESSAY TASK

The arts should be rejected in favour of more practical studies. Do you agree?

EXERCISE 2 Read the following two introductions to the Task II title you brainstormed in *Exercise 1*. Which one is better? Why?

a There are some who claim that studies involving the arts are insufficiently practical to pursue. Others argue that a value cannot be placed on education no matter what the discipline. I will argue in support of this latter point for a number of reasons.

b The arts should be rejected in favour of more practical studies. I do not agree with this. The arts have been studied for centuries. Many famous and well-respected people have studied the arts.

EXERCISE 3   Which of the following things do you agree with when writing an introduction to Task II?

You should...	Good idea	Bad idea
a ...give a general statement about the topic in the first sentence.		
b ...use as many words from the topic as possible.		
c ...typically introduce a contrast to the statement in the second or third sentence.		
d ...rephrase the question using your own words as much as possible.		
e ...write at least 70 words.		
f ...give a brief history to introduce the topic.		
g ...give an indication of what you are going to write about.		

EXERCISE 4   The eight sentences below are from four different introductions. Put them in pairs to recreate the introduction. *The first one has been done for you.*

1   Further education should be an opportunity for people to extend their knowledge of whatever appeals to them.
2   It seems clear, however, that studies with an arts-related focus often fail to train people for a specific job.
3   Many students of the arts are able to contribute as much to society as any other graduate regardless of career opportunities.
4   For most people, further education means an improvement in career opportunities.
5   Many people want to study a subject that has a definite value in the workplace.
6   Accordingly, they should not be made to feel that only practical education has any worth.
7   Thus arbitrarily limiting the courses available only to what is deemed 'practical' is unfair.
8   The arts should therefore be studied more for personal interest than as a course as such studies do not offer anything practical.

5	8						

POINT OF IMPACT   In your introduction, it is important to use parallel expressions or different word families to rephrase the question. However, avoid making your first sentence nothing more than a rephrasing of the title. For example, if the question was:

The arts should be rejected in favour of more practical studies.

Do you agree?

DO NOT write: Studying less theoretical subjects is better than studying arts. I don't agree with this.

It is better to add an opinion in the first sentence.
In my opinion, I do not think that studying more practical subjects is better than studying arts.
OR Some people believe that studying more practical subjects is better than studying arts.

EXERCISE 5 Transformation is very important when rephrasing the title. Complete the following table.

Verb	Noun	Adjective	Adverb
a	a culture	b	culturally
c	a solution	—	—
to improve	d	e	—
f	g	beneficial	—

EXERCISE 6 Rephrase the following statements using as much different vocabulary as possible, and then add a contrasting sentence. You should also include some opinion words.

Example: *So-called 'serious' arts such as theatre and opera are elitist, and do not interest the majority.*

Some people feel that more formal arts have no relevance to the general public and are intended only for a minority. However, others believe that such arts are available to everyone and are not exclusive.

1 Famous works of art should not be owned privately. They should be available to everyone.
2 Modern art is not really art at all.
3 Opera is irrelevant and has no place in modern society.
4 Nightly revision is beneficial for a good IELTS result.

EXERCISE 7 Read the following introduction. In what way is it different to *introduction* **a** in *Exercise 2*? Do you think it is better?

There are some who claim that studies involving the arts are insufficiently practical to pursue. Others argue that a value cannot be placed on education no matter what the discipline. There are points to be considered for both opinions, as I will now explain.

POINT OF IMPACT There are two ways you can begin an essay. After preparing a plan for your essay, you will often find it easier to present your opinion and then justify it (the opinion approach). Or you can present different viewpoints and then state your own opinion in the conclusion (the ideas approach). There are strengths and weaknesses to both formats.

EXERCISE 8 How would you begin to write an introduction to this question? *It often helps to plan the essay first, so you know which direction the introduction should aim.*

ESSAY TASK

In many countries, government sponsorship of the arts costs millions in taxpayers' money. There are many more important things to spend money on.

Do you agree?

Unit 4.12   Topic Card: Culture

POINT OF IMPACT   Every topic card has prompts about what you should say. The first two prompts are often simple, not requiring much information. Do not feel that you have to spend much time on these points. You can move on to the third and fourth point for most of your speech, or even away from the prompts if you have other things to say.

EXERCISE 1   Look at the topic card below. Which part is asking you to *compare* and *contrast*?

> Describe an important traditional festival from your country.
> You should say:
> * when it happens
> * why it is celebrated
> * what is special about it.
> You should also say why it is more important than other festivals.

EXERCISE 2   Now work with a partner and practise the interview. One of you should act as the candidate and the other should be the interviewer. The interviewer should make notes on the following.

* Have comparisons or contrasts been used?
* Has the speaker given a specific example?
* Does the speaker sound interested?

UNIT

5

Health matters

Unit 5.1 Reading for meaning

EXERCISE 1 What does the following sentence mean?

Public healthcare, on the other hand, has nothing like the resources available to those with private healthcare.

Public healthcare has
A more resources than private healthcare has
B very different resources from private healthcare
C fewer resources than private healthcare has.

POINT OF IMPACT There are many different ways of expressing the same information in English. One common example of this in the reading test is indirect sentences, where the meaning is not immediately clear.

EXERCISE 2 Circle the best answer for the following multiple-choice questions.

1 One thing that isn't true about X is that the weather is always bad.
   The weather in X is
   A never bad
   B always bad
   C sometimes good.
2 Y is a multicultural city. It's the biggest city in Z. Most people think it's the capital. This, however, is a common mistake.
   A Y is the capital.
   B Y is not the capital.
   C Y is not the biggest city.
3 It's highly unlikely that the government will reduce taxes.
   A Taxes are likely to increase.
   B The government will reduce taxes.
   C Taxes probably won't be reduced.

4 It's a popular misconception that chocolate gives you spots.
   A Spots are caused by eating chocolate.
   B Most people are unaware that chocolate gives you spots.
   C Spots are not caused by chocolate.
5 The number of private cars on the roads is getting bigger.
   A There are more cars being driven than before.
   B More and more private cars are getting bigger.
   C Bigger roads are becoming more common.
6 It's not unusual for most Japanese to clean themselves before having a bath.
   A Most Japanese don't clean themselves before having a bath.
   B Most Japanese clean themselves before having a bath.
   C Most Japanese find cleaning themselves before a bath very unusual.
7 Dr Johnson is not unlike his brother Dr Kerr.
   A Dr Johnson looks similar to Dr Kerr.
   B Dr Johnson doesn't like Dr Kerr.
   C Dr Johnson likes Dr Kerr.
8 Peter doesn't think you should think the worst of people.
   A Peter thinks you should think the best of people.
   B Peter thinks you should think the worst of people.
   C Peter doesn't think about the worst people.

POINT OF IMPACT   In complex and indirect sentences, the meaning in the sentence often involves prefixes.

EXERCISE 3   What do the prefixes mean in the following sentences?

1 *Mis*communication, even amongst speakers of the same language, can often lead to arguments.
2 Before going to war, governments should carefully consider the possible impact of *anti*-war protesters.
3 The Olympic Games first began in *pre*-Christian times, nearly 3000 years ago.
4 After completing university courses, some *post*graduates find themselves unable to get a good job.
5 Very few people can maintain a good relationship with their *ex*-husband or *ex*-wife.

EXERCISE 4   Do you know what the following prefixes mean? Write a sentence using the prefix.

Prefix	(a) Meaning	(b) Sentence
a inter-		
b micro-		
c pseudo-		
d psycho-		
e quasi-		
f eco-		
g narco-		

POINT OF IMPACT Remember that in academic writing, it is important to use varied sentences. It is a good idea to read articles not only from this book, but also in newspapers or in magazines, and see how linking words, complex sentences and prefixes are used.

EXERCISE 5 Read the text below and answer the questions that follow.

Student doctors

In comparison with the lives of other postgraduate students, the life of a student doctor is far from easy. Despite the heavy workload, it seems that the more you learn, the more you realise what you still need to study. As a result, it is not unusual for students to drop out. Misguided teachers attempt to simplify matters in an environment that demands the very best of its practitioners.

The situation is little better in the year or two years after qualifying. Poorly paid for such long hours, many junior doctors find themselves becoming disillusioned with medicine. The more depressed they become, the more likely they are to look elsewhere for a career, wasting up to seven years of training and education. An unfortunate statistic is that of those that qualify as doctors, 18% do not remain in the profession for more than three years.

Do the following statements agree with the views of the writer?

Write   **YES** if the statement agrees with the writer
         NO if the statement does not agree with the writer
         NOT GIVEN if the information is not given in the passage.

a   Medical courses are as difficult as any other postgraduate course.
b   For student doctors, the course becomes easier the more you learn.
c   A number of students do not complete the course.
d   Better teachers know how to simplify the course.
e   Once qualified, the situation for junior doctors slightly improves.
f   Junior doctors are poor.
g   Disillusioned doctors often move to another hospital to work.

The text below is a continuation of the article 'Student doctors'. Answer the questions that follow.

(continued ...)

The problem can be more clearly defined by considering specific examples. In New Zealand and Britain, for example, the exodus of medical graduates is leaving the remaining newly qualified doctors with responsibilities that are beyond their capacity. In statistics from 1998 over half the graduates from one medical school in New Zealand left the country immediately after qualifying, and hospitals are really beginning to feel the shortage. Certain hospitals in Auckland, for example, do not have enough staff to cover the timetable, and some of the newly qualified doctors are finding themselves on call for 48 hours straight. In Britain, the situation is equally bleak.

The structure of the health service itself is the most important factor to be taken into account when considering the number of migrating British medical graduates. Junior doctors are required to take mentors, more senior doctors (often consultants), to act as supervisors. They are entrusted with the educational supervision of doctors in their first year of practice and are responsible for ensuring the application of the principles of good medical practice. However, when interviewed, slightly less than 60% of junior doctors had any positive feedback on the relationship. The remaining respondents described situations in which a consultant was accused of making unreasonable demands, bullying, being unfair, or being sexist. In more extreme cases, the consultant was portrayed as incompetent, insensitive or negligent towards patients.

A healthy mentoring relationship is likely to provide the mental and moral challenges essential to continuing self-improvement. But such statistics may encourage junior doctors to conclude that role models may not be a dependable way to impart professional values, attitudes and behaviour. Indeed, a survey of just under 200 nearly qualified doctors highlights significant gaps in their knowledge and understanding of basic care. It was found that many junior doctors do not know the signs indicating a patient is critically ill, a third of respondents failed to answer a question on how to deal with someone who was unconscious and none of the trainees identified all of the steps involved in using an oxygen mask.

In New Zealand, the situation, although having essentially the same effect of fewer junior doctors, has different causes. There are two main factors which explain this mass migration of medical graduates from New Zealand. The first factor is the student loans system where a medical graduate can leave university having accumulated a loan of anything up to NZ$60 000 in the course of training. By leaving the country, such graduates have the option of at least delaying the repayment of those loans. The other reason is the long hours. The stories of working hours a week being almost in the three-figure mark are often not exaggerated, and this is a situation which is worsening the fewer junior doctors there are.

In New Zealand, at least, a solution is being sought at a student level. The New Zealand Medical Students Association (NZMSA) is a national body that aims to advance the long-term interests of medical students and act as their advocate on a political level. Composed of students elected from the Otago and Auckland Medical Schools, the NZMSA aims to find a balance between the demands of the profession and the expectations of junior doctors. At a recent conference, the Association concluded that increasing student numbers or attracting overseas doctors is too short term to be successful and the roots of the problem need to be addressed, specifically in the area of student debt.

Either way, there is no doubt that a solution is needed and needed quickly, not just in Britain and New Zealand, but in most countries.

Questions 1–10 are based on the text 'Student doctors'.

REVIEW   **Text completion (Unit 2.7)**

Complete the following text using *NO MORE THAN TWO WORDS* from the text.

A significant number of graduates from New Zealand and Britain are not remaining in the medical field. Poor relationships with **(1)** _____, student loan repayments and increasingly long **(2)** _____ are all contributory factors. The NZMSA is attempting to find an answer to the problem, but is wary of supporting ideas it perceives to be only **(3)** _____ solutions.

REVIEW   **TRUE, FALSE, NOT GIVEN-Style questions (Unit 4.7)**

Do the following statements reflect the views of the writer?

Write   **YES** if the statement agrees with the writer
            NO if the statement does not agree with the writer
            DOES NOT SAY if there is no information about this in the passage.

4   The majority of students had nothing positive to say about their mentors.
5   The root of the problem in New Zealand and Britain is essentially the same.

6 Many junior doctors are unable to repay their student loans.
7 The NZMSA has found a balance between expectation and reality.

REVIEW   **Short-answer questions (Unit 3.7)**

Answer the following questions using *NO MORE THAN TWO WORDS OR A NUMBER*.

 8 In which year did over 50% of newly qualified doctors from a medical school in New Zealand
    leave the country? _____
 9 How are members of the NZMSA chosen? _____
10 Where are two-day shifts not uncommon? _____

Unit 5.2   Describing illustrations

EXERCISE **1**   How would you describe the following illustration?

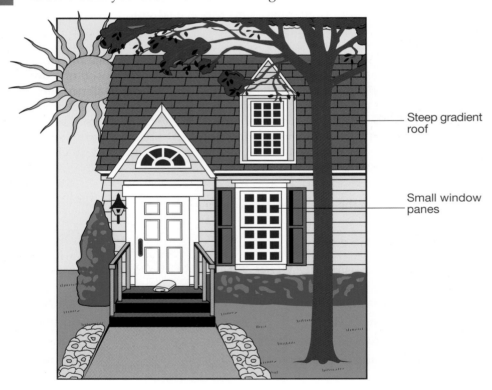

Steep gradient
roof

Small window
panes

POINT OF IMPACT   In Task I, you could be asked to do one of the following.
    1 Describe an illustration.
    2 Compare illustrations.
    3 Make comments on an illustration.

EXERCISE 2   How would you describe the rooms below?

1
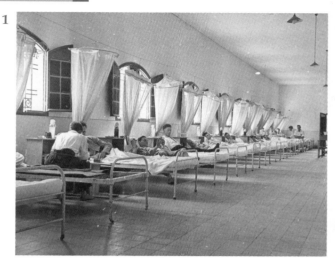

2

POINT OF IMPACT   There are Task I questions which may require you to describe similarities and differences between two pictures. This means you will need to use a variety of comparative constructions.

EXERCISE 3   The essay below compares two buildings. One building is in *Exercise 1*. Read the essay and sketch the other building from the description given.

The illustrations above show differences between typical houses in Britain and Spain.

There are two immediately notable differences between the buildings. The British house has two storeys, whereas the Spanish house has only one, and the roof of the Spanish house is considerably lower and therefore at much less of a gradient than that of the British house.

Again related to climate, it can be seen that although both buildings have the same number of windows, the window frames are wider in the Spanish house, allowing for greater ventilation in hot weather. Another difference can be identified in the size of the panes of glass. Where the windows in the British house have been constructed of smaller panes, the Spanish house has full-size windows with metal bars running vertically on the exterior of the building.

To summarise, both houses have been designed with climate and security in mind, yet their locations have led to different solutions. (153 words)

POINT OF IMPACT   Describing or comparing illustrations is actually very similar to writing about a graph or a chart – you are being asked to give a written description of what you can see. If you have to write an essay similar to that in *Exercise 3* imagine you are trying to describe the pictures to someone who can only read your description.

POINT OF IMPACT   In *Exercise 1* you saw an example of describing an illustration. In *Exercise 2* you saw an example of comparing. The third possible type of illustration is where you are asked to make a comment. This can share some of the skills you have learned for Task II, as you may have to give an opinion. Regardless of which type you may have, you should consider everything you can see on the illustration before you begin. Most, if not all, of the features have been added for a reason, and are often labelled. They should be included in your essay.

EXERCISE 4   You have been asked to decide which of the proposed sites would be more suitable for a hospital. How would you write 150 words on the subject?

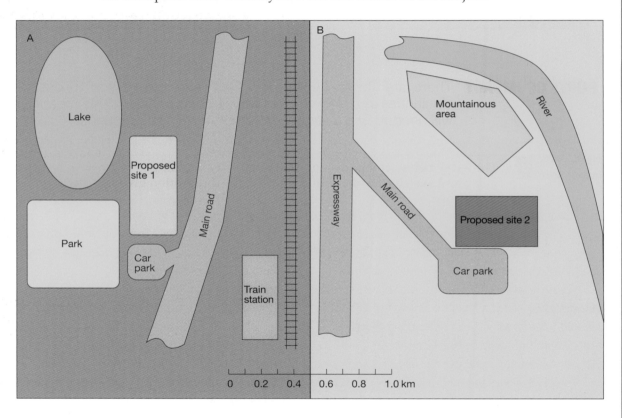

Unit 5.3   Food

EXERCISE 1   Write down some questions you could ask about someone's favourite food using the following question words: what, when, where, why, how.

| EXERCISE | 2 | Now ask a partner your questions. |

> **POINT OF IMPACT**　In order to give more detail to what you are saying, use a range of adjectives, as well as comparisons and contrasts.

| EXERCISE | 3 | Brainstorm for adjectives that could be used to describe the following categories. *Some adjectives may suit more than one category.* |

a　Food you love
b　Food you quite like
c　Food you do not really like
d　Food you detest

| EXERCISE | 4 | Compare and contrast your favourite food and your partner's. Consider the following areas. You should justify your opinions wherever possible. |

a　Healthiness
b　Ease of preparation
c　Taste
d　Cost

| EXERCISE | 5 | Connecting the topic of food with the theme of the unit (health), what questions do you think the interviewer may ask you? |

Unit 5.4 　Note taking (listening)

| EXERCISE | 1 | Look at the example test paper below. The candidate was able to answer the first two questions correctly, but then lost his place with the questions. Look at the notes made in the margin and make an educated guess about the remaining answers. |

Answer the following questions using *NO MORE THAN THREE WORDS*.

1　What was the project investigating? Stress-related illness
2　Why was some of the information misleading? Unreliable data
3　Does Dr Martinez hold himself responsible for the failure of the project?
4　Are there insufficient funds to start the research again?
5　Was any of the work useful?

Project leader – complained about data collection

Edwards – millionaire

not entire waste

POINT OF IMPACT   As well as keeping you focused on what you are listening to, note taking is a useful skill as there is the chance that in the test, you will lose your place with the questions. By taking notes, you have a chance of recording the relevant information and answering the question when the listening has finished.

EXERCISE 2   Listen to the recording. You will be given some questions later, but for this exercise make notes on whatever you think is important.

EXERCISE 3   Now compare your notes with a partner's. Did you both record the same information?

EXERCISE 4   Now look at Appendix A on page 219 and answer the questions.

POINT OF IMPACT   You can practise this skill by taking notes as you listen to the television or radio, then by checking your notes on the Internet, with other students or with your teacher.

EXERCISE 5   Answer the following questions. If you lose your place with the questions, take notes.

Question 1   Choose the correct letter A–C.

1 Helen became a vegetarian
   A sixteen years ago
   B because of family influences
   C for personal reasons.

Questions 2–4   Answer the following questions using *NO MORE THAN THREE WORDS*.

According to Helen,
2 what is the most important food source for vegetarians?
3 what do most countries do to vegetables?
4 what misconception do people have about vegetarians?

Questions 5–6   Complete the table below using *NO MORE THAN TWO WORDS OR A NUMBER*.

	World	Europe	America
Beef consumption per head (in kilograms per year)	less than 11	(5)____	(6) ____

Questions 7–10	Label the following diagram using *NO MORE THAN THREE WORDS*.

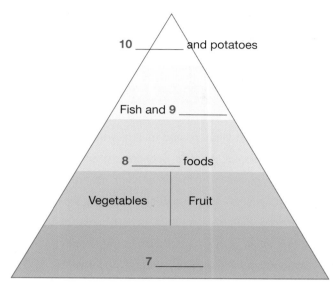

10 _____ and potatoes

Fish and **9** _____

8 _____ foods

Vegetables   Fruit

7 _____

Unit 5.5   Improving paragraphs

EXERCISE 1   What's wrong with the paragraph below? What do you think the question was?

No, I don't agree. I don't think we should worry about exercising. I think people should live how they want and thats it. Just a bit of running or something isn't going to help much. And nobody really has the time to do it regularly! it's more important to watch what you eat and drink, and get enough sleep.

POINT OF IMPACT   You have already studied the importance of register, punctuation, linking words and relative clauses when writing an essay. In this section, you will be putting all of this together to improve your paragraphs.

EXERCISE 2   Using the information in the Point of Impact above, identify ways to improve the sentences below.

1   Loads of people think smoking among teenagers is going down.
2   Legislation has attempted to control industrial pollution. It still continues.
3   Exercise videos allow people to keep fit at home. Exercise videos are becoming more popular.
4   most people prefer to drive rather than walk even if it is only to their local shop's

EXERCISE 3   Now rewrite the sentences above so they are more suitable for IELTS.

EXERCISE **4** Below is a brief review of some useful words you can use to link your paragraphs together. Put the headings in the correct place. *The first one has been done for you.*

Concession   For opposite examples   Cause and effect   For additional ideas

For giving examples   ~~Listing different points~~   For stress and emphasis   Time

Linking categories	Examples
Listing different points	the first feature, second, finally, to conclude
	another, in addition, related to, furthermore, moreover, not only ... but (also)...
	for example, for instance, such as, a good example of this is
	but, yet, however, on the other hand, nevertheless
	in fact, what is more, in particular, notably, indeed, of course
	therefore, thus, as a result of, consequently, because, for this reason, if so
	when, while, during, subsequently, before, after
	although, admittedly, even though, nonetheless

EXERCISE **5** Underline the *linking words* in the paragraph below.

When we think of lifestyles 100 years ago, we often think in terms of relative hardship, poverty and squalor. However, despite relatively primitive sanitation and concepts of hygiene, harmful pollution on the scale we experience today was unknown. Furthermore, there was a lack of awareness of long-term health effects and therefore there was little of the stress we worry about almost continually in the modern era. Admittedly, our life expectancy has notably increased, but we need to carefully consider whether we are in fact better off after all.

POINT OF IMPACT In Unit 1.2 you looked at different ways of linking your ideas together. This skill allows your essay to flow, but it also helps the paragraphs to have a natural *flow*. You can also use reference words such as those below (you will study referencing in more detail in Unit 6.1).

e.g. *it, they, this, that, those, her, him, us*

Despite better medical practices, heart-related illness has increased. This can stem from a number of factors including...

EXERCISE **6** Add more information to the following sentences using reference words.

Fatal car accidents are increasing.
Many people think smoking is declining among teenagers.
Heart attacks can happen at any age.

EXERCISE 7　Extend the points below into three full paragraphs. You can use *Exercise 6* to help you, but you should also add some ideas and support of your own.

a　Fatal car accidents are increasing. The government is not addressing the problem. Poor roads are partly to blame. Aggressive driving is also a factor.

b　Many people think smoking is declining amongst teenagers. Recent statistics show that smoking is increasing among teenagers. This suggests that anti-smoking advertising is not effective. Some new measures are needed to combat this problem.

c　Heart attacks can happen at any age. They are more common in elderly people. They are rarely fatal. The risks of a second heart attack can be reduced with appropriate medication. Rest is generally prescribed as a good means of recovery.

Unit 5.6　Giving instructions

EXERCISE 1　In what ways is this topic card different from the topic cards you have seen so far in the course?

> Describe how to cook a meal you like.
> You should say:
> * what it is
> * when you eat it
> * what you need to make it.
> You should also explain how to make it.

POINT OF IMPACT　Although it is not common, you could be given a topic card which asks you to describe how something is done. As with describing a process in the writing test, you should describe the sequence logically.

EXERCISE 2　In the answer below, the candidate is giving instructions. Complete the gaps with appropriate vocabulary. Try to guess the missing word from the context. (2) is the same word in both cases.

Well, I've been asked to describe how to use (1) _____, so I'm going to talk about something you may well be familiar with – a (2) _____. I use mine mostly for e-mails but also for word processing, especially when I'm writing essays. I find I can organise my ideas more clearly than with the traditional pen and paper. Although I do take it with me most days, I don't actually use it for very long at a time because the power doesn't last for more than a few hours if it's not plugged in.

Now, the (3) _____ in using a (2) _____ is quite obvious – you have to turn it on. This can take quite a while depending on the model. What you do next depends on the particular reason for using it, but I'm going to talk about connecting to the Internet. (4) _____ making sure that the phone line is attached, you should select the, umm, the small symbol that looks like an 'e', and wait for a connection. It might take a minute or two, but (5) _____ you should see a small notice on the screen telling you that you are now online – you know, connected to the Internet. (6) _____ , simply type in the website address you want, or if you are just surfing then type the word or words in the search bar. It's not at all difficult to use, but some people still have difficulty.

EXERCISE 3 Complete the topic below using the candidate's answer from *Exercise 2*.

Describe how to
You should say:
•
•
•
You should also explain how to

POINT OF IMPACT Notice how in speaking, unlike writing, we do not always use passive forms to describe an instruction or process.

EXERCISE 4 Spend one minute preparing notes for the topic card below, and then tell your partner.

Describe how to use a piece of equipment in your home.
You should say:
• what it is
• how often you use it
• where it can be bought.
You should also explain how to use it.

Unit 5.7 Labelling diagrams (reading)

POINT OF IMPACT As with the listening, prepositions, headings and other labels are important. However, unlike the listening, the text does not always give the answers in the order of the questions, so when you have pinpointed the relevant section remember to read up the page as well as down. Also remember that the vocabulary will often be difficult, but you will not be expected to have any specialist knowledge in order to complete the questions.

EXERCISE 1 Label the diagram on the right.

The left atrium is situated above two valves – the aortic and the mitral valve. Below these valves is the largest chamber of the heart, the left ventricle. On the opposite side of the heart is the right ventricle, which is separated from the right atrium by the tricuspid valve. The aorta is on top of the heart, curled around another artery.

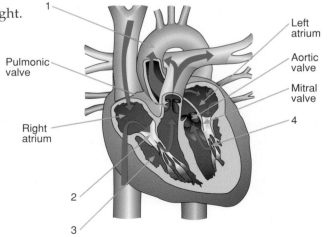

EXERCISE 2	What helped you label the diagram?

EXERCISE 3   Note down any prepositions of place and movement that you know.

Place	
Movement	

EXERCISE 4   Read the text below and complete the question that follows.

Gone in 60 seconds ...

By the time you have finished reading this article, your heart will have pumped blood all around your body at least once. In the normal adult, the heart pumps five litres of blood in a cycle which lasts 60 seconds as the blood moves from the heart into tubes called arteries, then into tiny tubes called capillaries and finally into the veins that lead back to the heart.

The process begins as blood moves to the left ventricle from the left atrium, passing through the mitral valve. As the left ventricle contracts, it pushes open the aortic valve and the blood is carried into the aorta, which distributes it to all other body organs including the heart by way of the arteries.

From this point, the blood begins its journey back to the heart, carrying with it wastes from the organs it has supplied. Entering the right atrium through the vena cava, the accumulated blood pushes open the tricuspid valve, allowing the blood to pass from the right atrium to the right ventricle. After the chamber fills, the heart contracts and the pulmonary valve opens and the blood then flows from the right ventricle into the pulmonary artery.

The pulmonary artery carries blood to the lungs, from where the capillaries take the blood to tiny air sacs and then into the pulmonary vein and back to the left atrium, where the cycle starts all over again.

Label the flow chart below using words from the box.

mitral valve	aorta	right ventricle	~~left atrium~~	body organs
right atrium	left ventricle	pulmonary artery	vena cava	pulmonary vein
~~tricuspid valve~~	pulmonary valve	lungs	aortic valve	

The components involved in blood flow through the body

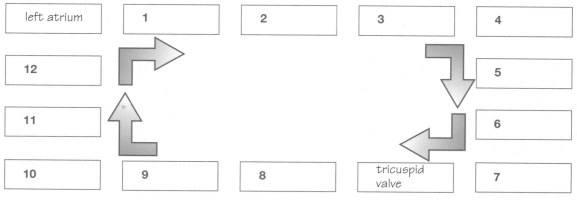

EXERCISE 5   Read the text below and answer the questions that follow.

Bionic bodies

A Robotics, the science of designing and operating robots, is well documented. What is perhaps less well known is the effect this has had on people. Today, the science of prosthetics – part medicine and part engineering – has made the fitting of elaborately functioning prosthetic limbs and joints commonplace. Orthopaedic surgeons routinely replace malfunctioning hips and knees when those joints wear out or succumb to disease. Surgery to fit artificial shoulders, slowly developed during the past 30 years, is no longer rare. What is new are the advances made in bionic prostheses – new limbs which can be attached to a patient's existing nerves and that work as hands, arms, legs or feet, no longer simply plastic replacements but functioning, useful appendages.

B For Campbell Baird, a Scottish hotelier, the news that he would have to have his arm amputated was devastating. He could no longer keep his job and drastic changes had to be made in how he lived. Given the accelerating rate of cancer that would have taken more than just his arm, Mr Baird had little option. Now, however, he has been offered a chance to recover some of his old abilities as a solution has arrived in the form of a robotic prosthesis – a new arm powered by complex electronics which permit the wearer to control movement through micro switches and pressure points. The new limb allows Mr Baird to carry out functions that for 16 years he had found impossible.

C Although admitting that the bionic arm was no match for the real thing, Dr David Gow, who has led the research project for 10 years, commented that bionic limbs are superior to more traditional limb replacements as they restore a biological function controlled by electronics rather than nerves. Bionic limbs require considerable electrical power to operate and it is only the development of advanced new motors in recent years that has allowed the researchers to make the step forward. With four basic functions, the limb Mr Baird was fitted with has been given an additional degree of realism by covering it with a thin, flexible covering the colour of skin. There are even wrinkles and fingerprints. At a cost of $32 000 it will take some time before such prostheses are available to the general public.

D Certainly an amazing story, but not perhaps as amazing as that of Denise Monroe, an 11-year-old American girl born without shoulders or arms. Before her operation, she used her feet to do everything, including, writing, eating, and even brushing her teeth. Revolutionary new technology allowed scientists to recreate shoulder sockets to which the bionic arms can be attached. The only problem that really remains is financial. For Denise, the $210 000 needed for her operation was raised by charity but there are many more people on the waiting list.

E Slightly less expensive is progress currently being made with regard to artificial internal organs. Although many versions are in early experimental stages, it is advancing fast, and some are already in general circulation. At least three new implanted heart devices are now undergoing clinical trials, and the eyes, the liver and other organs are all being researched.

F Bionic ears, or cochlear implants, have a long history, too. The first primitive versions were implanted in 1957 and thousands of hearing-impaired people are now using far more sophisticated versions. One of many such devices, the Clarion, has an external sound processor which converts incoming sounds to digital code, then transmits the code in sound waves to the 'bionic ear', sited beneath the skin at the side of the head. From there a thin internal electrode winds through the cochlea past the damaged hair cells, and sends the coded signals directly to the acoustic nerve at a million impulses a second.

Questions 1–15 are based on Reading Passage 1 'Bionic bodies'.

REVIEW   **Headings (Unit 1.7)**

Choose the most suitable headings for sections A–F from the list (i) to (ix).

List of headings

i	The leading authority
ii	Financial concerns
iii	Surgical implantation
iv	History of prosthetics
v	Commonplace miracles
vi	Other applications
vii	A perfect solution
viii	Improving realism
ix	A second chance

1   Section A
2   Section B
3   Section C
4   Section D
5   Section E
6   Section F

REVIEW   **Short-answer questions (Unit 3.7)**

Answer the following questions using *NO MORE THAN ONE WORD* from the text.

7   What was the reason for Mr Baird's amputation? _____

8   What is the main obstacle to using bionic limbs? _____

REVIEW   **TRUE, FALSE, NOT GIVEN-style (Unit 4.7)**

Do the following statements agree with the views of the writer?

Write   **YES** if the statement agrees with the writer
         NO if the statement does not agree with the writer
         NOT GIVEN if there is no information about this in the passage.

9   The difference between traditional prosthetics and bionic limbs is that they have not been subjected to such rigorous testing.

10 Many organs are now replaceable thanks to bionic technology and research.

REVIEW   **Labelling diagrams (this unit)**

The bionic ear

Label the diagram using *NO MORE THAN TWO WORDS* from the text for each answer.

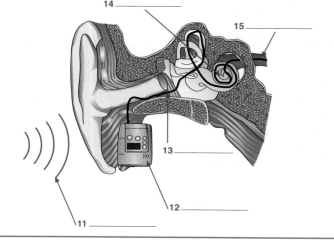

Unit 5.8   Tables

EXERCISE 1   What do you think is the biggest challenge when writing about Task I topics like the one below.

ESSAY TASK

The table below shows the average life expectancy in years of males and females in a number of countries and the world.

Write a report for a university lecturer describing the information shown below.

Country	Life expectancy (years)	
	Male	Female
Australia	77.22	83.23
Canada	76.12	82.79
China	68.57	71.48
Denmark	73.83	79.33
France	74.76	82.71
Germany	74.01	80.50
Japan	77.02	83.35
South Korea	70.75	78.32
Mexico	68.98	75.17
New Zealand	74.55	81.27
South Africa	52.68	56.90
United Kingdom	74.73	80.15
WORLD	61.00	65.00

EXERCISE 2   With so much information, it is sometimes difficult to see any striking trends. Practise by:

a   underlining the two highest numbers in each column
b   circling the two lowest numbers in each column
c   finding any patterns or trends.

POINT OF IMPACT   One possible Task I question asks you to describe information given in a table. Although you may be presented with a lot of data, do not panic. You should approach this in much the same way as you would with any other Task I report.

EXERCISE 3   Prepare a plan for the table above.

ESSAY TASK

The table below shows information regarding the percentage of the population in different age groups.

Write a report for a university lecturer describing the information shown below.

Percentage of people who are aged	World	Europe	North America	Asia
under 15	16	13	13	11
16–60	76	74	72	79
61+	8	13	15	10

EXERCISE 4   Follow the steps in *Exercises* 2 and 3 for the Task I title above.

EXERCISE 5   Read the answer below. How does it compare with your answer?

The table shows the percentage of the population divided into three age categories in three continents, namely Europe, North America and Asia, as well as the world.

For the three age groups, Europe and North America are within a 3% range. The widest difference between the two continents can be found in the population aged between 16 and 60. Another noticeable feature is that for the first two age groups, both Europe and North America vary by a maximum of 4% compared with the world figure, yet in the final age bracket there is a difference of up to 7%.

In contrast, the largest difference between the world population and the Asian population can be seen when comparing those aged 15 or under, where there is a difference of 5%.

To conclude, all three continents show disparities when compared with the world population. However, there is one uniform trend for all three continents in that approximately three quarters of the population are in the 16 to 60 age group.
(169 words)

Unit 5.9   Unexpected questions

EXERCISE 1   The interviewer has just asked you about a subject you have never thought about and you have no real ideas. What can you say?

POINT OF IMPACT   In this situation, the most important first step is not to panic. Avoid responding with 'I don't know'. There are a number of phrases you can learn that will give you some time to think of an idea.

1 Well, it's difficult to say, but ...
2 I don't have any personal opinions, but I suppose ...
3 That's an interesting point and I think I would have to say that ...
4 Mmm ... I'm not really sure, but ...
5 Actually, that's not something I've really thought about, but ...
6 I don't really know much about that, but ...

EXERCISE 2   The interviewer has just asked you the following questions*. Use the phrases to give yourself time to think.

a   What impact do you think power steering has had in reducing traffic accidents?
b   Do you think herbal cigarettes will ever become popular?
c   How can heavy industries be made to be more responsible for the health of their employees?

*These questions are to highlight the exercise. You will almost certainly not be asked anything so obscure.

EXERCISE 3   The candidate below could not think of anything to say about the question in *Exercise 2a*. How has he dealt with this problem?

Well, it's difficult to say but ... umm ... in my opinion the most effective factor in the reduction of traffic accidents is a result of stiffer punishments for poor driving. Although speeding is still a serious issue, other traffic offences such as drink driving have fallen because of the risk of heavy fines and even imprisonment. This has been reinforced by hard-hitting television advertisements highlighting driving while under the influence of alcohol.

POINT OF IMPACT   If you still cannot think of anything to say after a few seconds, you should focus on an aspect of the question you do know and move your answer onto related but more familiar topics. This is not ideal, but better than saying nothing at all.

EXERCISE 4   Try and talk about the unusual subjects on the following page for at least one minute.

The British Royal Family	Terrorism	Stamps
Insects	Donating blood	Video conference English classes
Nudist beaches	Aeroplane safety checks	Video piracy

Unit 5.10   Text completion (listening)

EXERCISE 1   What is the difference between the following pairs? Discuss with your partner.

A	Alternative/Herbal medicine	Western/Pharmaceutical medicine
B	Symptoms	Cause

EXERCISE 2   What do you know about the following topics? Brainstorm in groups.

Acupuncture   Chemotherapy
Osteopathy   Surgery
Reflexology   Paediatrics

EXERCISE 3   Listen to the recording and fill in the gaps using *NO MORE THAN THREE WORDS*. *Remember to use predicting skills before the recording begins.*

Amongst increasing **(a)**_____ pressure to quit, there is finally some good news for smokers. Research presented to the **(b)**_____ of Cardiology states that there are sufficient **(c)**_____ in two glasses of red wine to suspend the **(d)**_____ that smoking **(e)**_____ has on the functioning of arteries.

   Of course, the **(f)**_____do not suggest that drinking red wine allows you to smoke as much as you like, and it is still **(g)**_____ from finding any kind of drug that is capable of reversing the harmful effects of long-term smoking.

   The health effects connected with red wine are not really new. The Romans and **(h)**_____ all considered it as a form of medicine, possibly because of the abundance of polyphenols, naturally occurring chemicals which have a **(i)**_____ on the arteries.

POINT OF IMPACT   Text-completion questions in the listening test are the same as in the reading. They can be either in the form of a summary or as short sentences which you have to complete. With either type, you can expect some information on the recording that will not be required to answer the questions. This is a good opportunity to use your note-taking skills, just in case you miss anything. You will have a little time after the listening test (while you are transferring your answers) to complete any remaining answers.

EXERCISE 4   Now listen to the recording and complete the short sentences that follow.

1   The Health Sciences building is next to _____.
2   There are _____ each term.
3   In the first module, students will study health and safety _____.
4   Students will have to complete a _____ by the end of the course.
5   There will be speakers from various _____.

REVIEW   **Text completion (this unit)**

Listen to the final recording for this section and complete the questions that follow.

Complete the following sentences using *ONE WORD*.

1   East feels _____ therapy is a better word than 'alternative'.
2   Osteopathy involves the manipulation of _____ in order to remove stresses and strains.

REVIEW   **Short-answer questions (Unit 1.10)**

Answer the following questions using *NO MORE THAN THREE WORDS*.

3   According to Matthew East, what must be considered when treating a patient?
4   What was the original cause of the baby's discomfort?
5   How does East describe the use of drugs and operations?
6   How much does East claim natural remedies cost compared with western healthcare?

REVIEW   **Multiple choice (Unit 2.10)**

Circle the correct answer A–C.

7   East believes western medicine
    A is not suitable for the young
    B has not had sufficient trials
    C is overly influenced by pharmaceutical companies.

8   Natural remedies
    A are sometimes used indiscriminately
    B can be used with patients of any age
    C do not affect diet or lifestyle.

REVIEW   **Short-answer questions (Unit 1.10)**

Answer the following questions using *NO MORE THAN THREE WORDS*.

  9 What example does East give of the benefits of western medicine?
10 Who is next week's guest?

Unit 5.11   Staying on topic

EXERCISE 1   What are topic words? What are task words? Write a definition of each.

EXERCISE 2   Prepare a plan for the question below. Show your plan to your partner. Is there anything you think is not really connected to the topic?

People with health problems related to smoking, alcohol or drugs should not be allowed medical treatment. The money should be spent on people with natural and not self-inflicted illnesses.

Do you agree?

EXERCISE 3   What are your opinions on the student's answer that follows? Make a note of the positive and negative points.

With many natural causes of illnesses being stopped by modern science, an increasing proportion of illness is being attributed to personal bad habits. The argument as to whether people who become sick as a result of their addictions should be treated does not have a clear solution, but I suggest that the statement is wrong for the following reasons.

Everyone in this world even criminals have their own human right. Despite whatever objections people may have, people have the right to treat their body how they like within the boundaries of the law. As part of a progressive and modern society, we also cannot refuse to offer treatment to people purely because of their lifestyle choices. We should also consider our own personal reactions. For example, if one of our relatives or friends was very sick related to smoking, how could we stand aside and let them suffer? On this basis, we should therefore treat every human as equal regardless of the situation.

In the second place, addiction is not just people's fault. Sometimes society and community develop a bad effect in someone. People, especially teenagers, get bad information from places such as the Internet, television and music. Advertising increases younger people's awareness of products that can be harmful, but are selling them in a way that they seem only to be good. Educating society, and also not letting companies advertise things which can be harmful without clearly explaining the negative aspects, would help reduce the number of people suffering from self-induced illnesses.

To conclude, we will only be able to reduce the number of people seeking medical help as a result of their own addictions by treating the cause of the problem, not the effect. By educating and controlling, governments would be able to dramatically reduce a problem which is currently getting more.

POINT OF IMPACT   In Unit 1.5 you looked at brainstorming ideas then rejecting the points which were inappropriate for the specific question. Once you have prepared a plan and started to write your essay, it is very important that you *stay on the topic*. Keep referring to your plan, making sure it is *relevant*.

EXERCISE 4   Brainstorm the topic given in row A with as many connected ideas as possible.

A   Healthcare

EXERCISE 5   Your teacher will tell you what to write in rows B and C.

B

C

EXERCISE 6   You have now brainstormed ideas for the essay title 'Private healthcare is unfair'. Now prepare a plan using your ideas.

Unit 5.12   Topic Card: Health

EXERCISE 1   Use the Part One questions below and the topic card that follows to practise the first two parts of the speaking test.

Part One (use only three)

Talk about your hobbies.
What do you do?
Tell me about your family.
Talk about a typical day.
Can you describe your hometown?
Describe your house/flat.
What kind of food do you like?

SPEAKING

Part Two

> Describe your favourite way to relax.
> You should say:
> * what it is
> * when you started doing it
> * how often you do it.
> You should also explain how it relaxes you.

EXERCISE 2   Now work with a partner and practise the interview. One of you should act as the candidate and the other should be the interviewer. The interviewer should make notes about the following points.

* Part One comments.
* Part Two comments.

When you have finished, talk to your partner about your comments and then exchange roles.

UNIT 6

Back to school

Unit 6.1   Referencing (reading)

EXERCISE 1   Read the passage below. What do the underlined words refer to?

New Zealand is becoming an increasingly popular destination for overseas visitors. <u>It</u> attracts tourists and people on business, but the vast majority come as students. Mostly from Asian countries, <u>they</u> stay for anything from a few weeks to a few years or more, studying at language schools, colleges and universities. New Zealand can offer good homestay accommodation, a clean and beautiful environment and a reasonable cost of tuition. <u>These factors</u> attract an ever-increasing number of overseas students, accounting for millions of dollars in revenue for New Zealand.

It	
they	
These factors	

POINT OF IMPACT   An important part of understanding a text is being able to identify the reference words and their relationship to other phrases or sentences in the passage.

EXERCISE 2   Match a sentence from column A with a reference word from column B, then complete the sentence .

A	B
Professor Edwards has been lecturing for 16 years.	They
Overseas students often find university courses difficult.	It
The IELTS test is becoming increasingly popular.	He

POINT OF IMPACT   When talking generally, you may find that some singular nouns take a plural reference word. For example: *A teacher* should always be prepared. *They* should also be punctual.

EXERCISE 3   Read the text below.
a Find and underline all the reference words
b What do the reference words refer to?

Academic overdrive?

Student life is becoming increasingly difficult. Not only are students expected to perform and compete within the class, but also to devote time and energy to extra-curricular activities as well as struggle with an increasing load of homework. The push to get into the top universities has caused many overachieving students to take on heavier workloads and more challenging classes.

This push, however, doesn't end once students reach university. In fact, when they reach the top places they have worked so hard to get into, many students are forced to work even harder than they did in high school. Once in the top universities, the pressure is on to secure a place in the top graduate school. But it doesn't end there. Once students have graduated with the best results, they find that they must continue to overextend themselves in order to secure the top jobs in their particular field. Such is the emphasis on academic success.

There are many who claim that this entire system is wrong because it puts too much emphasis on measuring achievement and not enough on true learning. This in turn has inevitable effects on the students themselves. In such a high-pressure learning environment, those that find the pressure overwhelming have nowhere to turn. In an academic world measured only by academic success, many students begin to feel a low sense of worth, yet they fear to turn to anyone for help as this would be perceived as a signal of failure, an inability to cope with that which other students appear to have no problem. This can be particularly hard for foreign students as they find themselves isolated without familiar cultural or family ties in their new environment and thus they concentrate solely on their work.

Perhaps the main thing to remember is that although it is important to study hard, school life should also be fun.

POINT OF IMPACT   *Perhaps the main thing to remember is that although it is important to study hard, school life should also be fun.*
It is sometimes used as the **dummy subject** – it does not refer to anything specific.

EXERCISE 4   Read the sentences below. Is 'it' used as a reference word (RW) or a dummy subject (DS)?

a Look at those clouds. It's going to rain.
b Homework is essential. It allows students to review work they have studied in class.
c Admittedly, student depression is hard to investigate as few people are willing to talk openly about it.
d It can take up to four years to complete a degree.
e Otago is a very popular university. It was the first university in New Zealand.

EXERCISE **5**   Reference words are useful not only in the reading, but also in your writing. Use a reference word and a linking word to rewrite and extend the prompts below. *Remember that subject and object reference words can be used (e.g. they, them).*

Example	
Cost / university education / rising	Although the cost of university education is rising, this is not deterring increasing numbers of undergraduates.
a Some schools / better than other	
b Computer technology / used / classroom	
c Good student / takes / every opportunity / speak	
d Cambridge and Oxford / world-famous universities	

REVIEW   **Headings (Unit 1.7)**

Questions 1–15 are based on the reading passage that follows.

Questions 1–5   Choose the most suitable headings for sections A–F from the list below.

List of headings	
i	Why New Zealand?
ii	Course requirements
iii	Government funding
iv	Cost of further education
v	Further education options
vi	Overseeing authorities
vii	Specialisation
viii	Prestigious contribution
ix	Postgraduate choices

	1	Section A
Example		Section B *vi*
	2	Section C
	3	Section D
	4	Section E
	5	Section F

Read the text below, and answer the questions that follow.

READING PASSAGE **1**

Studying in New Zealand

A   A relatively small island with a population of less than a quarter of that of Tokyo, New Zealand has a huge overseas student population. With over half a million fee-paying foreign students, an ever-increasing range of academic, professional and vocational courses and English language services are being created or expanded. But why do so many people come from overseas to study in New Zealand? Primarily, there is the fact that it has an excellent education system, especially in English language teaching. With its many British connections as well as the adoption of language from America, New Zealand offers a very international language. Language students are also enticed to New Zealand as they can fully immerse themselves in the language. This is only possible in a country where English is the spoken language.

B   There are also strict government controls and standards on the quality of education offered. The government controls the education system, and it has appointed the New Zealand Qualifications Authority, a Ministry of Education and an Education Review Office, to license and control schools. These government bodies ensure that standards are as high in New Zealand as anywhere in the world. In addition, they decide whether or not language schools have the credentials and quality to operate. This allows students to have some peace of mind when choosing a school, but there are other reasons to choose New Zealand first. Independent reports have proven New Zealand to be the most cost-effective country in the western world for study fees, accommodation, cost of living, and recreation. It also has a reputation for safety and security, perhaps the best amongst western countries. Auckland City offers a multicultural and cosmopolitan place to shop, eat and be entertained. Less than an hour out of the city and you find yourself on beaches or mountains famous for their cleanliness and lack of pollution.

C Although a majority of international students spend some time in a language school, for those aged 13 to 18 New Zealand secondary schools provide a broad education. Other students take advantage of one of the many tertiary education institutions which form the New Zealand polytechnic system. These institutions are state-funded and provide education and training at many levels, from introductory studies to full degree programmes. University education was established in New Zealand in 1870 and has a similar tradition to the British university system. There are eight state-funded universities in New Zealand, all of them internationally respected for their academic and research performance. In addition to a centrally coordinated system of quality assurance audits at both institution and programme level, each university undertakes internal quality checks.

D All New Zealand universities offer a broad range of subjects in arts, commerce and science, but they have also specialised in narrower fields of study such as computer studies, medicine or environmental studies. Bachelor's, Master's and Doctorate degrees are offered by all New Zealand universities. A range of undergraduate and postgraduate diplomas are also available, along with Honours programmes (usually requiring an additional year of study). The first degree a student is able to gain in New Zealand is, as elsewhere, a Bachelor's degree. With a completed Bachelor's degree, a graduate may be able to go on to a number of other options. There are Postgraduate Diploma courses, Master's degrees, Doctorates and even research positions available.

E The Postgraduate Diploma course takes one year on a full-time programme and is designed for graduates building on the academic field of their previous degree. The Master's degree, like the Postgraduate Diploma, builds on a Bachelor's degree but can take up to two years, by which time a thesis must be completed. The Master's is the conventional pathway to the next level of education – the Doctorate. For this course, graduates are required to produce a research-based thesis as part of a course that takes a minimum of two years, and is by far the most challenging.

F Finally there is the possibility of research in New Zealand universities. Research is the main characteristic that distinguishes a university as opposed to a polytechnic or other tertiary education institution. New Zealand remains justifiably proud of the quality of its research as a large number of awards are presented to researchers from New Zealand universities.

REVIEW   **Short-answer questions (Unit 3.7)**

Answer the following question using *NO MORE THAN THREE WORDS* from the text.

6   In what field of study does New Zealand excel? _____

REVIEW   **Text completion (Unit 2.7)**

Complete the sentences below using *NO MORE THAN THREE WORDS*.

7   Full immersion learning can only happen in an _____
8   Educational standards are monitored by three _____

REVIEW   **TRUE, FALSE, NOT GIVEN-style questions (Unit 4.7)**

Look at the following statements and decide if they are right or wrong according to the information given.

Write   **TRUE** if the statement is true
FALSE if the statement is false
NOT GIVEN if the information is not given in the passage.

9 Most international students start their studies in a secondary school.
10 Postgraduate students undertaking a diploma course extend what they have learned during their Bachelor's degree.
11 All quality control at a tertiary level is done by the universities themselves.

REVIEW   **Labelling diagrams (Unit 5.7)**

Complete the flow chart below using *NO MORE THAN ONE WORD* from the text.

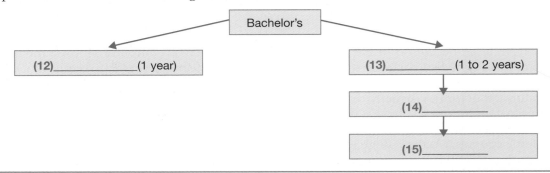

Bachelor's

(12)_____(1 year)

(13)_____ (1 to 2 years)

(14)_____

(15)_____

Unit 6.2   **Correlating data**

EXERCISE   1   Write a plan for the graph below.

1 Topic words?	
2 Tense?	
3 Axes?	
4 About?	
5 Trends(s)?	

ESSAY TASK

The graph to the right shows the number of students attending private schools in Britain.

Write a report for a university lecturer describing the information shown.

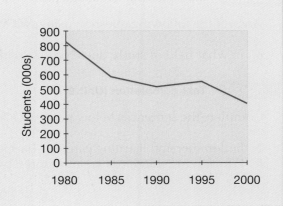

POINT OF IMPACT   It is common in Task I to have more than one set of data to describe. However, it is not sufficient to simply describe each set in turn – you should show the examiner that you know how the information **correlates** (the connection or effect they have on each other).

EXERCISE 2   Look at Figure A and Figure B below. It extends the data from *Exercise 1*. What correlation do the graphs show?

ESSAY TASK

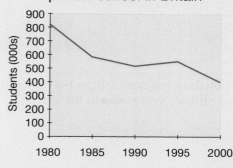

Figure A – Students attending private school in Britain

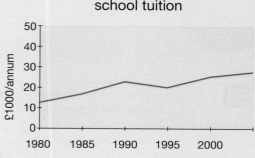

Figure B – Cost of private school tuition

Now you can add another row to the plan you made in Exercise 1.

6	Correlation?	

EXERCISE 3   Now look at the sets of data below. Why do you think they are together?

Set 1

The graph shows the employment status of six different age bands of New Zealanders.

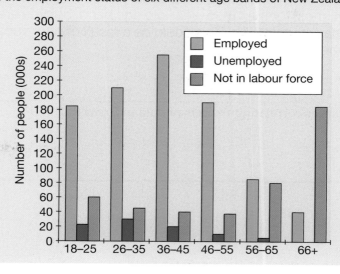

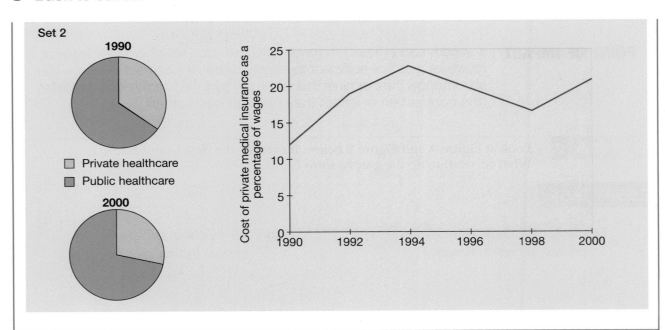

EXERCISE 4 Look at some of the language you can use when drawing correlations between sets of data. Add any other 'correlation' words or phrases you know to the list.

a (X) appears to have a direct impact on (Y).
b A rise in (X) causes an attendant increase in (Y).
c There is an inverse relationship between (X) and (Y).
d There is a direct relationship between (X) and (Y).
e There is a direct correlation between (X) and (Y).
f An increase in (X) resulted in a decrease in (Y).
g Closely linked to (X), it can be seen that (Y)...
h As a result of the decline in (X), (Y)...

POINT OF IMPACT Although writing about correlations is important when presented with different sets of data, do not feel that you have to think of an explanation as to *why* they might be correlated. For example, in *Exercise 3*, Set 1 you should observe that the level of unemployment is highest for the 18-25-year-old age band, but you are not expected to say anything like 'This could be a result of poor vocational training opportunities'.

EXERCISE 5 Write sentences correlating the sets of data in *Exercises 2* and *3*.

| **Unit 6.3** | **Likes, dislikes and preferences** |

EXERCISE 1   Which of the following do you think is the most effective method of learning English?

A   On your own.
B   In a group with a teacher.
C   One-to-one lessons with a teacher.
D   Living and working in an English-speaking country.

POINT OF IMPACT   When expressing preferences it is common to use concession words. For example:

I much prefer a group class. <u>Admittedly, you do get more personal attention in a private class</u>, but you can also learn from other students when you study together.

You may want to review Unit 1.2 for a list of concession words.

EXERCISE 2   Classify the following phrases as expressing:

A   likes
B   dislikes
C   preferences

   1   I'm not keen on (X)
   2   (X) is better
   3   I'm fond of (X)
   4   I like (X) more
   5   I detest (X)
   6   I'm into (X)
   7   I can't bear (X)
   8   I adore (X)
   9   I'd rather (X)
  10   (X) is far superior
  11   (X) is stunning
  12   I loathe (X)
  13   I can't stand (X)
  14   (X) is excellent
  15   I'd sooner (X)

EXERCISE 3   Express likes, dislikes and preferences on the following subjects. Express a concession wherever possible.

1   Learning languages
2   Reading novels
3   Fast food
4   Watching soap operas
5   Homework

Unit 6.4   Discourse markers (listening)

EXERCISE 1   Which is the best ending for which sentence? Why?

1   Computers can be useful in the classroom. However,

2   Computers offer an additional resource in the classroom. In addition,

a   being computer literate is becoming an increasingly important skill for students to learn.

b   they cannot replace the role of the teacher.

POINT OF IMPACT   In the listening test, the type of linking words you hear can help you predict the general direction of what you hear. You can tell if points are connected as:
*   comparisons
*   concessions
*   additions
*   sequences
*   opposites
*   cause and effect constructions.
Review Unit 1.2 and Unit 5.5 for different linking words.

EXERCISE 2   You will hear the first part of a sentence. What point (from the Point of Impact above) do you think it will be followed by? Write the linking word that helped you decide. *The first one has been done for you.*

Sentence	Next point	Linking word
1	opposite	Although...
2		
3		
4		
5		
6		

POINT OF IMPACT   Linking words in listening are only one example of **discourse markers** – the words and expressions used to show how speech is constructed. They are particularly useful for you in Sections 2 and 4 of the listening test as they indicate changes in the direction of a thought, idea or opinion. That means if you have a question asking about reading ability and the next question is asking about new additions to the school building, then you can expect to hear a discourse marker announcing the change of topic.

EXERCISE 3   What information do you think is given in the following discourse markers?

Discourse marker	Tells you	
First		
Like		
Anyway		
I mean		
So		
Moving on		
As I said		
To make myself clear		
Right		
To put it another way		
This isn't always so		
Now		
Talking about that		

EXERCISE 4   Put suitable discourse markers from *Exercise 3* into the text below.

(1)_____ I'd like to thank you all again for coming to this meeting, and to say that I have received apologies from Mrs Brownlow, who won't be able to attend today. (2)_____, I'd like to talk to you about our English language department. (3)_____ in the last meeting, we are looking for some of you to act as mentors for our international students arriving over the coming weeks. Although our college prides itself on having a welcoming environment in which international students can feel at home from the very first day, we know (4)_____. Feelings of homesickness, isolation and loneliness are somewhat unavoidable, but I would like, as much as possible, to reduce these factors by teaming new students with existing students who have been here some time. (5)_____, I am looking for volunteers to show the new students around, introduce them to people and generally ease them into their studies, so if any of you are willing to help, then please come to my office anytime during the week and let me know. (6)_____, I'd also like to talk to you about a temporary teacher who will be joining us for the next week or so. He will be teaching history and sociology, and substituting for Miss Kinsale until her recovery. (7)_____, if anyone wants to send her a card then just let me know by the end of the day as I will be going to the hospital this evening to visit her. (8)_____, unless there is anything else you want to add, we'll close the meeting. I hope to see some of you during the week.

EXERCISE 5   Now listen to the recording and check your answers.

POINT OF IMPACT   In addition to discourse markers, the intonation pattern of the speaker's voice can also indicate a change of topic. The tone of voice generally falls at the end of one topic, followed by a pause then starts on the next topic in a higher tone. Intonation and meaning will be studied in greater detail in Unit 8.4.

EXERCISE 6   Listen to the two sentences. In which sentences does the speaker's intonation suggest the topic will be resumed in the next sentence? In which sentence will the topic be different?

REVIEW   **Multiple choice (Unit 2.10)**

Listen to the recording and complete questions 1–10.

Circle the correct answer A–C.

1   The students were expecting
   A to hear a lecture on overpopulation
   B Mr Mackenzie
   C a guest speaker

REVIEW   **Table completion (Unit 3.10)**

Complete the table below using *ONE WORD OR A NUMBER*.

Statistics from USA
42 million adults **(2)** _____
50 million adults have the reading ability of a **(3)** _____-year-old.
Increasing by **(4)** _____ million per year.

Illiteracy costs

	Unemployment	Unrealised earnings	Literacy programmes
cost (in billions of dollars)	**(5)**	237	**(6)**

REVIEW   **Multiple choice (Unit 2.10)**

Circle the correct answer A–C.

7   Illiteracy is increasing because many young learners are
   A not being taught how to break words into sounds
   B given word lists which are too long
   C not challenged enough in the classroom.

REVIEW   **Text completion (Unit 5.10)**

Complete this summary using *NO MORE THAN TWO WORDS*.

English is made up of 26 letters, with 44 **(8)** _____ and 70 ways of **(9)** _____.
Unsuccessful teaching practices persist, however, because reading is **(10)** _____

Unit 6.5   Cause and effect

Further education has become more accessible for a wider range of people. As a result, an increasing number of people have degrees.

EXERCISE 1   Read the sentence above and answer the questions.

1   Why do more people have degrees?
2   What has happened because of the increasing accessibility of further education?
3   What words connect the answers to (1) and (2)?

POINT OF IMPACT   In the text above, the sentences can be broken down into cause, effect and connector.

Further education has become more accessible for a wider range of people is the **cause**.
... [A]n increasing number of people have degrees is the **effect**.
As a result is the **connector**.

Thinking of cause and effect allows you to extend your ideas and justify your opinions. Using a range of connectors will also make your essay more academic.

EXERCISE 2   Answer the three 'cause and effect' sections for each of the following statements.

A   Due to an obligatory level of education, illiteracy in many countries is low.
What is the cause?
What is the effect?
What is the connector?

B   Understanding the applications of technology has become increasingly difficult. Consequently, university courses are becoming increasingly specialised.
What is the cause?
What is the effect?
What is the connector?

C   Many overseas students find the first year of university courses difficult because of the language barrier.
What is the cause?
What is the effect?
What is the connector?

D   He did not get the required grade in his IELTS test and thus the university he had applied for rejected him.
What is the cause?
What is the effect?
What is the connector?

E   Teaching as a profession is not as prestigious as it was 50 years ago, in part a result of increasing problems in the education system.
What is the cause?
What is the effect?
What is the connector?

POINT OF IMPACT   The order of cause and effect or effect and cause depends on the type of connector you use. Make sure you are familiar with the different types as mistakes can make your point very unclear.

EXERCISE 3   Complete the table with a suitable connector in column B and an ending in column C.

	A	B	C
1	He finished the exam	so	he left the exam room.
2	He smoked 50 cigarettes a day		
3	The students always tried their best		
4	More and more students are studying abroad		
5	Degrees have become easier to obtain		
6	Private education has become increasingly expensive		
7	The school had neglected student recruitment		
8	He believed the key to success was good teaching		

POINT OF IMPACT   You can further extend cause-and-effect constructions by writing about secondary or root causes. Here are five common constructions:
(Z) has been directly affected by (X), as this allows for (Y).
As a result of (X) leading to (Y), (Z) has been possible.
(X), thus allowing for (Y), has resulted in (Z).
(X) results in (Y), which in turn leads to (Z).
Given (X), it follows that (Y) would mean (Z).

EXERCISE 4   Look at the diagram below and make some sentences using the constructions given in the Point of Impact. Add some more ideas to the mind map.

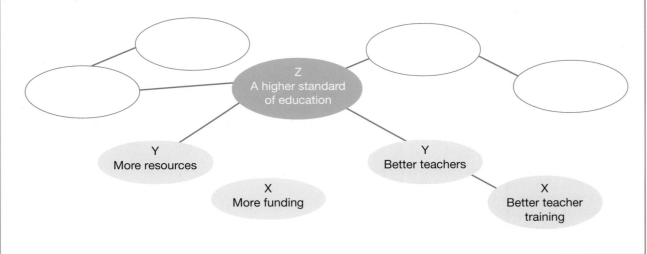

EXERCISE 5   Complete the essay task.

ESSAY TASK

You should spend about 40 minutes on this task.

What factors do you think are important in promoting a higher standard of education?

You should write at least 250 words.

Unit 6.6   School life

EXERCISE 1   What ages do you associate with the following?

High school	College
Kindergarten	Junior school
Polytechnic	Sixth form
Secondary school	Junior high
University	Nursery
Primary school	Intermediate

POINT OF IMPACT   The names of the educational level students are in at different ages can differ depending on what country you are in. In order to avoid confusion, it is useful to talk about the system used in the country in which you are taking the test.

EXERCISE 2   Read this description of school life in South Africa.

Well, you start your education at the age of seven. I think that's a little later than in most countries, but I thought it was great. After seven years in primary school, you move up to high school. That normally takes seven years again, but compulsory education ends once you're 16 so you only have to stay for the first four or five years. I really enjoyed high school – I had so many friends and it seemed so relaxed. Anyway, if you do complete high school and your grades are good enough, you can go to university.

Now write a similar description of the education system in your country.

EXERCISE 3   Prepare to answer the following topic card.

> Talk about your favourite subject at school.
> You should say:
> * when you studied it
> * what the subject was
> * what the teacher was like.
> You should also explain why it was your favourite subject.

Unit 6.7   Matching (reading)

EXERCISE 1   The sentences below have been divided into two. Match the columns to make two complete sentences.

A	B
1 This exercise is	a common example.
2 Putting sentence halves together is	an example of matching.

POINT OF IMPACT   Matching exercises come in a number of forms, but the most common are:
- matching headings to paragraphs (Unit 1.7)
- matching sentence halves
- matching cause and effect.

The skills you apply differ slightly depending on the type of matching question.

POINT OF IMPACT   When matching sentence halves, grammar and logic are important. If you are having difficulty finding the correct answer, begin by eliminating the options you think are wrong.

EXERCISE 2   Match the sentence halves below. *There is no text for this exercise.*

1 Further education is essential if ...	a	... you are hoping for a good job.
2 Degree-level study and beyond ...	b	... is part of building your English.
3 Good teachers ...	c	... is a very useful tool in the job market.
4 The ability to speak English ...	d	... should be self-funded.
5 Completing homework assignments ...	e	... have good students.

POINT OF IMPACT   Matching cause-and-effect sentences can be difficult as they often rely on reference words. Cause and effect will not always be in the same sentence with a clear connecting word. There are many ways of expressing cause and effect (see Unit 6.5).

EXERCISE 3   Think of a possible effect for the causes given. *One has been done for you.*

University enrolment has increased	More competition for places
High level of illiteracy in poor countries	
More universities accept IELTS	
Some schools have 40 or more students in one class	
A great demand for qualified teachers	

READING & LISTENING

| EXERCISE | 4 | Now think of a possible cause for the effect given. *The first one has been done for you.* |

technology is increasingly important in the workplace	specialised courses developed to train people
	parents sending children to private schools
	students become disillusioned with education
	weaker in the active skills of speaking and writing
	some students cannot cope with the pressure

POINT OF IMPACT When matching cause-and-effect questions, you will often find that the linking words and the grammar have been abbreviated, leaving almost note-form sentences. It often helps to build each cause or effect phrase into a complete sentence after you have matched them.

University enrolment has increased ⟶ more competition for places
As a result of increased enrolment in university, there is now more competition for places.

| EXERCISE | 5 | Read the text below and match cause and effect. |

READING PASSAGE 1

For many sufferers of dyslexia, the knowledge that they have this learning difficulty came too late to help. Having been through, and often dropped out of, the standard school system, they are left with a low sense of self-worth and the conviction that they are mentally below par. Yet in reality, dyslexics often have above-average intelligence. The problem, it appears, is that they have trouble translating language into thought and thought into language. The two-dimensional world of reading and spelling is a constant source of frustration, and those suffering from dyslexia need more time and help in reading and spelling. Undiagnosed, children see a difference between themselves and their peers but don't know how to express it to others and continue quietly struggling to compete in a world for which their mind is not geared. Teachers and even other students push them to simply 'try harder' or 'just concentrate and you'll get it'.

Moving from childhood to adolescence, the situation becomes worse. Young teenagers are academically left even further behind, and this is often noticed by fellow students, an embarrassing situation for people already going through hormonal and biological changes. Anxiety and anger build from repeated failures, low school results and an inability to follow the flow of lessons that other students seem to comprehend with relative ease.

Motivation then becomes a problem as these young teens are mislabelled 'lazy', or 'emotionally disturbed', and some schools then probe into the home life of a student in order to uncover causes for these problems. This inevitably adds pressure to an already tense situation.

Fear of humiliation combined with an unimpressive academic record often combines to discourage students from continuing to university or further education. For those that do pursue an academic path, they often find college just as hard, if not harder. Finding some solace in menial jobs which do not require the academic skills they could never master, many intelligent people with dyslexia never get to explore their true abilities and so are left with low self-esteem that follows them throughout their adult life.

Cause	Effect
1 Symptoms not recognised in childhood	a Lack of ambition
2 Peer pressure	b Feeling of inferiority begins
3 Incorrectly diagnosed	c Chronic low self-confidence
4 Fear of further humiliation	d Deeper investigation into the wrong areas
5 Never realising full potential	e Additional stress at an already difficult age

Unit 6.8   Bar charts and pie charts

ESSAY TASK

You should spend about 20 minutes on this task.

The graph shows the percentage of primary and secondary schools with Internet access in New Zealand from 1991 to 1999.

Write a report for a university lecturer describing the information shown.

You should spend about 20 minutes on this task.

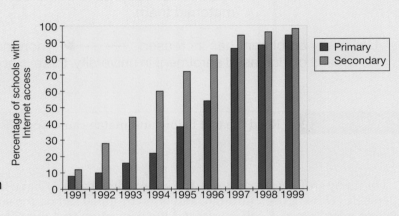

EXERCISE   1   Look at the bar chart in the essay task above. What are the main trends?

EXERCISE   2   Why are the bar chart and the pie charts together?

The graphs below show the percentage of primary and secondary schools with Internet access in New Zealand from 1991 to 1999 and the percentage of households with Internet access in 1991 and 1999.

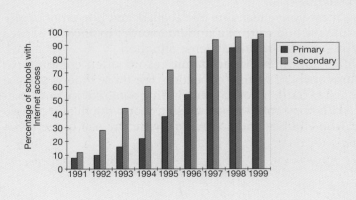

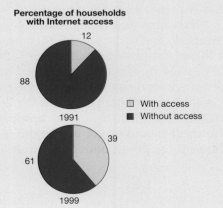

EXERCISE	3	Prepare a plan and write an essay based on *Exercise 2*.

EXERCISE	4	Below are two possible answers to the Task I title from *Exercise 2*. Match each essay with a comment.

1 The bar chart illustrates the number of primary and secondary schools with access to the Internet between 1991 and 1999 in New Zealand. The horizontal axis represents years and the vertical axis is percentages. Furthermore, there are two pie charts which show the percentages of families with Internet access.

In 1991 the percentages of primary and secondary schools with Internet access were 6% and 12% respectively. After a year, the second one suddenly doubled. After another year, it nearly doubled again to reach a total of 45%. During the same period, the primary one increased slightly. However, its use increased dramatically in the next few years to nearly 90% while the secondary one continued its sharp increase to over 90%.

From 1997 to 1999 the percentages of primary and secondary schools climbed slightly, peaking at 90% and 98% respectively.

From the pie charts, the percentage of households with Internet access was 12% in 1991. It tripled from 1991 to 1999.

To conclude, the percentage of households, primary and secondary schools with Internet access in New Zealand increased dramatically between 1991 and 1999.

2 The bar chart illustrates the percentage of New Zealand primary and secondary schools which had Internet access from 1991 to 1999. The pie charts show Internet access in the home for 1991 and 1999.

The most striking trend of the three charts is that in all areas, Internet access increased. The most rapid increase came in secondary schools, which rose to nearly all schools within the eight year period. Although a rising trend was maintained throughout the period, it became increasingly less dramatic over the years.

Despite having a similarly increasing overall trend, the number of primary schools with Internet access increased slowly for the first three years, then sharply accelerated from 1993 to 1997. From this point, the increase became considerably less marked.

In 1991 the number of households with Internet access was higher than primary or secondary schools. However, in 1999 the number of household with Internet access was less than half the percentage of Internet access of either primary or secondary schools.

To sum up, the trend for all areas was increasing, with secondary schools being followed by primary schools. Households also increased during the period.

A The candidate has presented a thorough and logical description of the graphs, correlating the information and highlighting general as well as specific trends. The candidate has also made good use of extended sentences, although there are some areas which lack clarity. However, more data would have supported the points. Overall, a very good attempt that is worth a high level result.

B Although the trends are expressed, the candidate has taken data directly from the graph without using a variety of structures to present the information. There is only a cursory explanation of the pie charts, and no correlation is drawn between the bar chart and the pie charts. Generally clear, some of the language used is a little below the academic standard required for a high level result. The candidate has reached the required word limit, but the report seems considerably more hurried towards the end.

Unit 6.9   Talking about changes

EXERCISE 1   In your country, what are the trends in the following areas? Write *I* for increasing, *D* for decreasing and *NC* if there has been no real change in recent years.

a Employment
b Price of electrical goods
c Birth rate
d People living alone
e Young mothers

f House ownership
g University graduates
h Reading books
i Immigration
j Emigration

POINT OF IMPACT   In Part Three of the test, you could be asked to talk about changes either in your country or in international trends. You have already studied much of the vocabulary in the writing course. Remember that a full answer will require you to justify and support what you say.

EXERCISE 2   Write down the words/phrases the candidate has used to express changes.

Q Tell me about recent changes in university graduation in your country.

A Well, not only in my country but also around the world, there is a marked increase in the number of university graduates. I can't speak for the rest of the world, but in my country this is partly due to subsidised study costs. Only 10 or 15 years ago, the option of going to university was open only to those that were wealthy enough, but now people from all backgrounds have an equal chance. I think this is definitely a step in the right direction, although there are still some potential students that still don't have the means.

EXERCISE 3   a Make short notes on three of the subjects in *Exercise 1*. Remember to use structures that express changes.
            b Now talk about the subjects.

Unit 6.10   Matching (listening)

POINT OF IMPACT   Matching questions in the listening test use many of the skills you have already practised. The most common types ask you to match a diagram with a description or decide who said something.

EXERCISE 1 What skills would you use if you were answering the following questions? *There is no recording for this exercise.*

1 Which is Fiona's favourite painting?

2 Who states the following? Write (M) for Mark and (B) for Belinda.

Language students from different countries have different weaknesses.
Cultural differences are the most common reason for a student not learning.

POINT OF IMPACT With matching questions, the answers are often logically marked (Write (M) for Mark and (B) for Belinda). However, you should be very careful when transferring your answers to the answer sheet.

EXERCISE 2 Listen to the recording and answer the following questions.

To whom do the following phrases relate? Write J for Joe and A for Alana.

1 Is not that interested in the ceremony.
2 Thinks the occasion should be celebrated.
3 Which diagram best illustrates what Alana is describing?

A   B   C   D

REVIEW   **Matching (this unit)**

Listen to the recording and answer the following questions.

Circle the correct letter A–C.

		South Africa	Australia	New Zealand
1	Children start later	A	B	C
2	Has intermediate school	A	B	C
3	Few religious private schools	A	B	C
4	Doesn't have correspondence education	A	B	C
5	Home schooling	A	B	C
6	Compulsory extracurricular activities	A	B	C

REVIEW   **Text completion (Unit 5.10)**

Complete the notes below using *NO MORE THAN THREE WORDS*.

New Zealand boarding school dress code

Dress had to be one inch below the knee when **(7)** _____

A hat had to be worn at all times when **(8)** _____

Socks had to be **(9)** _____

Your **(10)** _____ had to be worn at all times.

Unit 6.11   Writing a conclusion for Task II

EXERCISE   1   Do you think these are good points in a conclusion?

		Yes	No
a	It should be at least 70 words.		
b	It should include a general statement about what you have written.		
c	You can speculate or make a recommendation.		
d	A short conclusion of two or three sentences is unacceptable.		
e	There are a number of set phrases you can use in a conclusion.		

EXERCISE   2   Here are some conclusions. What do you think the title may have been about?

A Title:

To conclude, technology has presented us with many advantages in a learning environment, yet total reliance on computers is not a suitable replacement for a teacher. Despite the precision that technology may be able to offer, a human atmosphere offers a much broader scope of education, and a combination of the two would provide the most effective solution.

B Title:

Generally speaking, therefore, it would seem to be counterproductive to raise the cost of higher education. Although there are some students who do not fully exploit the opportunities offered, making university financially inaccessible is not an effective solution. In addition, reducing the number of university-educated citizens would have a detrimental impact on both society and the future of the workplace.

POINT OF IMPACT   Your conclusion should review the main points of your essay. It is also good practice to end your essay with some form of speculation or recommendation. In the examples in *Exercise 2* conclusion A makes a recommendation and essay B speculates on potential implications.

EXERCISE 3   Look at the table below and decide if they are recommendations (R) or speculations (S).

		S/R
a	To sum up, although cutting unemployment benefits presents a short-term resolution, the provision of free or subsidised training offers the best and most far-sighted solution to the problems of unemployment.	
b	Ultimately, the argument comes down to this: unless students choose to take full advantage of all the opportunities they are offered, their English ability may suffer even to the point of finding themselves regressing to a lower level.	
c	In the final analysis, children should be guided by their parents and their teachers until such time as they are old enough to decide the course of education that best suits them. Otherwise they may well lack a fully developed understanding of their options when they grow up.	
d	Overall, as career opportunities are becoming increasingly dependent on more specialist skills, it would be logical for governments to provide and promote appropriate training and education at an early age, allowing the workforce to diversify into many areas of specific expertise.	

EXERCISE 4   Now think of some recommendations or speculations that you could add to the comments below.

1   The number of people in higher education has increased fourfold in the past 50 years.

2   Some schools cannot afford modern equipment.

3   An increasing number of people who studied specialist courses are finding they do not have the broad scope of knowledge essential for job mobility.

4   IELTS teachers are not very well paid.

EXERCISE 5 In *Exercise 2* and *Exercise 3* a number of ways are given to signal to the reader that you are beginning your conclusion. What are they? Do you know any more?

POINT OF IMPACT There are different opinions on the use of *In conclusion* .... Although it is grammatically correct, some feel that it has been used to excess, and alternative phrases show a wider degree of vocabulary. Remember, you only have 250 words in Task II to demonstrate your ability to the examiner, so make every word count.

ESSAY TASK

A course of study that has no direct employment opportunities serves no purpose.

To what extent do you agree with the above?

EXERCISE 6 Make a plan for the essay task above. Try to write a conclusion based on your plan.

Unit 6.12 Topic Card: Education

POINT OF IMPACT As you prepare for your IELTS test, you may use a number of different questions and topic cards that are similar. Make sure that you talk about the question you were asked, and not something you have already prepared. Make some notes on the topic card before you begin.

EXERCISE 1 Use the topic card and the Part Three questions to practise the last two parts of the speaking test.

Part Two

Describe the most important thing you learned at school.
You should say:
- what it was
- when you learned it
- how you were taught.
You should also say how it has been important to you in your life.

Part Three (use only two)

1   Do you think too many subjects are taught at school?
2   Have there been any major changes in the education system in your country?
3   What are the most important factors of a good education?
4   Should everyone be entitled to go to university?
5   Do you think school uniforms are important?

EXERCISE 2	Now work with a partner and practise the interview. One of you should act as the candidate and the other should be the interviewer. The interviewer should make notes under the following headings.

- Part Two comments.
- Part Three comments.

UNIT

7

In the papers

Unit 7.1   Facts and opinions (reading)

EXERCISE 1   Do the sentences below express facts or opinions? Underline the words that helped you decide.

1   Text messaging is a convenient way of keeping in touch with people.
2   Statistics have shown that an increasing number of people are using the Internet.
3   Some people claim that statistics can be used to prove anything.
4   Recent research has revealed that tabloid newspapers are more popular than broadsheet newspapers.
5   It is commonly accepted that we cannot believe everything we read in the newspapers.
6   The workers have told the press that if they are not given a pay rise, then there will be a strike.
7   Capital punishment is an effective way of reducing serious crime.
8   Seatbelts have been proven to prevent fatalities.

EXERCISE 2   Read the text below. Underline the facts and circle the opinions.

I personally believe that there are such things as UFOs. The first recorded sightings were in 1600 BC, and since then many other incidents have been reported. Many people exaggerate or misinterpret what they see, but it seems that there certainly are genuine cases. Statistically it is very likely that there is life on other planets – I mean, in my view, it would be egocentric to believe we were the only life in the universe.

POINT OF IMPACT   A writer's opinion is sometimes expressed in easily identifiable phrases or in the vocabulary used, especially adjectives. For example, if the writer tells you something is 'tasteful', you can tell that his or her opinion is positive.

EXERCISE 3   Look at the prompts in the table at the top of the next page. Write one fact and one opinion about the subject. *An example has been done for you.*

	Fact	Opinion
Poor inner city living standards	Statistics show that inner cities have higher crime rates.	Living conditions can sometimes be shocking.
The rainforests		
Tabloid newspapers		
Digital music		
Nuclear power		
IELTS		

EXERCISE 4　Read the text below and answer the questions that follow.

The price of your newspaper

The average family buys two newspapers and a magazine every week, in addition to receiving up to three pieces of junk mail. Multiplied by the global population, this amounts to a lot of paper, and therefore a lot of wood. Although the rise of the home computer has gone a long way in reducing this excessive use of paper, the demand is still considerable.

Social and economic concerns have over-ridden environmental common sense, and in many western countries, the woods and forests that once covered the land have long since been cleared away. A shocking example can be found by looking at the United States, which now has less than two per cent of its original forest. Other areas, predominantly tropical countries, are now following the same destructive path. In 1995 over one million hectares of forest in Brazil were cleared, a disturbing statistic but nonetheless inevitable as timber and other related raw materials are important exports for countries that often have little other way of supporting themselves. They provide employment for those who harvest the wood, extract rubber or make products using available materials. With one third of the world depending on wood for fuel, it is very tempting, though shortsighted, for poorer countries to exploit the market.

It could be argued, then, that countries with rich wood resources should be fully entitled to exploit them. However, there are less destructive alternatives for generating an income from the rainforests. The forest environment provides a popular setting for ecotourism, which includes hiking, camping, bird watching and other outdoor adventure or nature study activities. International travel is becoming increasingly popular, making the rainforests accessible for the more adventurous holidaymaker.

No matter what the solution, the rampant spread of deforestation has to be halted. Surveys in Cameroon, the Ivory Coast, Ghana and Liberia found that forest wildlife accounted for 70 to 90 per cent of the total animal protein consumed, thus arguing that some indigenous peoples are completely dependent on forests for food. In many of these countries, wood harvesting is carried out on a considerably more sensible scale. There appears to be the realisation that selling the wood is a temporary solution that would inevitably lead to worse problems for the future. Not only would the traditional food source be gone, but the trees which protected the soil against erosion would be gone. Landslides would become more common and rainwater would not be absorbed so easily into the ground, leading to a shortage of freshwater supplies. There is also the global impact, not only from the burning of the wood but also because trees provide an important role in the recycling of carbon dioxide and the production of oxygen. Estimates based on the current rate of deforestation have predicted a 15 per cent rise in the greenhouse effect.

In order to combat the problem of deforestation, it is important to consider its causes in greater detail. In Brazil, we should look at the unequal and unfair distribution of land – 4.5 per cent of landowners hold 81 per cent of the country's farmland, and 70 per cent of rural households are landless. With either no legal claim to the land or ownership of so much, deforestation is inevitable as land owners profit from the land. This is the point in which the situation is in the hands of government, yet often the landowners have shown their ability to sway official regulations regarding timber harvesting.

In order to effect a serious reversal of the damage, some governments are taking a more active role in forest management to protect the environment and employment. The interests of its citizens and its future must be considered, with policies of replantation and protection. In addition, individuals can make a difference by practising green consumerism. Recycled paper is readily available, and we can all make an effort to purchase the most ecologically sensitive products. Demanding alternative products, such as clear-cut free paper and eco-certified lumber, is important in convincing companies that markets exist for such products.

None of these activities can occur without the raising of public awareness to inform consumers about the environmental effects of their products, and this is not an easy task. Many people are too entrenched in their habits or too lazy to change, yet one of the most important ways for a person to have a positive effect is to reduce his or her consumption of forest and related products. An increase in the participation of the public in, and the accessibility and productiveness of facilities for, reducing, reusing and recycling is not only necessary, but also a duty. So next time you buy a newspaper, just consider the cost.

What are the writer's attitudes to the following points? Use *NO MORE THAN THREE WORDS* from the text.

Write   **P** if his opinion is **POSITIVE**
         N if his opinion is **NEGATIVE**
         NG if his opinion is **NOT GIVEN**.

a   The degree of deforestation in the USA.
b   Less developed countries profiting from their natural resources.
c   The approach taken by countries like the Ivory Coast.
d   The distribution of land in Brazil.
e   The attitude of landowners in Brazil.
f   The reaction of the general public.

EXERCISE 5   Write a short article presenting both facts and opinions. *Choose a subject you know some facts about.*

POINT OF IMPACT   The exercises you have done throughout the reading course often practise skills you can use in your writing test. *Exercise 5* above is a good example. However, remember that in your writing you are presenting a report, which means you should avoid **extreme** expressions of opinions and **justify** what you write.

Unit 7.2   Passives

EXERCISE **1**   Which of the sentences below best describes the graph?

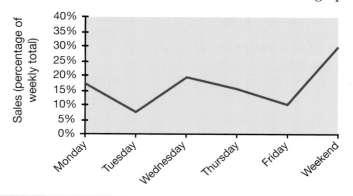

A   I can see from the graph that sales are at their lowest on Tuesday and Friday. More people purchase newspapers at the weekend than during the week.

B   As can be seen from the graph, sales are at their lowest on Tuesday and Friday. More newspapers are purchased at the weekend than during the week.

POINT OF IMPACT   A common way of making your writing more formal in Task I and Task II is to use **passive** constructions. The passive is commonly used when:
    a   the object is the focus
    b   the agent is not known
    c   giving a general instruction
    d   the agent is obvious
    e   a process is described
    f   the subject is long.

EXERCISE **2**   Why is the passive used in the sentences in column A below? Use the Point of Impact above to help you.

A	Sentence	B	Construction	C	Passive name
1	My car has been stolen!		am (is) are + past participle		present continuous
2	Taxes will be raised to pay for the new road.		modal + be + past participle		future
3	His medal is being presented by the mayor tonight.		have/has been + past participle		present/future modal
4	Letters should be kept confidential		am/is/are + being + past participle		past simple
5	Finally, the newspapers are delivered to retailers		will + be + past participle		present perfect
6	Many people were surprised by the government's decision to keep interest rates low despite the current economic climate		was/were + past participle		present simple

| **EXERCISE** **3** | Match a passive sentence to a construction (column B) and tense (column C). *The first one has been done for you.* |

| **EXERCISE** **4** | Change the following sentences from the active to the passive. |

1 They print the weekend papers on Friday night.
2 Newspaper editors do not always verify the truth of their articles.
3 We should allow freedom of the press.
4 Internet news sites will replace newspapers.
5 People have been publishing magazines for over 100 years.

ESSAY TASK

The task should take about 40 minutes.

Journalists often claim that people have the right to know everything. Are there any situations in which the freedom of the press should be limited?

Write a minimum of 250 words.

| **EXERCISE** **5** | Complete the essay task above. |

Unit 7.3   Film and TV

| **EXERCISE** **1** | Talk about TV, video and the cinema using the following pointers. |

a Comparison
b Contrast
c Likes and dislikes
d Personal preferences

| **EXERCISE** **2** | Write a film genre that connects all of the adjectives in each group. |

a Amusing, funny, hilarious
b Frightening, terrifying, scary
c Imaginative, realistic, inventive
d Heartwarming, touching, tragic
e Exciting, thrilling, action-packed

EXERCISE 3 If the interviewer asks you which type of film you like, how can you extend your answer? Discuss your ideas with a partner.

POINT OF IMPACT If you are asked a question about television or the cinema, you can extend your answer by giving a specific example.

Well, I much prefer going to the cinema because the screen is bigger than any television, and the sound is really good. For example, I thought the film Titanic was great because the music was so romantic, and it just wouldn't have been the same played at home on a normal television.

EXERCISE 4 Imagine the interviewer has just asked you whether you watch many DVDs. In your answer, consider the following points.

1　comparison and contrast
2　likes, dislikes and preferences
3　justifying your answer with a specific example

Unit 7.4 Recognising speakers (listening)

EXERCISE 1 Listen again to the recording you heard in Unit 3.10 (*Exercise 3*). Makes notes about what each person says.

Sam	Mary	John

EXERCISE 2 When do you think it will be important to differentiate between speakers? Consider specific question types and sections of the test.

POINT OF IMPACT Some questions, especially matching, require the ability to distinguish between speakers. Often this is not a problem as you normally hear one male and one female. However, when there are more than two speakers, you need to listen carefully.

EXERCISE 3 Listen to the recording. How many speakers are there? What are their names?

EXERCISE 4 Now listen to the conversation again and write a name beside the following points.

	thinks mobile phones are annoying.
	suggests that they can be useful sometimes.
	agrees that they can be useful.
	believes people do not respect privacy anymore.
	does not agree that people do not respect privacy.
	feels that the media in general have become too invasive.
	claims that the public have a right to know information.

POINT OF IMPACT   Read the question closely to make sure that you know not only *what* but also *who* you are listening for.

Unit 7.5 Predictions

EXERCISE 1   Read the sentence below. Is the speaker confident in his prediction?

'Within the next ten years, traditional newspapers will be replaced by more environmentally friendly alternatives.'

How likely do *you* think the prediction is?

POINT OF IMPACT   Expressing predictions is a useful IELTS skill. Not only does it apply to writing a conclusion, but there is also the possibility of having an essay title that asks you to predict. Verbs, adjectives and adverbs can all be used when writing a prediction.

EXERCISE 2   Put the following headings in the correct column.

Adjectives of prediction   Verbs of prediction   Adverbs of prediction

a	b	c
I think/don't think ... I anticipate... this will... I strongly suspect this will... I believe ... In my opinion/view ... Some people hold that this will...	It is probable that... It is likely that... It is possible that... It is unlikely that...	This will undoubtedly lead to... This will certainly lead to... This will definitely lead to... This will probably lead to... This will possibly lead to... This would lead to... This would possibly lead to... This might lead to...

POINT OF IMPACT　**Predictions** are just like any other opinion in a Task II essay. After you have stated them, you should justify and support them.

EXERCISE 3　Use some of the language from *Exercise 2* to write predictions using the following prompts. Write a second sentence justifying your prediction.

1　Newspapers / become less popular / Internet / news websites
2　Journalists / less interested in the lives of famous people
3　Tabloid newspapers / become more widely read than serious newspapers
4　Newspapers / become interactive / within ten years
5　I / read a broadsheet newspaper / every day from now on
6　I / get / 8.5 / IELTS test

POINT OF IMPACT　In addition to verbs, adjectives and adverbs, nouns can also be used to express predictions:
- In all probability, ...
- There is a strong possibility of ...
- There is little likelihood of ...
- There is only a remote chance that ...

EXERCISE 4　Write sentences for each of the phrases in the Point of Impact above. *They do not necessarily have to be about the topic of this unit.*

EXERCISE 5　Complete the essay task below.

ESSAY TASK

The task should take about 40 minutes.

As we move into the digital age, books and newspapers are becoming less important. Within the next 20 years, computers will have entirely replaced any other such form of media.

To what extent do you agree with the above?

Write a minimum of 250 words.

Unit 7.6　Explaining effects

EXERCISE 1　What is the difference between these two topic cards?

> Describe a relative you like.
> You should say:

> Describe a relative who had a great impact on you.
> You should say:

POINT OF IMPACT　Some topic cards may ask you to talk about the impact someone or something had on you. With this kind of question, you need to talk about the **effect** this had.

EXERCISE 2　On the left are some common expressions for talking about effects. Make some sentences using the situations on the right.

It was then that I saw the value of ...
It taught me how to ...
I realised the importance of ...
From that point on, I've always ...
I was touched because ...

Your first girlfriend/boyfriend
Receiving your first wage cheque
A friend you knew at school
A teacher that influenced you
A movie that inspired you

EXERCISE 3　Prepare to talk about the following topic card.

> Describe an important book you have read.
> You should say:
> * what it was about
> * why you read it
> * when you read it.
> You should also explain the impact it had on you.

Unit 7.7　Multiple choice (reading)

EXERCISE 1　Answer the following questions. Look back at Unit 2.10 if you need to.

a　How many types of multiple-choice questions are there?
b　How many possible answers are you given for each question?
c　Why are multiple-choice questions particularly hard?
d　What should you do to help you with multiple-choice questions?

POINT OF IMPACT   In Unit 2.10 you looked at multiple-choice questions in listening. The skills for this question style in the reading test are basically the same. However, the questions may be longer and more complex

EXERCISE 2   Read the text below and answer the question that follows.

The majority of people read a newspaper at least once a week, but an increasing number are turning away from traditional broadsheets with their serious journalism to simpler, and often less factual, newspapers. This is in part due to the time it takes to read the more serious newspapers, but perhaps more worryingly because we are becoming increasingly fascinated with trivia.

According to the text, broadsheet newspapers
A are becoming more popular than tabloids
B take longer to read than tabloids
C are boring
D often have trivial stories.

POINT OF IMPACT   Remember that multiple-choice questions give options that might be directly contradicted, indirectly contradicted, or not exactly what is stated, as well as the right answer. However, do not always expect that there will always be one of each answer for every multiple-choice question.

REVIEW   Read the text below and answer the questions that follow.

The development of the magazine

In almost every kind of waiting room you can imagine, be it a dentist's or a car showroom, you will find them. No matter how much of a minority sport, interest or hobby you may have or take part in, you will almost certainly find one devoted to it. Over the past 20 years, magazines have become so popular that they are now outselling most newspapers.

The forerunners of magazines were nothing like the glossy, colourful affairs they are now. They were small printed pages announcing forthcoming events and providing a little local information. They became popular during the seventeenth century, when the idea was exported around Europe. Magazines became thicker, and were not only informative but also entertaining. In addition, literary magazines began to publish short literary works. Indeed, many classic authors of the period first published their material in magazines such as *The Tatler* and *Gentleman's Magazine*. However, they remained more of a hobby than a business, generating only enough income to cover production costs.

The *American Magazine*, first published in 1741, was the aptly named first magazine to be available in America. Launched in Philadelphia, it was available for only a few short months, and was soon replaced by more popular (although still not profitable) magazines including *Lady's Book*, the first to be aimed exclusively at women.

In the early nineteenth century, the nature of magazines changed as illustrated magazines and children's magazines made their appearance. The illustrations were immediately popular, and within a few years every magazine was brightening its pages with them.

The Industrial Revolution that hit Europe around this time also had a great impact. With the advent of better quality printing processes, paper and colour printing techniques, magazines became lucrative as local businesses began to pay previously unimaginable prices for advertising space. This heralded a new era within the industry as magazines now represented a significant source of income for publishers.

Towards the end of the nineteenth century, better standards of education were resulting in a higher degree of literacy, and this of course meant that there was an increasing number of markets to be exploited, and with better transportation, the means developed with which to reach these markets.

The most conclusive factor, however, in the rise of magazines came about with the rise of national advertising. Previously, advertising in magazines had remained relatively local, but with the birth of the concept of national markets, where goods could be delivered to almost any destination and at previously unheard-of speeds, advertisers were willing to pay for as wide a coverage as possible in as many magazines as they thought would usefully promote their products.

Competition inevitably increased and this led to the development of new magazines. In the following years, magazines became more specialised, significantly rivalling newspapers as the dominant form of media and paving the way for the wealth of choices available today.

It was at this point that magazine owners and editors found another area which would guarantee a wider circulation. Attributed to Samuel S. McClure, editor of the American magazine *McClure's*, the early 1900s saw the advent of the gossip column, in which the private lives of prominent political or social figures was investigated by those who became known as 'muckraking journalists'. They would invade the privacy of anyone they thought would interest the public, exposing secrets or even fabricating stories in order to raise the circulation of their magazine.

As the circulation of magazines increased, they began at first to reflect, then to influence, popular opinion. This led to them being heavily used by both sides during World War I and World War II as propaganda, inspiring people to join and fight against the enemy. Most people have, at some time in their life, seen the ubiquitous picture of the British General Kitchener pointing out of the poster with the slogan 'Your Country Needs You!' printed below, exhorting people to join the army during World War I. It was in magazines that this picture had such wide coverage.

In the 1950s, magazines took a heavy blow at the hands of the new medium of advertising – television. With sound and pictures now on offer, many magazines lost business and faced collapse as advertisers took their business to television studios. Magazines became even more specialised, hoping to still find new markets, and that is why today we find so many obscure titles on the shelves.

There is no doubt that the magazine has come a long way from its humble beginnings, but when you can buy magazines devoted to the art of Body Painting or informing us of the latest Caravan Accessories, or read about the latest gossip from another Hollywood star, you have to wonder if magazines have actually come a long way in the right direction.

REVIEW   **Multiple choice (this unit)**

Circle the correct answer A–D.

1 The earliest magazines
   A had a number of similarities with modern magazines
   B were intended for women
   C focused on hobbies
   D were very different from magazines today.

2 Magazines became a highly profitable business when
  A they were exported around Europe
  B they began including illustrations
  C advertisers began paying more for space
  D they included short stories.

3 How have magazines retained their popularity despite increased competition?
  A By influencing popular opinion.
  B By specialising.
  C Because of the war.
  D Through cooperation with television.

4 *McClure's* magazine
  A was a respected political and social publication
  B was the first publication to specialise in invasive journalism
  C was the most popular American publication of 1900
  D had the highest circulation of any magazine.

REVIEW   **TRUE, FALSE, NOT GIVEN-style questions (Unit 4.7)**

Look at the following statements and decide if they are right or wrong according to the information given.

Write   **TRUE** if the statement is true
           FALSE if the statement is false
           NOT GIVEN if there is no information about this in the passage.

5 *Lady's Book* was written by women.
6 After the Industrial Resolution, magazines sold more copies than newspapers.
7 Better education supported the rise of magazines.
8 Magazines began to influence popular opinion.

REVIEW   **Short-answer questions (Unit 3.7)**

Answer the following questions using *NO MORE THAN THREE WORDS*.

 9 With what form of journalism did Samuel McClure guarantee more sales of his magazine?
10 What allowed the exploitation of new markets in the late 1800s?
11 Whose picture was in many magazines during World War I?
12 What stopped the increasing rise of magazines?

Unit 7.8　Processes and diagrams

EXERCISE 1　What process is the diagram below explaining? Look carefully at the labels given.

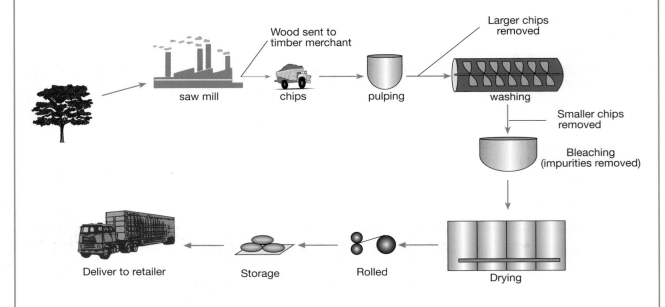

EXERCISE 2　Read the short description of the process from *Exercise 1*. What is important about the words: **in bold?** *in italics?* that are underlined?

> **After** the trees *have been cut down* and *taken* to a saw mill, two products remain. There is the timber which *is sold*, and there is the wood chip. The wood chip *is* **first** *pulped* and **then** *washed* ...

POINT OF IMPACT　When describing a process, remember the following.
* The passive is the most common construction.
* Sequencing words are essential.
* Relative clauses can help avoid repetition.

e.g. Saw the trees into timber. Send the timber to the timber merchant. Becomes: The trees are sawn into timber, which is then sent to the timber merchant.

EXERCISE 3　Use a **variety** of sequencing words to make full sentences about the prompts.

first	the first step	then	next	the next step	the third step	after that
before	after (+ *ing*)	as	while	when	meanwhile	soon afterwards
from then on	the last step	finally	in the process of			
in the course of	once X has *happened*, Y can *happen*					

1 Tree / cut / take / saw mill
2 Wood / send / timber merchant
3 Chips / pulp / wash
4 Pulping / washing / larger chips removed
5 Bleach / impurities removed
6 Bleached pulp / dry / roll
7 Store / deliver to retailer

EXERCISE 4 Before you begin, as with any IELTS writing, you should *plan*! The plan for a process is a little different from other Task I essays. What is each point asking you to do?

1 Topic words?	
2 Tense?	
3 About?	
4 Begins?	
5 Paragraph stages?	

EXERCISE 5 Prepare a plan based on the following process then write the essay. This exercise should take about 20 minutes (minimum 150 words).

The diagram below shows the process of publishing a book.

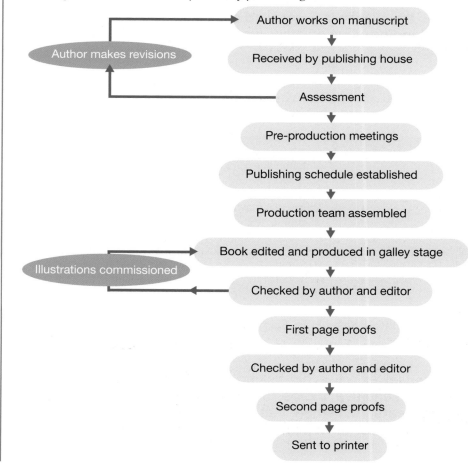

Topic words?	
Tense?	
About?	
Begins?	
Paragraph stages?	

Unit 7.9   Looking at both sides

EXERCISE 1

The short dialogue below comes from Part Three of the speaking test. How could you improve and extend the candidate's reply?

Examiner: Do you believe there is too much violence on television?
Candidate: Yes, there is far too much violence on television and we should consider the effect this is having, especially on younger viewers. We must find something more suitable to watch.

POINT OF IMPACT   With less than a quarter of an hour to demonstrate your speaking ability to the examiner, every word counts. By being less dogmatic and **balancing** your opinion, you show a better control of the language.

EXERCISE 2

Look at the words and phrases below. Add more to each column.

Less dogmatic	Balanced
I feel ... In my opinion ... Well, personally I ... I believe/I have always believed ... To my mind ...	Although some might not agree with/that ... Admittedly ... Granted, ... Although it may be true that ... Of course, this is only an opinion.

Using fewer imperative modal verbs will also make you sound less dogmatic.

must ————▶ should

EXERCISE 3

Improve the candidate's answer in *Exercise 1* with words or phrases from the columns above.

POINT OF IMPACT   The interviewer will avoid asking particularly argumentative or culturally sensitive topics, but will be listening for how you **communicate**. Remember that the best communicators are those that can consider other points of view as well as their own.

EXERCISE **4**   Practise using less dogmatic and more balanced opinions by considering the following topics:

1 Extinction is a natural process of evolution.
2 Film-makers only make violent programmes because that is what people want.
3 Tabloid newspapers should be banned.
4 The Internet will replace all other forms of media.

Unit 7.10   Gap filling (listening)

POINT OF IMPACT   Some questions require you to fill in gaps. This is more a combination of question types than a question type in its own right. Gap filling is a common form of text completion, but can also be used for completing tables or short sentences.

EXERCISE **1**   Below are some examples of different gap-fill questions. Which number:

a   could be lecture notes?
b   is probably a hospital?
c   describes some kind of sales procedure?
d   is connected to business?
e   is probably a menu?
f   could be for a university 'open day'?

1	2	3
Burger and chips _____ _____ £2.50 Orange/apple/_____ juice £2.10 Sandwiches £2.90–£3.70	Meeting at _____ Discuss implications of _____ _____ proposal Representatives _____ to Head Office	Visiting hours: Morning 8:00–10:00 Afternoon _____ –4:00 Maximum __ visitors per bed

4	5	6
1. Customer completes order form 2. Send to _____ 3. Wait ____ working days 4. Receive goods 5. Sign _____ Any problems ph: (09) 263-8666	Famous leader in _____ Fought _____ War had effect on _____ Implications now: _____	_____ University Day and date: _____ Place: _____ Entry requirements: _____ Courses offered:_____ Come and meet_____

POINT OF IMPACT   As with any question type, predicting the topic and possible answers or answer types will give you an idea of what the listening is about. For example, for number 3 in *Exercise 1* the listening is probably something connected with hospitals or hospital regulations.

EXERCISE 2   What do you think the place or situation is for the other five examples in *Exercise 1*? *Write as much as you can.*

1	
2	
3	A hospital, hospital regulations, a noticeboard for visitors not patients, probably not a private ward (maximum visitor numbers and strict visiting times), probably not intensive care (visitors allowed)
4	
5	
6	

POINT OF IMPACT   With gap-fill questions, the answer sometimes comes in the form of specific information such as a time or a price which cannot be precisely predicted. However, there are occasions when the answer comes in the form of a general idea which can be more easily and logically anticipated.

EXERCISE 3   Listen to the recording and write the word you hear before and after the words given below.

a younger people
b buy or even read a
c taken from the
d great harm in

e a general decline in
f such pursuits have long since
g of a book before
h older generation, this

i is entering
j technological
k any of the classic works of

EXERCISE 4   Now listen again, and write any additional information you hear.

EXERCISE 5   Now rewrite the passage as closely as you can to the original. You should use logic and grammar to write about anything you missed.

EXERCISE 6   The following exercise uses a recording script from a previous unit. Predict as much of the missing vocabulary as you can before listening to the recording. Use *NO MORE THAN THREE WORDS OR A NUMBER*.

Emiliano   Hello my name is Emiliano. I am a student here and I would like to rent a house (1)_____.

Rental agent	Okay, well you have come to the right place! We specialise in short-term rental. First of all I would like to get a few details from you. Can you give me (2)_____please?
Emiliano	Yes. It's Emiliano Nespola.
Rental agent	And can you tell me your present address, please?
Emiliano	Yes. It's 17 Meadow Way, Penrose. I'm living with a homestay family at the moment.
Rental agent	That's great! Now do you have (3)_____with you? Oh, and we will need (4)_____from someone who knows you here. Maybe your homestay family?
Emiliano	Yes, okay. Here's my passport and the card from (5)_____. My referee can be Mrs Alice Thompson, she's my homestay mother and she won't mind, I'm sure. You can contact her at the same address as me of course.
Rental agent	Okay. If we need to contact you, should we (6)_____with your homestay?
Emiliano	No, you can speak to me directly. My cellphone number is 021 548 3534.
Rental agent	Great. Now, do you have (7)_____? You will need to pay your rent by (8)_____ – you know, it will come out of your account automatically every month.
Emiliano	Okay. I don't have my bank account details with me now but I can get them and bring them back later today.
Rental agent	That's fine. Now can you tell me what (9)_____you are looking for? Do you want to rent by yourself?
Emiliano	No. I'm looking for a (10)_____ ... I want to rent with (11)_____. I'll bring them in to see you later today.
Rental agent	Okay. And what areas are you interested in renting in?
Emiliano	Well, here's a map. Can you see my school? I don't have a car so I need to take some kind of (12)_____to school and I don't want to travel for more than (13)_____each way. Do you think you have anything which is suitable?
Rental agent	Yes we do. Look, here is a list of (14)_____. I'll highlight the ones that could be of interest to you. Look at the map and go and have a look at the houses with your friends. Do you have a friend (15)_____?
Emiliano	Yes I do.
Rental agent	Good. So go and look outside the houses, it will give you an idea of what the area is like, but remember don't go (16)_____ or knock on the door. If you want to go in and have a look let me know and we can arrange an appointment.
Emiliano	Okay. Can you give me an idea of price?
Rental agent	Yes. If you look at the list, you can see the (17)_____written next to the house address.
Emiliano	Oh yes, I can see it now. Do I need to pay anything else?
Rental agent	Yes, you need to pay (18)_____which you will get back when you move out and you have to pay a non-refundable (19)_____which is equivalent to one week's rent. You will have to pay your bills when they come every month too, of course.
Emiliano	Okay, well thank you very much for your help. What time should I come back with my friends and my bank details?

Rental agent	How about **(20)**_____this afternoon?
Emiliano	That sounds good. Thank you for your help. I'll see you later.
Rental agent	Thank for coming in. Goodbye ...

Unit 7.11   Solutions

EXERCISE 1   Read the Task II essay title below. What is it asking you to do?

Children watch too much television. As a result they are losing important social skills. What can be done about this?

POINT OF IMPACT   In Task II essays, you may be asked to do one or more of the following: present and justify an opinion, compare and contrast evidence or consider a problem and either evaluate possible solutions or suggest a solution of your own. For problem/solution essays, it is obviously very important to identify the *problem*.

EXERCISE 2   What is the problem presented in the Task II title in *Exercise 1*? It will help to rephrase the question.

EXERCISE 3   Identify the problem and brainstorm some solutions to the problems below.

1   Journalists no longer respect people's privacy. What steps can be taken to address this problem?
2   Old newspapers and magazines often end up in landfills when they could very well be recycled. How could people be encouraged to recycle such materials?

POINT OF IMPACT   When presenting opinions or solutions, use suitable vocabulary and make concessions. By admitting your ideas may not be the only answer, you avoid being dogmatic.
Useful language for presenting a solution
a   A possible solution (to this) is ...
b   We might be able to ...
c   This could perhaps be resolved by ...
d   It should be possible to ...
e   One suggestion could be to ...
f   An alternative (to this) could be ...
g   Perhaps (X) would be better.

A very useful academic way of presenting a solution is to use conditional structures. This structure also allows you to extend your answer to include the possible results of your solution.

'If parents limited the time their children spent watching television, there would be more time for more family-centred activities.'

Remember that indirect structures can be used to add some variety to your sentences.

'Should parents limit the time they allow their children to watch television, it would allow more time for more family-centred activities.'

EXERCISE 4   Make sentences using the vocabulary from the Point of Impact above to present your solutions to *Exercise 3*.

POINT OF IMPACT   If you are required to present solutions in a Task II essay, think carefully about how you are going to paragraph your ideas before you start writing. You could consider:
- having one solution and its implications in each paragraph
- giving more than one solution in the first body paragraph and then considering the implications of each in the following paragraphs
- concluding your essay with the solution you think is strongest.

EXERCISE 5   Select one of the titles from *Exercise 3* and extend your answer into a paragraph by considering the **potential effects** of your solution.

EXERCISE 6   Complete the essay task below.

ESSAY TASK

The task should take about 40 minutes.

Children watch too much television. As a result they are losing important social skills.

What can be done about this?

Write a minimum of 250 words.

Unit 7.12   Topic Card: The media

EXERCISE 1   Do you prefer watching TV or reading books? Discuss with your partner.

POINT OF IMPACT   Remember that with some questions you can extend your answers by talking about preferences as well as comparing and contrasting. A topic card that focuses on books, for example, can be balanced with a few opinions about other media such as television or the Internet.

EXERCISE 2   Ask your partner some Part One questions before moving on to the topic card.

> Describe a movie that had a great impression on you.
> You should say:
> * what type of movie it was
> * why you saw it
> * what it was about.
> You should also say why it made such a strong impression on you.

As your partner speaks, make some notes under the following headings.
* Areas in which the speaker is strong (e.g. intonation).
* Areas in which the speaker is weaker (e.g. tenses).

UNIT

8

On the road

| Unit 8.1 | Timing (reading) |

POINT OF IMPACT Looking at headings, skimming, scanning and reading topic sentences are all essential skills, but you also have to be able to read parts of the texts in detail to answer some questions.

EXERCISE 1 Complete this brief review quiz by answering TRUE or FALSE.

a You should read every word of the text.
b You should spend 20 minutes on each text.
c Skimming the text should take less than five minutes.
d You should scan for specific details.
e You should answer each question before moving on.
f 60 minutes is enough time to complete the reading test.

EXERCISE 2 Skim the following short texts for a general idea of what each one is about. You should take no longer than half a minute on each paragraph.

A The traditional stereotype attached to female drivers is slowly being reversed, arguably as a result of increasingly conclusive statistics which prove women are safer and more considerate than men. Data compiled from insurance claims reveals that men between the ages of 40 and 60 represent the greatest risk.

B In many countries, the incidents of driving whilst under the influence of alcohol have significantly declined. Explicit and often shocking advertising appears to have enforced the opinion that drink-driving is socially and morally wrong. It is perhaps significant that the majority of offenders are 35 or older, whereas those under 35, raised on a diet of television, have understood the message.

C In relative terms, the cost of international travel is getting cheaper by the year. Flights, which were previously the biggest expense of an overseas holiday, are now almost thrown in with a hotel package deal. It has also become possible to travel between almost any two points on the globe within 24 hours. It is surprising, therefore, that so few people take advantage of these opportunities to explore new parts of the world, often preferring to travel within their native country or continent.

EXERCISE 3 Now close your books and reproduce as much of the information as you can remember for each of the three passages.

POINT OF IMPACT Given time for skimming the text, reading the questions and transferring your answers, you have about one minute to answer each of the 40 questions. So it follows that if you are taking more than a minute or two to answer a question, then you are wasting time. Even if you get the answer right after five minutes of close reading, you are losing time and may lose more points rushing through the remaining questions at the end of the test. If you cannot answer a question, put a clear mark beside it and move on. If there is time at the end of the test, go back and try again. No matter what you do, in the last seconds of the test put an answer on the answer sheet even if it is just a guess – points are not deducted for a wrong answer.

EXERCISE 4 Complete the questions based on the reading passages below. Follow the time given on the stopwatches to the right.

Questions 1–13 are based on Reading Passage 1.

READING PASSAGE 1

Migration – the incredible journey

Twice a year, certain species of birds make immense journeys, often in excess of ten thousand miles, spending the summer months in a temperate climate and the rest of the year in more tropical climates. This migration is a long journey which many birds do not complete, yet it is an essential part of their natural pattern.

4 minutes
You should have skimmed the first text for general meaning.

Many reasons can be given for this migration. Some argue that it is a result of some birds being unable to withstand extremes of temperature, especially the cold weather, explaining why many birds migrate to Africa during the European winter. It has also been suggested that this migration is a result of travelling instincts of millennia ago, before the continents drifted apart. As the land mass spread, birds continued to travel the required distance back to the area they knew was a good source of food or protection. The primary cause, however, is considered to be the search for food, particularly for their chicks. Staying in one place, the food sources would become increasingly scarce.

In preparation for their long journey, migratory birds undergo a number of physical and chemical changes. These changes are triggered by the rising or falling daylight and result in a considerable increase in the birds' appetite (up to 40% more than during other times of the year). This food is stored in fat deposits and in some long-distance migrants, this fat becomes 30–50% of their weight, ready to be released gradually to fuel their journey. In addition, they are also considerably more active at night, influenced by chemical changes preparing them for their long-distance haul. Most birds travel long distances overnight, partly as migratory flight generates considerable heat that needs night-time temperatures to dissipate.

The speed at which migratory birds travel varies depending on species. Some birds can reach speeds of nearly 90 kilometres an hour, while others travel at a more sedate pace. Ducks and geese can fly between 60 and 80 kilometres an hour where herons and hawks travel at less than 40 kilometres an hour. Many smaller birds are capable of travelling at considerably faster speeds for short periods in order to escape predators, but cannot maintain these speeds for the distances required for migration. Another difference between species is that for some, the males migrate first, arriving at the breeding grounds early in order to establish territories before the female arrives to choose a suitable site for a nest.

One of the most impressive aspects of this migration is how birds can maintain a direction. Most migrating birds return to the same nesting areas year after year. Theories to explain precision of travelling such distances without getting lost have considered landmarks on the Earth's surface, the sun and the stars, even wind direction and an acute sense of smell. Yet these theories do not explain how some birds can travel thousands of miles on windy and wet nights and still arrive in the same area year after year.

Naturally, given the dangers involved, migration is a dangerous journey. Untold thousands of smaller migrants die each year from storms and attacks by predators. Mortality during migratory flight, of course, is one of the several costs that are covered by the increased production of offspring that migrants obtain by nesting in locations where food is more abundant and competition for most resources is lower. Flying at night, lighthouses, tall buildings, monuments, television towers, and other aerial obstructions have been responsible for destruction of migratory birds who simply do not detect the problem before it is too late. There is also the simple matter of exhaustion, particularly for smaller birds with less energy reserves. Birds flying for up to 48 hours straight can run into adverse winds and find the last of their energy depleted before they reach land. Flying lower and lower as fatigue sets in, these birds fall into the sea.

The most recent challenge to migration is, however, man. Slow climatic and environmental changes have always occurred, but not on the grand scale people have been responsible for. Extensive forests have been burned or cut away, and open fields have been claimed for agricultural purposes. Urban expansion has further encroached on the birds' natural habitats, and pollution, particularly in the form of acid rain, has damaged many of the remaining fields, mountains, lakes and forests. Wetlands that were once home to many species of birds are increasingly drained or filled as land is needed for new housing developments. After overcoming all the trials and risks involved in migration, many birds find that their homes of the year before are now unrecognisable and they are forced to find new grounds on which to breed, often straying into areas defended by larger and aggressively territorial birds.

6 minutes You should have skimmed questions 1–12.

18 minutes You should have answered all the questions you can.

Questions 1–3   Circle the correct answer A–D.

1 The main reason birds migrate is
   A the demands of their new-born
   B to avoid cold weather
   C because of an instinctive homing impulse
   D because of a scarcity of food.

2 Birds prepare for migration by
   A gradually burning fat deposits
   B shedding up to 50% of their body weight
   C becoming more nocturnal
   D travelling long distances.

3 Birds that die during migration
   A often drown
   B balance the number of new-born birds
   C are generally old
   D waited too long to begin their journey.

Questions 4–8   Do the following statements agree with the views of the writer?

Write   **YES** if the statement agrees with the writer
NO if the statement does not agree with the writer
NOT GIVEN if there is no information about this in the passage.

4   Migratory habits vary between species.
5   There are a number of complete theories to explain the navigational abilities of migrating birds.
6   The female of the species often flies slower than the male.
7   Smaller birds are at greater risk than bigger birds.
8   People's relationship with the land is the biggest danger for migrating birds.

Questions 9–12   Complete the following summary using *NO MORE THAN TWO WORDS FROM THE TEXT*.

Not only are cities becoming larger, new housing is being built on areas reclaimed from
(9) _____. In addition, migrating birds are also at risk from a number of different
(10) _____ which cannot be seen in the dark. Smaller birds are particularly
vulnerable as they are at risk from **(11)** _____ and **(12)** _____.

Questions 13-25 are based on Reading Passage 2.

19 minutes
You should have transferred answers 1–12 and be starting Reading Passage 2.

READING PASSAGE 2

A In 1913 an American industrialist named Henry Ford employed an innovative system in his factory that changed the nature of American industry forever – the production line. Instead of a group of workers constructing a complete product, Ford's production-line techniques relied on machine parts being moved around the factory on a conveyor belt, passing each employee who had a single task to

perform before the component moved down the line. This saved time in that employees were not required to move around, collect materials or change tools; they simply stood in one place and repeated the same procedure over and over again until the end of their shift. In this way, Ford was able to mass produce the now famous Model-T car for only 10% of traditional labour costs.

23 minutes
You should have skimmed for general meaning.

B Working on a production line was monotonous work, undoubtedly, but it was not in the production line alone that Ford was something of a pioneer. In 1913 the average hourly rate for unskilled labour was under $2.50 and for such low wages and repetitive work, the labour turnover in Ford's factory was high, with many employees lasting less than a month. In order to combat this problem, he took a step that was condemned by other industrialists of the time, fearful that they would lose their own workforce – he raised wages to $5 an hour. The benefits were twofold. Not only did Ford now have a stable and eager workforce, he also had potential customers. It was his intention 'to build a motorcar for the great multitude', and the Model-T car was one of the cheapest cars on the market at the time. At $5 an hour, many of his employees now found themselves in a position to feasibly afford a car of their own.

Ford's production practices meant that production time was reduced from 14 hours to a mere 93 minutes. In 1914 company profits were $30 million, yet just two years later this figure had doubled. Until 1927 when the last Model-T rolled off the production line, the company produced and sold about 15 million cars.

25 minutes
You should
have skimmed
the questions.

C Although Ford was without doubt successful, times changed and the company began losing its edge. One problem came from the labour force. Ford was a demanding employer who insisted that the majority of his staff remained on their feet during their shift. One error meant that the whole production line was often kept waiting, and Ford felt that workers were more attentive standing than sitting. Yet the 1930s saw some radical changes in the relationships between employer and employee, as an increasing number of industries were forming Labour Unions. Ford flatly refused to get involved, employing spies in the workplace to sabotage any plans for a union within his factories. Eventually a strike in the early 1940s forced Ford to deal with unions. Another example of Ford being unable to adapt came from his unwillingness to branch out. Ford's competitors began operating the same systems and practices, but also introduced the variety Ford was lacking. The Model-T had remained essentially the same, even down to the colour, and by the time he realised his error, he had already lost his pre-eminence in the industry. Subsequent involvement in aeroplane manufacturing, politics and publishing was a failure. Leaving the company to his grandson in 1945, he died two years later leaving an inheritance estimated at $700 million.

38 minutes
You should
have
answered all
the questions
you can.

D Yet the legacy of Fordism lives on. The development of mass production transformed the organisation of work in a number of important ways. Tasks were minutely subdivided and performed by unskilled workers, or at least semiskilled workers, since much of the skill was built into the machine. Second, manufacturing concerns grew to such a size that a large hierarchy of supervisors and managers became necessary. Third, the increasing complexity of operations required employment of a large management staff of accountants, engineers, chemists, and, later, social psychologists, in addition to a large distribution and sales force. Mass production also heightened the trend towards an international division of labour. The huge new factories often needed raw materials from abroad, while saturation of national markets led to a search for customers overseas. Thus, some countries became exporters of raw materials and importers of finished goods, while others did the reverse.

E In the 1970s and '80s some countries, particularly in Asia and South America, that had hitherto been largely agricultural and that had imported manufactured goods, began industrialising. The skills needed by workers on assembly-line tasks required little training, and standards of living in these developing countries were so low that wages could be kept below those of the already industrialised nations. Many large manufacturers in the United States and elsewhere therefore began 'outsourcing' – that is, having parts made or whole products assembled in developing nations. Consequently, those countries are rapidly becoming integrated into the world economic community.

Questions 13–17   Choose the most suitable headings for sections A-E from the list below. Use each heading once only.

List of headings

i	Effect on modern industry
ii	New payment procedures
iii	Labour problems
iv	The Model-T
v	Creating a market
vi	Revolutionary production techniques
vii	The Ford family today
viii	Impact on the global economy
ix	Overseas competition

13 Section A
14 Section B
15 Section C
16 Section D
17 Section E

39 minutes
You should have transferred your answers accurately.

Questions 18–22   Answer the following questions using *NO MORE THAN TWO WORDS*.

18 What was the main saving of production line techniques?
19 What level did Ford cut production costs down to compared with more traditional methods of the time?
20 When was the last Model-T Ford produced?
21 What did Ford unsuccessfully oppose the organisation of?
22 What is the name given to the principles of mass production and associated practices?

Questions 23–25   Complete the following summary using *NO MORE THAN THREE WORDS FROM THE TEXT*.

One of the long-term effects of Ford's business practices was that many developing countries became industrialised as a result of **(23)** _____. The skills for **(24)** _____ were easily acquired and **(25)** _____ was minimal.

40 minutes
You should have made sure you have transferred all your answers accurately and put an answer (even if it is just a guess) for every question.

Unit 8.2   Error correction

EXERCISE   1   Look at the incorrect sentences in A to H below. Complete the second two rows for each one.

A	Incorrect sentence	The graph shows that the percentage of total travellers using four types of transportation in three different periods.
	It should be ...	
	Why?	

B	Incorrect sentence	There was a sharply increase in the number of people who attended university in 1989.
	It should be ...	
	Why?	

C	Incorrect sentence	The number of people who visited museums accounted for the least percentage.
	It should be ...	
	Why?	

D	Incorrect sentence	The beach was chosen by nearly three quarters of respondents, which was the most popular.
	It should be ...	
	Why?	

E	Incorrect sentence	From 1995 to 1998, the population was increased by 20% to reach nearly 150 thousand.
	It should be ...	
	Why?	

F	Incorrect sentence	Least popular was other, which only accounted for 8%.
	It should be ...	
	Why?	

G	Incorrect sentence	It can be found that coal production dropped dramatically over the next ten years.
	It should be ...	
	Why?	

H	Incorrect sentence	There was a dramatic increase in hydro electric.
	It should be ...	
	Why?	

EXERCISE 2 Make a list of other mistakes you think are common when writing a Task I essay.

EXERCISE 3 Write a short report on the strengths and weaknesses of the report that follows the graph.

ESSAY TASK

The graph shows the number of people using different modes of transport to travel to work in 1990, 1995 and 2000 in Melingen City.

Write a report for a university lecturer describing the information shown below.

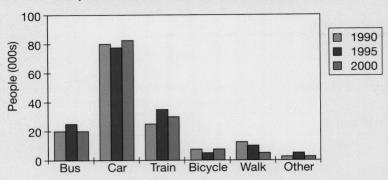

Modes of transport used to travel to work in Melingen City, 1990–2000

This illustration shows the number of citizens who used different transportation to work in 3 separated years, namely 1990 1995 and 2000 in Melingen City. The vertical axes represent the number of people from zero to 100 in thousands. The horizontal one stands for 6 different modes of transport: buses, cars, train, bicycles and other.

The number of people who drive to work was dramatically higher than the others. The number of citizens who went to work by bus was 20 000 in 1990 it rose to 25 000 in 1995 then dropt to 20 000 in 2000. In contrast the number of people who travelled by train was slightly higher than the people travelled by bus. The number was approximate 26 000 in 1990. The number of people who travelled by train which was 36 000 was the highest.

The number of people who transported by bicycle was not high.

To sum up, the bar chart shows that cars were the most popular form of transport over the 3 years and less people went to work on feet.

(174 words)

EXERCISE 4   Compare your report with a partner's and rewrite the essay.

Unit 8.3   Travel

EXERCISE 1   Write a list of possible questions the interviewer could ask you about 'travel' in Part One of the test.

POINT OF IMPACT   Remember that you will be asked about subjects which should be familiar to you in Part One of the test. Deeper questions such as 'What are the advantages of travelling at a young age?' may come up in Part Three.

EXERCISE 2 Match the sentence halves to create full questions.

1	How has travel changed
2	What's your ideal
3	What do you do
4	What is the road system
5	Do you
6	What countries would
7	How does travel here and

a	enjoy travelling?
b	on holiday?
c	in your country over the past 20 years?
d	in your country compare?
e	you like to visit?
f	kind of holiday?
g	like in your country?

POINT OF IMPACT Remember that in Part One of the speaking test, there may be an opportunity to use a number of different skills.
A talking about habits or routines
B giving a description
C expressing likes, dislikes and preferences
D making comparisons
E expressing opinions
F talking about future plans
G talking about changes

EXERCISE 3 Which questions from *Exercise 2* test the skills in the Point of Impact? *The first one has been done for you.*

Skill A = 3 What do you do on holiday?
Skill B =
Skill C =
Skill D =
Skill E =
Skill F =
Skill G =

EXERCISE 4 Read the dialogue below. How has the candidate expressed **changes?**

Interviewer: How has travel changed in your country over the past 20 years?
Candidate: Well, the first thing is that there are more and more cars on the road, so traffic congestion is becoming a serious issue. We used to have a good public transport system, but fewer people use it now so the services have been reduced.

EXERCISE 5 Now ask and answer the questions in *Exercise 2*. *Extend your answers as much as possible.*

Unit 8.4   Meaning and intonation (listening)

EXERCISE 1   Read the gap fill below and predict possible answers.

It's (1)_____ for passengers on an aeroplane, particularly first-time flyers, to feel trepidation prior to getting on the aircraft, and nervousness during the flight, particularly on long-haul flights such as Australia to the UK. Yet the belief that flying is dangerous is a (2) _____. Flying, (3) _____ sky diving, is statistically much safer than many other daily activities like driving a car or even crossing the road.

EXERCISE 2   Now listen to the recording. Were you correct?

POINT OF IMPACT   In Unit 5.1 you looked at indirect sentences in the reading. There is also the possibility of indirect sentences in the listening. Make sure you listen closely for meaning.

EXERCISE 3   Listen to the recording. Which is correct (A or B)?

1 A Lyn likes the T-shirt.   B Lyn doesn't like the T-shirt.
2 A The speaker should have booked.   B There is plenty of seating available.
3 A Steve agrees with the first speaker.   B Steve doesn't agree with the first speaker.
4 A He is happy with their travel arrangements.   B He is not happy with the travel arrangements.
5 A He feels the advertisement was misleading.   B He is satisfied with the product.
6 A The speaker is annoyed.   B The speaker was misheard the first time she spoke.
7 A The food was good.   B The food wasn't very good.

POINT OF IMPACT   In the listening test, you may need to consider more than just the language the speakers use. Listen closely to the meaning in the intonation the speakers use. This will help you understand even if you are not sure of the vocabulary. By now, you should be able to identify speakers, interpret discourse markers and understand meaning from intonation in order to build a comprehensive understanding of the listening.

EXERCISE 4   Give your opinion on the following. *Your intonation can be as important as your vocabulary.*

1 Candidates aged 10 to 12 taking the IELTS test.
2 The salaries of top sports stars.
3 Life on Mars being discovered tomorrow morning.
4 A company developing fish-flavoured ice cream.
5 Raising old-age pensions by three times the current amount.

EXERCISE 5   Listen and complete the 10 questions that follow.

REVIEW   **Multiple choice (Unit 2.10)**

Choose the correct letter A–C.

1   The travel agent:
    A thinks Europe is a good destination
    B can personally recommend Vancouver
    C does not think America is a good choice.

2   The customer:
    A is going to Europe next year
    B knows people living in Canada
    C wants to go to the warmest place.

REVIEW   **Text completion (Unit 5.10)**

Copy and complete the form using *NO MORE THAN TWO WORDS OR A NUMBER*.

The Travel Depot flight reservations	
Customer's name: Jim **(3)**_____	Flight number **(5)**_____
Address 10 Allen Road, Oldham	Destination: Vancouver, Canada
Contact number: 0151 **(4)**_____(home)	Length of stay (nights): **(6)**_____

Copy and complete the following using *NO MORE THAN TWO WORDS*.

Travel insurance is **(7)**_____ for peace of mind. There are two types of cover, but the best is the **(8)** _____. With this policy, you are insured for any accident or injury that may happen on your holiday.

REVIEW   **Table completion (Unit 3.10)**

Copy and complete the table below using *NO MORE THAN THREE WORDS*.

	Cost	Main attraction
Theatre	**(9)** $_____	Shakespeare play
Museum	free entry	Japanese armour

REVIEW   **Matching (Unit 6.10)**

Answer the following question.

Write   **M** for Museum
         T for Theatre
         N for Neither of the above.

10 What events does the customer sound interested in?

Unit 8.5 Commonly confused words

EXERCISE 1 Read the pairs of sentences below. What is the difference between the words in italics?

a There are *so* many small roads in the city.
   It is *such* an easy place to get lost in.

b Pollution would be reduced if there were *fewer* cars.
   Improvements in the service offered by public transport would result in *less* pollution.

c Of all life on earth, only *humans* build machines to travel.
   Most *people* have a driving licence by the time they are twenty.

d The government plans to introduce new *economic* policies early next year.
   Diesel is more *economical* than petrol.

e Over sixty *per cent* of families in New Zealand have at least one car.
   The *percentage* of two-car families is increasing.

f Good grammar *knowledge* is important for your IELTS test.
   Information about the IELTS test can be found on a number of websites.

g The changes in IELTS testing policy were *effected* in September.
   These changes concerned the administration of the test and did not directly *affect* students.

h Pollution has caused *global* changes in climate.
   A number of *international* bodies have been formed to consider potential solutions to this.

EXERCISE 2 Complete the text below using an italicised word from *Exercise 1*.

The accelerating rate at which modern technology is produced is causing problems. Products which are state-of-the-art one moment are becoming almost obsolete within a few years or sometimes even months, and with a_____ short shelf lives b_____ are finding it more c_____ to rent instead of buy. Inevitably, this is having a direct d_____ on the economy as an increasing number of companies compete for a e_____ of the market. In addition, we are becoming less able to keep up with an almost endless flow of new products and their applications.

   One solution is to create f_____ products but increase their quality, therefore not leaving consumers with such a bewildering choice.

POINT OF IMPACT When using formal words, you often find that there are very subtle differences between them. If you are unsure about a word, check in your dictionary, write some example sentences and ask a native English speaker to check them for you. When you are in the test, it is better to use vocabulary you are confident with, rather than a more academic alternative you are not sure about.

EXERCISE	3	Write down some more words which you often confuse. Pass your list on to another student and ask him or her to explain the differences in meaning.

EXERCISE	4	Write an essay on the topic below using words from *Exercise 1* and *Exercise 3*.

ESSAY TASK

The task should take about 40 minutes.

Traffic congestion in major cities is an increasing problem, yet there is an environmental impact to be considered when building new roads.

What can be done about this problem?

Write a minimum of 250 words.

Unit 8.6   Recounting an experience

EXERCISE	1	Try to recall a time in your life when you felt

a   very happy
b   very lucky
c   very angry
d   very embarrassed.

Tell your partner.

EXERCISE	2	In what way could this topic card be considered easier than the other topic cards?

Describe the best holiday you have had.
You should say:
• where you went
• what it was like
• what you did.
You should also explain why it was the best holiday you have had.

Write a few notes about your answer.

POINT OF IMPACT   In many ways, topic cards that ask you to recount an experience are the easiest as you will probably talk about something you have told quite a few people. Just relax, picture the situation or occasion and speak. As with most speaking topics, adjectives are very important. With topic cards like the one in *Exercise 2*, you will be able to use a number of superlative and extreme adjectives or intensifiers.

EXERCISE 3   Read the candidate's answer to the first two prompts of the topic card. Underline the words that tell you how the candidate felt.

The best holiday I have ever been on was a three-week trip to the south of Spain. The people were very friendly and the weather was absolutely fabulous, with bright blue skies every day. It was one of the cleanest environments I've ever experienced – there didn't seem to be any pollution, and that's a welcome change compared with my hometown.

EXERCISE 4   Put a suitable adverb in front of each group of adjectives.

A	B	C	D
fabulous	useless	damaged	sorry
priceless	destroyed	injured	late
amazing	healed	weakened	expensive

EXERCISE 5   Practise the language in *Exercise 4* by talking about the following.

a The best film you have seen.
b The worst meal you have eaten.
c The friendliest place you have been to.
d The most uncomfortable journey you have taken.
e The most frightening experience you have had.
f The most exciting experience you have had.

Unit 8.7   Classifying (reading)

EXERCISE 1   Match the sentence halves. There is no text for this exercise, but the subject is *transport*.

1 Being tied to a timetable and schedule, it ...
2 It offers a freedom some argue ...
3 Its advantage is that it ...
4 Despite the restrictions, ...
5 An increasing number of households ...

a ... is often inconvenient.
b ... have two, despite the cost.
c ... cannot be found with four wheels.
d ... this is the most environmentally friendly option.
e ... can seat the average family quite comfortably.

EXERCISE 2   Classify the questions from *Exercise 1* as referring to

cars (C)   motorbikes (M)   public transport (PT)

You may use any answer more than once.

	Category heading (C/M/PT)
Sentence 1	
Sentence 2	
Sentence 3	
Sentence 4	
Sentence 5	

POINT OF IMPACT   **Matching** questions ask you to put one point with another. **Classifying** questions ask you to categorise points under different headings.

EXERCISE 3   Make notes from the text below for each of the categories given in *Exercise 2* (Cars, Motorbikes and Public Transport).

There are a number of tangible reasons not to travel by public transport. There is the rigidity of the timetable and the inflexibility of destination. Then there are concerns about getting a seat, waiting at bus stops or train stations, having the correct change, keeping our tickets. Yet there are deeper reasons why many of us shy away from public transport – our own set of perceived prejudices and opinions that private transport ownership symbolises more than just convenience.

To varying degrees, we are all slaves to images sold to us by retailers. Car advertisements enforce the notion of freedom, and motorcycles are offered as a way to recapture our lost youth. Our first reaction on seeing a middle-aged man on a bus is not to think that he may not have his own transport, but to assume he has other motives for using public transport – his car is being repaired, for example. The impact of advertising can also be seen when we see motorbikes. Admittedly, they are less common and less polluting, but they are hardly practical. The rider is open to the elements, is at greater risk, has no practical carrying capacity or the luxury of a heater or CD player. But again, there are many who would still see this as superior to public transport.

It is these reactions, these feelings that we must have our own transport whatever the financial or environmental cost, that is putting us right into the middle of a moral dilemma. We have been warned and are aware of the damaging increase in traffic pollution, yet very few people are actually willing to change these habits.

EXERCISE 4   Look at the question below. Is it a 'classification' question? *There is no text for this exercise.*

Which four of the following factors are mentioned in the text?
1   Cars are sold not for their practical points, but on the number of gimmicks.
2   A majority of people drive if they have to travel a distance of over 500 metres.
3   Safety features have had a dramatic influence on road fatalities.
4   Cars are becoming less environmentally damaging.
5   Car pool schemes have proved successful only with planning.
6   One solution being presented is that cars should have a much shorter road life.

POINT OF IMPACT   With some classification questions, the categories you are supposed to use are not clear. In *Exercise 4* although you are not actually required to **classify**, you are being asked to put the points into two **categories – mentioned** or **not mentioned** in the text.

EXERCISE 5   Which other question type asks you to put things into categories? Hint: There are always three categories for this type of question.

POINT OF IMPACT   Classifying questions may ask you to classify according to object (as in *Exercise 3*) or classify who said what. In either type, you will have to carefully consider how **referencing** words have been used.

EXERCISE 6   Quickly scan the passage below. What do you think you may be asked to classify?

Travelling overseas

Over the last decade or so, the number of young people travelling overseas, usually for a relatively short period of time, has been on the increase. Yet the motivation for this temporary migration is under debate. Dr John Unwin, a psychologist from the Institute of Migration Studies, insists that travelling overseas is not usually for education or professional purposes, but for the hedonistic purpose of freedom and experiencing something untried and exotic. According to Unwin, improvements in technology have broken down many of the barriers that previously existed and have given many younger people some idea of what even the most remote areas of the globe are offering. Developments in the aviation industry mean that long-haul flights are no longer financially out of the reach of the average person and tour companies have grown and established themselves specifically on the market of these new adventurers, offering camping, trekking and exploring packages to travellers who, a generation ago, might never have even heard of their destination.

Dr Margaret Love, who has researched the phenomenon from an Australasian aspect, claims that many young people now visit places in Europe and beyond because of a more relaxed official stance to international travel. Reciprocal agreements with a whole host of countries including the UK, Canada and Japan, mean that New Zealanders and Australians under the age of 30 are allowed to work in the host country on a temporary basis (and vice versa) through the Working Holiday Visa scheme. This allows young people to truly experience the culture of another country on a different level and depth to that of a two-week package holiday as those who take advantage of the scheme can mix with locals and find out more about true life in that country. Dr Love believes that as a government-directed move, it provides 'an enriching experience as young people can learn more about cultural differences, acceptance, self-reliance and tolerance. This, in turn, will allow for better relationships to build between countries which can only prove beneficial in the long run'.

Research from America on the same subject has had some similar results to that of Dr Love. Sociologist Dr Darren Moore has analysed the impact of working holidays on future employment prospects and has found the data to be encouraging. Usually undertaken by people who have just completed a significant period of study, either after high school or university, Dr Moore believes that those who go overseas before university are often expected by professors to be of a more mature outlook after their return commenting that 'employers will often welcome a graduate who has experience overseas as a potentially more mature employee with a wider international perspective'.

Yet not all the research was so positive. In a study lasting seven years, Professor Ewan Marks's conclusions about travelling overseas suggested that they had a negative impact on some individuals. Marks links extended travelling to 'an inability to focus on the daily world of work' on their return. 'Having spent so much time without the real responsibilities inherent in pursuing a career and instead simply working in menial jobs without intellectual stimulation, some university graduates are never satisfied following the career path they studied for during their degree.' He claims that a few of these travellers go abroad again, often to stay, whilst others either return to university to complete postgraduate courses or find jobs beneath their level of education.

Although research and opinions are divided, there is one thing that seems very clear – the 'overseas experience' is unlikely to stop.

EXERCISE 7 Classify the following opinions as being from:

JU   Dr John Unwin
ML   Margaret Love
DM   Darren Moore
EM   Ewan Marks

1 We should be wary of lengthy working holidays.
2 People that have travelled overseas are more sought after in the workplace.
3 Extended visits to a country offer far more than traditional holidays.
4 International travel can lead to permanent migration.
5 A better cultural understanding is a positive effect of travel to foreign countries.
6 International agreements have made overseas travel easier.
7 Lower costs have encouraged people to travel more extensively.
8 Travel can lead to job dissatisfaction.

Unit 8.8   Appropriate language

EXERCISE 1 What is your impression of the paragraph below?

It is often said that the exploration of space is very expensive. Rockets are expensive, as well as rocket fuel, and all of this raises the cost of missions into space. Although the cost is very important, we should continue paying. Simply because it is expensive is not a good enough reason to stop.

POINT OF IMPACT Throughout the course you have been brainstorming and planning. Make sure that in the final exam, you do not write sentences or paragraphs that do not actually contain any information. In the paragraph above, all the writer has really expressed is that space exploration is expensive.

EXERCISE 2 Rewrite the following paragraph to make it more **concise**.

People are often in a hurry to get somewhere. They buy the fastest cars and drive beyond the speed limit simply to avoid being late. People also drive very fast even if they are not in a hurry. Speed has become important to us. We do not like having to wait for anything. You can see just how irritating most of us find delays simply by watching people caught in a traffic jam. They are often excessively agitated or angry. This has given rise to the phenomenon of road rage.

POINT OF IMPACT Throughout the course, you have studied a number of sentence structures and phrases. Remember that although you should aim for varied sentences and vocabulary, a clear, simple structure is better than a more complex but inaccurate sentence. Do not think that phrases you have learned can freely apply to any situation. For example:

In modern society, many students find that homework can improve their ability.

There is actually no connection between modern society and homework. Avoid using phrases you have memorised but not really learned.

No native speaker of English thinks on an academic level that it rains cats and dogs, or that there is any place in academic writing for a coin with two sides. Avoid writing phrases that English speakers themselves no longer use.

EXERCISE 3   The five sentences below are inappropriate for IELTS. Why?

a   Many people are worried about the environment. They think we should do something to make it better. For example, instead of using fossil fuels we can use the sun's heat to make electricity. Or we can use the wind to make electricity. We can also use water.
b   I want to tell you my views on public transport.
c   Although computer games can be entertaining, beware! They can also cause aggression in younger children.
d   Many people wonder – is television a negative or positive influence? Should we spend so much time in front of the television?
e   Encouraging and providing better facilities for traditionally neglected areas by employing more teachers and equipping the school with the most modern technology is one way of improving education levels.

POINT OF IMPACT   Here is one final tip about structuring academic sentences – inversion.

Journalists are rarely sympathetic to their interviewees.   ⟶   Rarely are journalists sympathetic to their interviewees.

EXERCISE 4   Invert the following sentences. *The sentences are not related.*

a   Those who sell drugs are seldom caught and punished.
b   The situation is becoming so serious that governments are enforcing ever stricter penalties.
c   The environment will not repair itself without a concerted effort.

EXERCISE 5   Write an essay on the following topic. Pay particular attention to sentence construction and the use of **academic** writing.

ESSAY TASK

The task should take about 40 minutes.

The number of car accidents is increasing annually. This is the result of poor driving habits.

To what extent do you agree?

Write a minimum of 250 words.

Unit 8.9   Speculating

EXERCISE 1   What do you think would happen if:

a   passports were abolished?
b   the government tried to ban private car ownership?
c   language ability could be surgically implanted?

EXERCISE 2   What do you think will happen if:

a   deforestation is allowed to continue?
b   the number of IELTS candidates doubles next year?

EXERCISE 3   What is the difference between the following conditional sentences?

a   If passports were abolished, ...
b   If deforestation is allowed to continue, ...

POINT OF IMPACT   Using conditional sentences is very important when speculating, but they must be applied appropriately. Make sure you are using the correct conditional structure to express your point. Remember also to **justify** your statements, but avoid being too **dogmatic**. For example:

If passports were abolished, it would *almost certainly* lead to domestic problems in a country **as governments would be unable to identify and provide for their citizens**.

EXERCISE 4   How could you use the following language to speculate? Write a sentence using each one.

a   highly likely to
b   could lead to
c   has the potential to
d   runs the risk of (+ ing)

EXERCISE 5   Make speculations based on the prompts below.

a   Cheaper public transport
b   14-year-olds were allowed to drive
c   Subsidies for car-pooling (people in the same workplace rotate responsibility for collecting their colleagues)
d   An alternative source of fuel to replace petrol is found

Unit 8.10   Labelling maps and plans (listening)

EXERCISE 1   Look at illustrations A and B below. What are they?

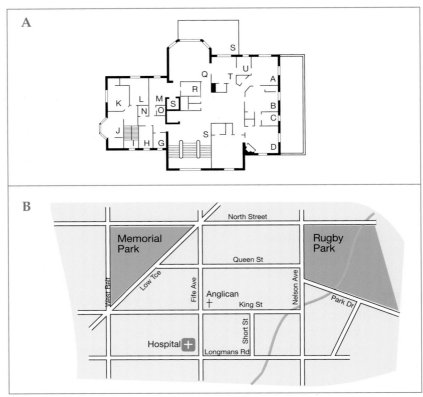

EXERCISE 2   What kind of language do you think is important when describing maps or plans?

EXERCISE 3   Look at the map below and describe the location of the buildings.

Westmore University Campus

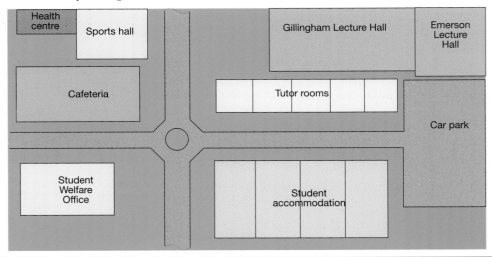

POINT OF IMPACT   Maps and floor plans use the same basic skills. One way to help you is to put your pen on the point where the recording begins, and then draw what you hear. For example, if the speaker says 'turn left', then draw a line to the left on the question paper. This will help you follow what the speaker is saying.

EXERCISE 4   Listen to the recording and label the rooms on the plan using words from the box.

a   Reception
b   Theory test room A
c   Theory test room B
d   Processing office
e   Waiting area
f   Practice test area
g   Toilet

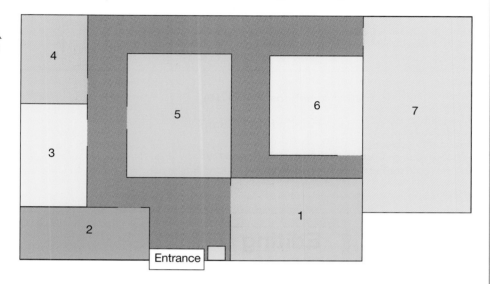

EXERCISE 5   Now write a sentence describing where each place is. Start your sentence from the entrance. (e.g. Take the first left and it's immediately on the left (Room 2)).

REVIEW   The following recording is unusual in that it gives a lot of information very quickly. This is to test your ability to concentrate as you write.

Listen to the recording and answer the questions using *NO MORE THAN THREE WORDS OR A LETTER*.

REVIEW   Short-answer questions (Unit 1.10)

1   What is Gillian's relationship to Joanna?
2   Is this Joanna's first visit to the university?
3   What does Gillian think can be difficult at first?
4   Is Gillian enthusiastic about the teaching staff?
5   What's Joanna's major in?

REVIEW   Multiple choice (Unit 2.10) and Labelling maps and plans (this unit)

6   Which diagram best illustrates where the social sciences block is?

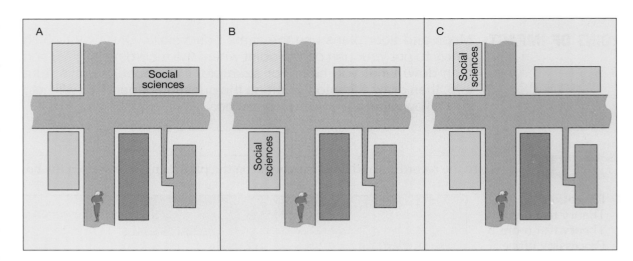

Short-answer questions (Unit 1.10)

7 Where can Joanna normally find Gillian?
8 What does she do on Mondays?
9 Why does Gillian recommend the party?
10 What time are they going to meet?

Unit 8.11 Editing

Imagine ... after all your studying, practising skills and writing essays, you have finally finished your Task II essay. There are only two minutes left on the clock, so why not relax, sit back and congratulate yourself? What else could you do with only 120 seconds remaining?

POINT OF IMPACT   Use the last few minutes of the writing test to read through your essay again, editing for errors. Be sure you have written what you intended and that there are no important ideas missing. Simple spelling or grammar errors can add up, and a few minutes of error correction can make a difference.

EXERCISE 1   Complete the tables for each sentence.

Incorrect sentence	Fining industries that are guilty of polluting the atmosphere is not the only.
It should be ...	
Why?	

Incorrect sentence	The most beautiful future will come to those who are worthy.
It should be ...	
Why?	

Incorrect sentence	In my opinion, nuclear power becomes the main source for our energy needs.
It should be ...	
Why?	

Incorrect sentence	In the future, developments in the medicality will greatly extend our life span.
It should be ...	
Why?	

Incorrect sentence	During a war, many public buildings are devasted.
It should be ...	
Why?	

Incorrect sentence	Developments in the computer industry continue to accelerate, almost to the point of being beyond our ability to continually learn and assimilate these new technologies and therefore unless we make a conscious effort to reduce the quantity and instead invest more in the quality we will find ourselves entirely swamped with a mass of almost instantly obsolete hardware and software ...
It should be ...	
Why?	

Incorrect sentence	Nuclear power, which is used widely throughout the world, has many positive and negative aspects and we should consider them all before we pursue a particular course of action because there are alternatives and furthermore, these
It should be ...	
Why?	

POINT OF IMPACT The changes above all improve your writing, but it is better to be a little informal than attempt to be over-formal and make major errors.

EXERCISE 2 Here are a few points that may help, but first they need to be corrected.

a Verbs has to be in the correct person.
b And don't start a sentence with 'and' or 'but'.
c Avoid clichés, even if every coin has two sides.
d No sentence fragments.
e Make sure you are clear when you are not using no double negatives.
f Be careful, not to, overuse, commas in your, writing.
g DO NOT emphasise your opinion with capital letters.
h Should rhetorical questions be used?
i Exaggeration will not make your essay a billion times better.
j Edit carefully in case have forgotten something.

EXERCISE 3   Which of the following pairs of short paragraphs is best?

	A	B
1	There is no doubt that robotics have literally saved our lives. Without automation, especially in mass production industries like the car industry, businesses would not be able to operate. But on the other hand, automation has created the unemployment problem.	There is little doubt that automation has improved the quality of our lives. Without automation, mass production industries would have considerably more difficulty operating. However, automation has had a negative impact on employment.
2	There are many who hold that the money spent on space exploration could be better used in more practical areas, such as healthcare or education.	There is some people who believe that space exploration are costing money that could be better spent on education or healthcare. We should therefore NOT direct so much money in this direction.
3	In our technologically motivated society, who can argue that computers have little use? From business to education, most industries rely to some degree on the use of computer technology for even the most basic purposes.	It is undeniable that computers have become an essential part of our workplace, with many industries relying on computer technology for the most menial tasks.
4	Although the current economic climate may not be so nothing to underestimate, retraining programmes and employment schemes mean there is light at the end of the tunnel.	Although we should not underestimate the current economic climate, retraining programmes and employment schemes are creating more opportunities for the future.
5	Along with advancements in technology, computer games have evolved and have become a major industry of their own, despite some opinions claiming games to be a misdirected use of technology.	Advancements in technology. Along with this, there has been an equal evolution of computer games. Many people believe this, is a misdirected use of resources, yet entertainment has become a major industry, and it is inevitable that companies will exploit this market.

EXERCISE 4   There are two errors from *Exercise 2* in each of the weak paragraphs above. What are they?

POINT OF IMPACT   Study the checklist for editing. It lists points to think about when checking your essay. Become familiar with the list so that you will know what to check for in the actual IELTS Writing Module.
Have you ...
1 checked your grammar (plural and third person 's')?
2 used a range of structures?
3 used appropriate vocabulary?
4 checked your spelling?
5 considered topic sentences and paragraphing?
6 used a variety of connectors and linking words?
7 justified and supported your opinions?
8 shown a clear point of view?
9 stayed on topic?

EXERCISE **5**   Read the essay below, and use the guide from the Point of Impact on the previous page to make any necessary changes. You may need to rewrite sections of the essay.

ESSAY TASK

As the number of private cars has increased, so too has the level of pollution in many cities.

What can be done about this?

As the number of private cars <u>increases</u>, so has the level of pollution. Overreliance on ⟨has increased⟩ cars at the expense of public transport have made this problem even bigger, causing many concerned citizens to look for a solution to the problem.

One potential solution to the problem is to discourage the use of private cars by raising taxes. If the cost of petrol was increased, then many people will consider using alternative forms of transport or even walking. Admitedly, there would be a number of complaints from car drivers, but these would not be worthy when balanced against the environmental benefits

Another solution could be to look at more specific causes of the problem. Modern cars are fitted with cleaner burning engines and catalytic converters. Furthermore, they do not cause as much of an environmental hazard as some older cars. In Japan, for example, cars are heavily taxed once they've been on the road for three years or more, encouraging people to buy new cars which pollute less. By heavily taxing older vehicles from the road, some of the worst pollution making vehicles will be taken off the road. Admittedly, this would not really be fair to those who cannot afford a new car with such regularity.

An improvement in the quality and effishiency of public transport would also encourage people to use these cars less. In London, a system has been operating for some time in which people are allocated days of the week when they can use their cars. On days what they are not allowed to drive, public transport is taken. London is also a difficult place to get around, especially for visitors. London taxi drivers have a worldwide reputation for their ability to navigate the main roads and the back streets with equal ease, the result of having to take an extensive test based on the local road system.

Although these are potential solutions to the problem, none of them are perfection. Only by a concerted effort by both the government and the public can this situation truly be resolved.

Unit 8.12   **Topic Card: Transport**

EXERCISE **1**   What skills could you use to talk about a *memorable journey*?

EXERCISE **2**   Spend one minute making notes on the following topic card.

Describe your favourite way to travel.
You should say:
- what it is
- when you first did it
- how often you do it.
You should also say why it is your favourite.

EXERCISE 3   **Student A:**   Talk about the topic card.
                   Student B: Listen to your partner. Tick the skills you hear used. Add other skills to the list if you hear them.

opinions	
justification	
recounting an experience	
likes and dislikes	
preferences	
comparatives and superlatives	

UNIT

9

Looking ahead

Unit 9.1	Review of reading skills

POINT OF IMPACT   As this is the last unit of the book, you should spend some time between now and your test reading through previous units, skimming the articles and reviewing the Points of Impact.

EXERCISE 1   Make notes on the part of the reading test you think will be the most difficult and state why.

POINT OF IMPACT   You should have just enough time before your test to focus on areas you feel you still need to work on. Do not waste time panicking or thinking you need to work on *everything*!

EXERCISE 2   Without referring back to sections of the book, answer the following questions.

a   How many sections are there in the reading test?
b   Will you have to answer every question style you may have practised?
c   What should you do if you cannot find the answer to a question?
d   Are you given any additional time to transfer answers?

EXERCISE 3   The following questions are from the two reading passages on pages 194–196. Before you read the texts, look at the questions and decide what skills you would use. *An example has been done for you.*

Reading Passage 1

Question type	The skills I am going to use

Questions 1–3   Look at the following statements and decide if they are right or wrong according to the information given.

Write   **TRUE** if the statement is true
FALSE if the statement is false
NOT GIVEN if the information is not given in the passage.

1 A better understanding of the causes of amnesia has allowed researchers to find cures.
2 Older people are more likely to suffer from amnesia.
3 Some forms of amnesia are self-induced.

Questions 4–8   Match a type of amnesia with a description.

4 Anterograde
5 Retrograde
6 Transient global
7 Lacunar
8 Korsakoff

a   more isolated than other forms
b   failure of short-term or recent memory
c   clear memories only since the onset of amnesia
d   the result of the sufferer's habits
e   possibly a result of temporary blood-flow problems

Questions 9–10   Circle the correct answer A–D.

9 Most amnesiacs
A   recover all their memories
B   recover older memories first
C   suffer from transient global amnesia
D   have suffered a head injury.

10 Diagnosis of amnesia
A   has now been perfected
B   depends on a patient's general health
C   can sometimes be made with a brain scan
D   is easily made.

Reading Passage 2

Question type	The skills I am going to use

Questions 1–4   Label the diagram below using *NO MORE THAN TWO WORDS.*

Banned or controlled performance-enhancing substances (purpose and examples)

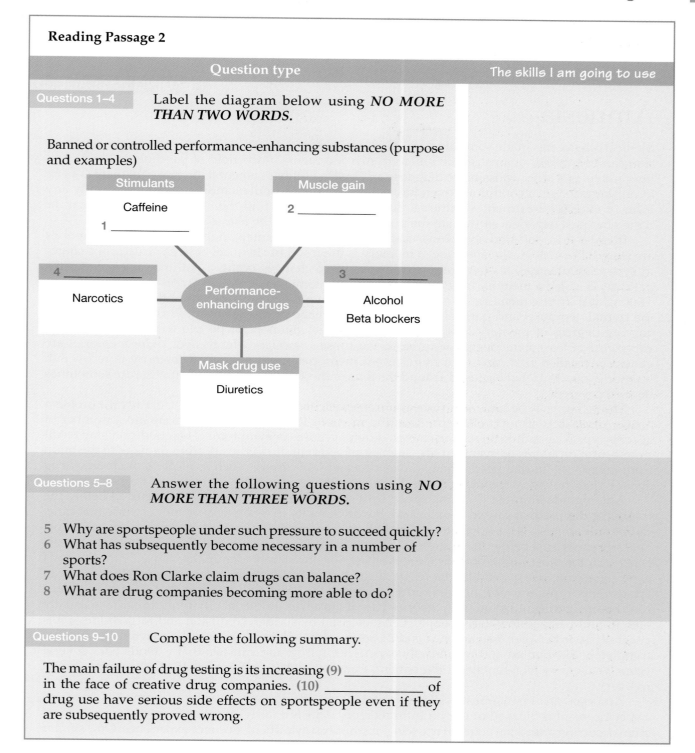

Stimulants

Caffeine

1 _____

Muscle gain

2 _____

4 _____

Narcotics

Performance-enhancing drugs

3 _____

Alcohol

Beta blockers

Mask drug use

Diuretics

Questions 5–8   Answer the following questions using *NO MORE THAN THREE WORDS.*

5   Why are sportspeople under such pressure to succeed quickly?
6   What has subsequently become necessary in a number of sports?
7   What does Ron Clarke claim drugs can balance?
8   What are drug companies becoming more able to do?

Questions 9–10   Complete the following summary.

The main failure of drug testing is its increasing **(9)** _____ in the face of creative drug companies. **(10)** _____ of drug use have serious side effects on sportspeople even if they are subsequently proved wrong.

EXERCISE 4   Now read the texts and answer the questions.

Amnesia

Medical science has made some amazing discoveries over the past century. Nerves can be repaired, skin can be grafted, organs can be replaced. Advancements in the field of psychology are no less impressive, as it is now possible to diagnose and treat a number of mental illnesses. Yet there is a gap in our knowledge, a condition which has as yet defied true understanding and consequently any form of effective treatment – amnesia. Sufferers of amnesia find themselves unable to recall or remember past experiences, even to the point of not knowing the names of their own family.

In order to understand how amnesia affects us, it is important to understand how our memories are stored. Physiologically speaking, a memory is the result of chemical or even structural changes in synaptic transmissions between neurons. As these changes occur, a pathway is created. This pathway is called a memory trace. Signals can travel along these memory traces through the brain. Making and storing memories is a complex process involving many regions of the brain, including the frontal, temporal and parietal lobes, and it is damage or disease to these areas that results in varying degrees of memory loss. For this reason, it is common for people with head injuries to experience at least some degree of amnesia. For those amnesiacs who recover, older memories are generally recalled first, and then more recent memories, until almost all memory is recovered. Memories of events that occurred around the time of the accident or onset of amnesia are sometimes never recovered.

Though we may be some way from a cure, research has allowed us to at least identify the problem areas. Amnesia is an umbrella term covering memory loss in general and there are a number of specific types depending on related causes, different causes or symptoms. This condition may result from health problems or events in life, such as an accident. It may result from damage to the brain from injuries, including head injury, stroke, or a result of disease, such as alcohol, or chronic drug abuse or psychological trauma or stress. For each of these causes, there is a distinct form of amnesia.

Anterograde amnesia is characterised by a complete recall of events that occurred before the trauma or disease that caused the amnesia, but an inability to retain new memories since that time. Retrograde amnesia is the opposite, in which short-term memory functions perfectly well, but events or experiences from before the trauma or disease can no longer be recalled. Transient global amnesia is perhaps the most frightening, as there is as yet no consistently identifiable cause. Some theorists have suggested that it could be the result of small strokes which can occur when a blockage in an artery temporarily prevents oxygen supply to part of the brain. Others argue that intense migraines could be a significant factor. Both theories base themselves on the fact that this amnesia is usually seen in middle-aged to elderly people. Characterised by sudden confusion and forgetfulness, this generally lasts between half an hour and 24 hours, although in severe attacks a victim can become completely disoriented and may briefly experience retrograde amnesia that extends back several years. While very frightening for the patient, transient global amnesia has the highest rate of total recovery.

Amnesia can also manifest itself in other, more specific, forms such as lacunar amnesia, in which a specific event is blocked or erased from memory. This is a fairly common form of amnesia, most often occurring after a particular harrowing or emotionally difficult event or experience. On a similar note, temporary memory loss can be induced through psychological trauma leading the victim to suffer from emotional or hysterical amnesia. There are some forms of amnesia that are self-induced. Korsakoff syndrome, familiar in its mildest form to many, is memory loss stemming from excessive alcohol consumption. In extreme cases of alcohol abuse, days or even weeks of memory may disappear.

Diagnosing amnesia and its cause is still far from an exact science. If amnesia is suspected, patients undergo a physical examination during which doctors look at several factors. During a physical examination, the doctor enquires about recent traumas or illnesses, drug and medication history, and checks the patient's general health. For cases where a problem appears to be manifesting itself, psychological examination may be able to determine the extent of amnesia and the memory system affected. The brain can also be scanned to reveal any evidence of damage, and blood can be tested to check for any diseases that may be present. Yet it should be remembered that for the most part, amnesia is often temporary and very limited. Some types of amnesia, such as transient global amnesia, are completely resolved and there is no permanent loss of memory. Others, such as Korsakoff syndrome, may be permanent, but no matter what the cause, a degree of rehabilitation is almost always possible.

READING PASSAGE 2

A running controversy

In 1988 Canadian athlete Ben Johnson set a new world record for the 100 metres sprint and set the Seoul Olympics alight. Just a few days later, he was stripped of his medal and banned from competing after having failed a drug test, highlighting what has since become an international problem – drug use in sport.

Those involved in sports face enormous pressure to excel in competition, all the more so as their careers are relatively short. By the time most sportspeople are in their forties, they are already considered to be past their prime, and as a result they need to earn their money as quickly as possible. In such a high-pressure environment, success has to come quickly and increasingly often drugs are playing a prominent role.

There are a number of specific effects that sportspeople are aiming to achieve by taking performance-enhancing drugs. Caffeine and cocaine are commonly used as stimulants, getting the body ready for the mass expenditure of energy required. In addition, there are those who are looking to build their body strength and turn to the use of anabolic steroids. Having worked so hard and needing to unwind, sportspeople may misuse other drugs to relax, cope with stress or boost their own confidence. Alcohol is common on such occasions, but for sportspeople something more direct is often required, and this has led to an increase in the use of beta-blockers specifically to steady nerves.

Increasingly accurate drug testing is leading to ever-more creative ways of avoiding detection, and there are a range of banned substances that are still taken by sportspeople in order to disguise the use of other, more potent drugs. Diuretics is a good example of this: in addition to allowing the body to lose excess weight, they are used to hide other substances.

Drugs or not, the working life of the average sportsperson is hard and often painful. Either through training or on the field, injuries are common and can lead to the use of narcotics simply to mask the pain. There are examples of champion motorcyclists taking local anaesthetics to hide the pain of a crash that should have seen them taken straight to hospital, and though this is not directly banned, use is carefully monitored.

Drug testing has since become an accepted feature of most major sporting events, and as soon as a new drug is detected and the user is banned from competitive sport, then a new drug is developed which evades detection. Inevitably, this makes testing for such banned substances even more stringent, and has in recent years highlighted a new and disturbing problem – the unreliability of drug tests.

Recent accusations of drug use have seen sportspeople in court attempt to overthrow decisions against them, claiming that they were unaware they had taken anything on the banned list. A test recently carried out saw three non-athletes given dietary substances that were not on the banned list, and the two who didn't take exercise tested negative. However, the third person, who exercised regularly, tested positive. This, of course, has left the testing of sportspeople in a very difficult position. Careers can be prematurely ended by false allegations of drug abuse, yet by not punishing those who test positive, the door would be open for anyone who wanted to take drugs.

The issue is becoming increasingly clouded as different schools of opinion are making themselves heard. There are some that argue that if the substance is not directly dangerous to the user, then it should not be banned, claiming that it is just another part of training and can be compared to eating the correct diet. Ron Clarke, a supporter of limited drug use in sport, commented that some drugs should be accepted as 'they just level the playing field'. He defended his opinion by pointing out that some competitors have a natural advantage. Athletes born high above sea level or who work out in high altitudes actually produce more red blood cells, a condition which other athletes can only achieve by drug taking.

Others claim that drug use shouldn't be allowed because it contravenes the whole idea of fairly competing in a sporting event, adding that the drugs available to a wealthy American athlete, for example, would be far superior to those available to a struggling Nigerian competitor.

Governing bodies of the myriad of sporting worlds are trying to set some standards for competitors, but as drug companies become more adept at disguising illegal substances, the procedure is an endless race with no winner. In the face of an overwhelming drug and supplement market, one thing is certain – drugs will probably be a significant factor for a long time to come.

Unit 9.2   Review of Task I skills

EXERCISE 1   Prepare a plan for the following Task I title. You should take no more than three minutes.

ESSAY TASK

The charts below show different causes of death in the USA for two different years.

Write a report for a university lecturer describing the information shown below.

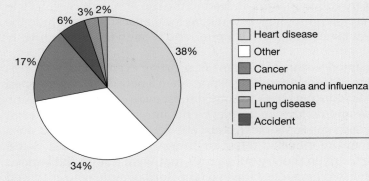
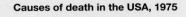
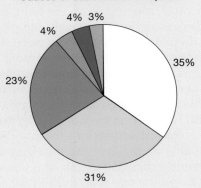

EXERCISE 3 Prepare a plan for the following Task I title. You should take no more than three minutes.

ESSAY TASK

The table below shows the percentage of different-aged cars in four countries.

Write a report for a university lecturer describing the information shown below.

Age Country	New to 3 years	4 to 5 years	6 to 8 years	9 to 12 years	13 years or more
New Zealand	26	32	34	6	2
Japan	79	16	3	1	1
USA	39	24	21	11	5
Britain	35	36	24	2	3

EXERCISE 4 Prepare a plan for the following Task I title. You should take no more than three minutes.

ESSAY TASK

The graph below shows the percentage of university students studying arts degrees over four different decades in three continents.

Write a report for a university lecturer describing the information shown below.

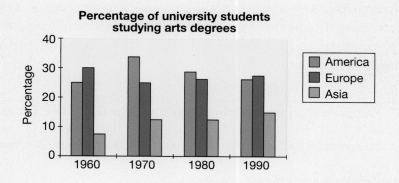

Percentage of university students studying arts degrees

EXERCISE 5 Prepare a plan for the following Task I title. You should take no more than three minutes.

ESSAY TASK

The picture below shows the interior of a caravan.

Write a report for a university lecturer describing the information shown below.

Unit 9.3   Plans and ambitions

EXERCISE 1 'Will' and 'going to' are the most common ways of talking about the future. Which is the most common for talking about future plans and ambitions?

EXERCISE 2 What other language is used in the paragraph below to refer to plans and ambitions?

Well, I'd love to get a job working with children, so I'm planning to take a teacher training course. I wouldn't mind working abroad for a while, but I expect that will have to wait until I get some experience. I'd love to do some voluntary work though – that would give me an opportunity to travel as well as get some experience of a different culture. I'm hoping to complete the course within the next year because I want to start work as soon as possible.

EXERCISE 3 Prepare a short presentation on you and the IELTS test. For example:

I expect to feel a little nervous just before the test, but I'm going to review all the skills I have learned ...

Spend one minute making notes before you speak.

EXERCISE 4 Now talk about your long-term plans for the future.

Unit 9.4   Review of listening skills

EXERCISE 1   What do you think is the most important listening skill? Consider the following and rate the top three (one being the most important). Compare your answers with a partner.

a   Predicting and anticipating
b   Word families
c   Synonyms and antonyms
d   Recognising speakers

e   Listening to intonation
f   Note taking
g   Discourse markers
h   Spelling

POINT OF IMPACT   A major problem for IELTS candidates is that despite everything they have studied and practised, they feel there will not be enough time to apply these skills in the test. It is very important that you read the question carefully in the time you are given, predicting and anticipating as much as possible.

EXERCISE 2   Before you listen to the recording, read the questions below and predict as much as you can.

Questions 1–2   Answer the following questions using **NO MORE THAN THREE WORDS**.

1   What is the name of Dr Philipps' book?
2   How does Dr Philipps describe the interviewer's attitude?

Questions 3–4   Circle the correct letter A–D.

3   Dr Philipps was surprised at
   A   the number of reported sightings
   B   the impact that the media has had
   C   how similar witnesses' descriptions were
   D   how many countries reports have come from.

4   Dr Philipps' book
   A   provides irrefutable evidence
   B   is a mixture of fact and fiction
   C   is very objective
   D   has been plagiarised.

Questions 5–7   Complete the summary below.

(5) _____ is the name of an army installation in New Mexico made famous by (6) _____, a farmer who claimed to have recovered pieces of (7) _____.

Questions 8–10   Answer the following questions **USING NO MORE THAN TWO WORDS OR A NUMBER**.

8   What term does Dr Philipps use to describe people with unreliable or exaggerated information?
9   What area is not covered in the book?
10   How much does the book cost?

EXERCISE	**3**	What do you think the recording will be about? How many speakers do you think there will be?

EXERCISE	**4**	Now listen and answer the questions in *Exercise 2*.

EXERCISE	**5**	Before you read the questions below, close your books and take notes on the second recording.

EXERCISE	**6**	Try to answer as many of the questions as you can using your notes, what you can remember and what seems logical.

Complete the following form *USING NO MORE THAN THREE WORDS OR A NUMBER*.

BIOLOGY FIELD TRIP

(1) _____ assignments must be completed on the day.

Dress (2) _____

You must have (3) _____ and a waterproof jacket.

(4) A _____ is recommended

You will be on the marsh for about (5) _____

A light lunch is (6) _____

Be outside the college by (7) _____ at the latest.

Dropped back at the college at 9.00 p.m. (or later, depending on (8) _____)

You will need to bring (9) _____ to complete the assignments (do not bring anything expensive)

Do not disturb (10) _____

Unit 9.5	**Review of Task II skills**

EXERCISE	**1**	Number the following skills as they should be done. *The first one has been done for you.*

	Start writing
	Identify the topic
	Brainstorm for ideas
	Divide the question into two parts (if appropriate)
	Identify the task words
	Remove irrelevant ideas
	Edit your work
	Organise your ideas into paragraphs
1	Read the question

EXERCISE	2

Follow the first seven points from *Exercise 1* for the title below.

ESSAY TASK

Television and computer games are an increasing aspect of many young people's lives. Do you think that modern forms of entertainment are making us less sociable?

EXERCISE	3

Below are two possible answers to the essay in *Exercise 2*. Decide which paragraph is better in each case. *There may be no grammatical or academic differences – it may simply be personal choice.*

Candidate A	Candidate B
1 There is little doubt that both television and computer games have became common forms of entertainment for many people, yet the claim that they are making us less sociable is not entirely accurate. There are points of view for both sides, as I will discuss.	Television and computer games occupy an increasing part of our leisure time and some people feel that this is making us less sociable. I will present my opinions.
2 Against the statement, it could be said that more traditional forms of entertainment were no better. Children at least have some common ground when playing computer games, and could find themselves making friends simply on the strength of a conversation about the popular game of the time.	In opposition to the argument, it could be said that more traditional forms of entertainment such as reading were equally unsociable, as they did not involve others. In addition, many children find that by playing computer games they have a ready source of conversation between friends, and as such it is promoting interactive behaviour.
3 It should not be overlooked that television is often used as a method of bringing families together, and as such is a perfectly sociable event. I personally remember when my family and I all used to gather around the television, watching quiz programmes. Computer games can also be seen in this light as many computer games offer a multiplayer function, inviting people to share their entertainment.	Not only are popular forms of entertainment just as valid as more traditional forms, there is another argument that suggests simply because people watch television, does not make them less sociable. In fact, many parents use the television as a focal point for getting families together. Admittedly, this often involves little more than discussing the programme that they are watching, but it can still be considered a sociable activity. A similar observation can be drawn from computer games, although to a lesser extent. There are

computer games that involve more than one player and as such provide a sociable environment for people to play together.

4   In support of the opinion that computer games and television are essentially anti-social, it could be argued that those who play or watch to excess do become more isolated. Those who spend their entire night playing games or watching television become tired by day, and as a result are less inclined to behave sociably. Moreover, they may find their conversation limited by their hobbies, further isolating them from others.

Yet the other side of the argument should also be considered. Like most things, the problem comes with excessive behaviour. Too much time in front of a television or playing games, and people lose their social abilities. This is something of a concern, as 'serious gamers' are becoming less and less rare.

5   To sum up, there is an argument for each side. The final answer comes down to a matter of personal choice, but the decision should be made with a consideration for other people.

In conclusion, as with most pursuits, the forms of entertainment that we enjoy should be used in moderation. Neither television nor computer games cause us to lose our social skills if we balance them with other pursuits.

Unit 9.6   Review of speaking skills

EXERCISE 1   Throughout the course, you have studied and practised extending answers to include a number of different functions. Review by considering the following topic and make short notes using the prompts.

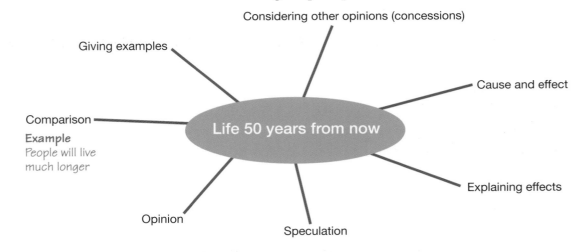

Considering other opinions (concessions)

Giving examples

Cause and effect

Comparison
Example
People will live
much longer

Life 50 years from now

Explaining effects

Opinion

Speculation

EXERCISE 2   Now talk about the topic with your partner.

Unit 9.7   Test

IELTS test: Listening

You will be given time to transfer your answers at the end of the test.

The test is divided as follows:

Listening Section 1   Questions 1–10
Listening Section 2   Questions 11–20
Listening Section 3   Questions 21–30
Listening Section 4   Questions 31–40

You should answer all the questions.

Section 1

Questions 1–5

Complete the table using *NO MORE THAN TWO WORDS OR A NUMBER*.

Northern Rental Bookings

Name: William **(1)** _____

Contact number: **(2)** _____

Address: 10 **(3)** _____ Nelson

Payment by **(4)** _____

Card No. 4550 1392 8309 3221

Card expiry date: July 20XX

Rental period: **(5)** _____ days

Questions 6–10

Answer the following questions *USING NO MORE THAN TWO WORDS OR A NUMBER*.

6 How much is the car per day?
7 What does the price include?
8 Who will he be visiting?
9 What kind of car does the agent recommend?
10 What does he need to collect the car?

Section 2

Questions 11–15

Complete the table below. If there is no information given, write X.

	Distance/km	Highlight	Time/hours
Overlander	(11)	3 volcanoes	11
Transalpine	223	(12) 16 _____	(13)
Transcoastal	(14)	(15)	5

Questions 16–20   Complete the summary below *USING NO MORE THAN TWO WORDS OR A NUMBER.*

Taking three days to complete, the **(16)** _____ is one of the world's longest train journeys. The Ghan is shorter, passing through towns built by the **(17)** _____. There is also a sculpture designed to mark the laying of the **(18)** _____ sleeper. The Overland was the first train to travel between two **(19)** _____ and it is also the oldest journey of its kind on **(20)** _____

Section 3

Questions 21–25   Circle the correct letter A–C.

21 Lyn is having difficulty completing her project because
    A she doesn't have enough information
    B she can't organise her presentation
    C she doesn't have enough time.

22 Her presentation is going to focus on
    A solar power in America
    B solar-powered water heaters
    C alternative energy technology.

23 Why does Lyn think we should be looking for alternative sources of energy?
    A Fossil fuels are expensive.
    B Fossil fuels have an impact on the environment.
    C Fossil fuels are limited.

24 Solar power is a good form of alternative energy because
    A it can be harnessed with simple technology
    B it is infinite
    C it can be applied equally well in any country.

25 Which graph best indicates what Lyn is describing?

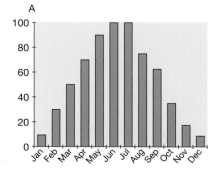
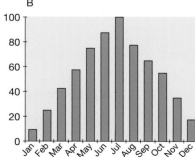
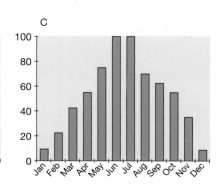

Questions 26–30   Label the following diagram.

minimum tank capacity: **(26)** _____

(29) _____ degrees

80 mm (30) _____
insulation

40 degrees

(28) _____ degrees

(27) _____

Section 4

Questions 31–40   Complete the lecture *USING NO MORE THAN THREE WORDS*.

Lecture on **(31)** _____
Examples: tourism and **(32)** _____
Common misconception is that marketing points to **(33)** _____ in what is being provided.
Marketing is actually essential in maintaining **(34)** _____
Selling a product is easier because it is **(35)** _____ and customers do not have such different **(36)** _____ .
Aim: offer service beyond hopes of **(37)** _____
Important to   (a)   keep informed
            (b)   **(38)** _____
One way to achieve this: **(39)** _____
(40) _____ must always be available for any queries or problems.

IELTS test: Reading

All answers must be written on the answer sheet by the end of the test.

The test is divided as follows:

Reading Passage 1   Questions 1–15
Reading Passage 2   Questions 16–26
Reading Passage 3   Questions 27–40

You should answer all the questions.

TIME ALLOWED: 60 MINUTES

You should spend about 20 minutes on Questions 1–15 which are based on Reading Passage 1 below.

A very brief history of time

These days, time is everything. We worry about being late, we rush to get things done or to be somewhere and our daily schedules are often planned down to the minute. Of course, none of this would have been possible without the humble clock. The internationally accepted division of time into regular, predictable units has become an essential aspect of almost all modern societies yet the history of time keeping is almost as old as civilisation itself. Nearly 3000 years ago, societies were using the stars in order to keep track of time to indicate agricultural cycles. Then came the sundial, an Egyptian invention in which the shadow cast by the sun was used to measure the time not of the seasons but of the day.

The first manufactured clock, believed to have come from Persia, was a system which recreated the movements of the stars. All the celestial bodies which had been used to tell the time of year were plotted onto an intricate system in which the planets rotated around each other. Not being dependent on either sunlight or a clear night, this was one of the earliest systems to divide a complete day. Although ingenious for its time, this method suffered from incorrect astrological assumptions of the period, in which it was believed that the Earth was the centre of the universe.

The Greeks were next to develop a more accurate clock using water to power a mechanism that counted out the divisions of the day. The simplest water clock consisted of a large urn that had a small hole located near the base, and a graduated stick attached to a floating base. The hole would be plugged while the urn was being filled with water, and then the stick would be inserted into the urn. The stick would float perpendicular to the surface of the water, and when the hole at the base of the urn was unplugged, the passage of time was measured as the stick descended farther into the urn.

Then, for nearly one thousand years, there was little in the way of progress in time keeping until the European invention of spring-powered clocks in the late fourteenth century. Unreliable and inaccurate, the early models of these clocks were useful in that they gave direction to new advances. In 1656 Christiaan Huygens, a Dutch scientist, made the first pendulum clock, which had an error of less than one minute a day, the first time such accuracy had been achieved. His later refinements reduced his clock's error to less than 10 seconds a day. Some years later, Huygens abandoned the pendulum for a balance wheel and spring assembly which allowed for a whole new generation of time piece – the wristwatch. Still found in some of today's wristwatches, this improvement allowed portable seventeenth-century watches to keep time to 10 minutes a day.

While clock making and musical chime clocks became increasingly popular, it was the invention of the cuckoo clock, designed and made by Franz Anton Ketterer, which really caught people's imagination. The design was not particularly complex. The clock was mounted on a headboard, normally a very elaborate carving reflecting the tastes of the artist. Many of the original cuckoo clocks are still kept today because of the artwork on the headboard. Using the traditional circular pendulum design, the clock could run accurately for up to a week, using a weight to keep the pendulum in motion. Again, the weight was often carved with a design making it as much an art form as a timepiece. The most innovative feature of these cuckoo clocks, as the name implies, is that a small carved cuckoo came out of the clock to chime the hour. Particularly ingenious was the placement of bellows inside the clock, which were designed to recreate the sound made by the bird, although later models included a lever on the bottom of the clock which could be used to stop this hourly chime.

Refinements to this original pendulum concept meant that by 1721 the pendulum clock remained accurate to within one second per day by compensating for changes in the pendulum's length due to temperature variations. Over the next century, further refinements reduced this to a hundredth of a second a day. In the 1920s, a new era of clock making began which is still popular today – the quartz clock. When under pressure, quartz generates an electric field of relatively constant frequency, and it was discovered that this electric signal was sufficient to power a clock. Quartz crystal clocks were better because they had fewer moving parts to disturb their regular frequency. Even so, they still rely on a mechanical vibration and this depends on the size of the crystal, and as no two crystals can be exactly alike, there is a degree of difference in every quartz watch.

Comparing performance to price, it is understandable that quartz clocks still dominate the market. Yet they are no longer the most accurate. Scientists had long realised that each chemical element in the universe absorbs and emits electromagnetic radiation at its own specific frequencies. These resonances are inherently stable, thus forming the basis for a reliable system of time measurement, all the more so because no moving parts are needed to record these resonances. Yet the cost of these atomic clocks mean that such timekeeping precision is a long way from becoming common.

Questions 1–8   Match a type of clock with a description.

1	Quartz clock	A	Relied on basic scientific principles
2	Cuckoo clock	B	was the first to replace the pendulum
3	Sundial	C	Is the most common method of timekeeping
4	Persian clock	D	Is the most accurate clock
5	Wristwatch	E	Is the earliest known method of measuring time during the day
6	Pendulum	F	Was inaccurate because of misconceptions of the age
7	Atomic clock	G	Was often highly ornamental
8	Water clock	H	Had only a 10-second margin of error per day

Questions 9–12   Label the diagram using words from the text.

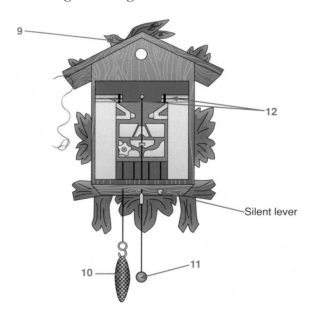

Silent lever

Questions 13–15   Complete the following summary using **NO MORE THAN TWO WORDS**.

Although quartz clocks are **(13)** _____, the atomic clock is the most **(14)** _____ as it does not rely on any **(15)** _____.

You should spend about 20 minutes on Questions 16–27 which are based on Reading Passage 2 below.

Holiday blues

The holiday season has always been a cause for celebration around the world. The opportunity to take a break from work, be frivolous, go on holiday, meet family and friends – all good reasons to look forward to the holidays with enthusiasm and anticipation. Or at least that is what we are led to believe.

A Research carried out in America suggests that these feelings of euphoria may be somewhat misplaced. A study recently carried out by New York University Child Study Centre has concluded that one in three people of varying ages suffer 'holiday blues' to varying extents, from a mild feeling of sadness to severe, sometimes even suicidal, depression. The effects can manifest themselves in many ways, such as an inability to sleep or sleeping too much, overeating or undereating, headaches or drinking too much. The report also concluded that not only are there a number of complex causes that can trigger such depression (psychological and biological), there are an equal number of opinions as to the best solution.

B According to Dr Frank Pittman, a leading family psychiatrist, the most significant cause for holiday depression actually stems from our concerns about our family. During the holiday season, families meet, often for the first time since the last holiday season, and try to make these reunions 'perfect'. In fact, says Pittman, we count on the holidays to compensate for the rest of the year. He himself comments that 'I wanted to make up to the family for not having been a good enough father and uncle all year'. However, such good intentions are often thwarted by old family arguments, feelings of not being appreciated or being used, all of which result in holiday stress. It seems that the idyllic picture of our family we wish to build in our minds cannot be sustained in reality.

C Although Pittman holds family to be the source of much of the problem, others point to a more general social context. Gift shopping, for example, does not help reduce tensions – crowded shops, long queues, the pressure of choosing just the right present – all of these things contribute to a feeling of stress and anxiety. On the other end of the scale, there are those without family who experience a sense of extreme loneliness and isolation throughout this period, often spending the long holidays alone. Any feelings of inadequacy they may harbour throughout the year can often become unbearable at a time when friends are unavailable and enjoying an apparently cosy break with their loved ones. In fact, such is the extreme nature of this isolation that many organisations have been established to offer some help and support to those who feel most alone over what should be the 'festive' season.

D Others, however, argue that more scientific explanations carry an equal weight in explaining holiday blues. Seasonal Affective Disorder, or SAD as it is more commonly known, is also held responsible for winter depression. A natural reaction to falling levels of sunlight, the pineal gland secretes the hormone melatonin, which has the effect of slowing the body down. When days get shorter, more of the hormone is released causing sufferers to become lethargic and miserable. From being industrious people with plenty of energy, SAD sufferers find themselves increasingly weary and unable to sustain any prolonged activity, a situation which often leads to depression. In addition, for many people this has a major impact not only on their personal life but also on their professional life, as employers often see this lack of productivity in terms of laziness or unwillingness to work. As a result, SAD has been linked directly to the high rate of suicide in a number of Scandinavian countries during winter months, when there are often a few hours of sunlight a day.

E The good news for SAD sufferers is that there is a cure, and as far as many medical cures go this is relatively simple. As the cause is lack of bright light, the treatment is to be in bright light every day. This can obviously be achieved by staying in a brightly lit climate, explaining why skiing holidays are so popular as they allow people to get plenty of sunlight as well as providing a stimulating activity. Another method is by using light therapy, in which patients sit in front of a lamp which acts in the same way as sunlight. To be more specific, the light should be about as bright as early morning sunshine, and the user should allow the light to reach the eyes for anything up to one hour a day in order to alleviate the symptoms. There are a number of companies currently manufacturing these lights as a health aid and they are even being prescribed by some doctors. In addition, they can be bought at considerably less than the cost of a holiday.

Whatever fundamental reason underpins holiday depression, it seems reasonable to argue that the phenomenon does indeed exist. Voluntary support services, offering counselling services to those who need the unbiased and friendly voice of a stranger to help them work through their unhappiness, report a significant increased demand for their services during holiday periods such as Christmas and the New Year.

Questions 16–17   Circle the correct answer A–C.

16 Research has shown that
   A we become more depressed during the holidays
   B poor diet can lead to depression
   C simple things can lead us to feel varying degrees of depression.

17 Dr Pittman believes holiday depression comes from
   A feelings of inadequacy
   B being alone
   C over-compensation.

Questions 18–21   Answer the following questions using *NO MORE THAN THREE WORDS*.

18 What is the chemical cause for lethargy in SAD sufferers?
19 Why is the Scandinavian suicide rate so high in winter?
20 What daily treatment can SAD sufferers benefit from?
21 For whom are the holiday periods the busiest time?

Questions 22–26   Choose the most suitable headings for sections A–E from the list below. Use each heading once only.

List of headings		
i	Family cures	22 Section A
ii	Addressing the problem	23 Section B
iii	Impact of personality	24 Section C
iv	Psychological factors	25 Section D
v	Biological factors	26 Section E
vi	Avoiding stress	
vii	Manifestations of depression	
viii	Depression in children	
ix	Pressures of the holiday period	

You should spend about 20 minutes on Questions 27–40 which are based on Reading Passage 3 below.

Weakness of the school system

A By attempting to fit in as much as possible, the school day is continually being added to. In many ways, this would appear to be a good idea, as our knowledge and understanding of the world is always growing and it would seem logical to incorporate this into schools. The reality, however, has some decided drawbacks. There is a growing feeling amongst many that the modern school curriculum, in an effort to teach as many varied subjects as possible, is actually teaching students less. It seems that by constantly adding to what should be taught in the classroom, the classes are less focused, not offering the deeper learning that institutions perhaps should.

B With classes sometimes only 30 minutes long, the overwhelming amount of information teachers are required to present often only gives students time to learn facts, not to think in any great detail about what they are being presented with. The problem is that students are not getting the opportunity to absorb what they are being taught as the curriculum expands in order to keep what has already been taught and supplement it with everything new that comes along. The weaknesses of such a system are clear – well informed though such students may be, there is the risk of an increasing number of graduates who have no real creative or intellectual ability. By denying students the opportunity to sit and think their way through problems, or even consider their own opinion, some schools are not always providing a truly educational atmosphere. There are, of course, certain aspects of education which need to be taught by simply inputting the information. Basic mathematics, for example. But there are many other subjects which could be best learned by having an opportunity to think and discuss what is being taught. Literature, writing and the social sciences are good examples of subjects which cannot be considered as 'covered' by a mass of information without the opportunity to discuss, debate or consider meaning or implications. There are also important social skills to be learned during such periods of open discussion, skills which are not addressed by an endless flow of teacher-centred information.

C Teachers themselves have also voiced concerns about the amount of information they are required to impress upon their students. There is a feeling in many educational establishments that students are no longer being educated, but taught how to pass tests. In a world where academic success is too often measured by examination results, this is a serious concern. If there is too much information to simply be memorised and not enough time to truly assimilate it, what happens to students who fail to meet the grade? By current standards, they are failures, yet they may have great potential in areas not covered by the test and there are many students who, despite clear intellectual ability, simply do not perform well in tests. Again, the problem is one of focus, as education authorities are looking at the outcome of schooling rather than the content presented in the class.

D It is here that many teachers feel the situation could be addressed at a local level. By giving more discretion to teachers, school courses could be tailored to suit the students rather than tailoring students to meet ever-expanding course requirements. In addition, by running a curriculum that gives options rather than defines an entire course, considerably more freedom would be possible. As it is, progression through most primary and secondary schools is regimented, and there is little room for students to identify and develop their own skills and strengths. If material could be chosen on the basis of its merits rather than simply because it has been put in the curriculum, then what is selected may be taught to a depth that would serve some purpose. There is, of course, a counter-argument, which claims that such open guidelines could lead to vast differences in standards between schools. What one teacher may see as essential for a student's education, another may see as irrelevant, and this will result in students with widely different educational strengths.

E With such a high-pressure learning environment, there are also a number of social aspects to schooling which need to be considered. The increased student workload cannot be covered in the classroom alone for the simple reason that there is not enough time in the average school week, and much of this extra workload has been pushed into the realm of homework. At its best, homework should be the opportunity to look in greater detail at what has been studied. In other words, to actually think about it and its relevance. The reality, however, is often very different. Concerned parents and overextended students are finding that homework is taking an increasingly large part of a student's evening, cutting into time many feel should be spent as part of a child's social education. Other social pressures have compounded the situation, as many of the areas of educating a young child which should be the responsibility of the parents have ill-advisedly become the school's responsibility. Drug awareness and health issues, for example, are occupying an increasingly large part of the school day.

F Many people believe that we should be teaching less, but teaching it better, and it is here that they think a solution can be found. Yet the process of rewriting a curriculum to incorporate only that which is essential but can be well learned would take far longer than most educational authorities have, and would be considered by many to be a 'regressive' step. Changes in the curriculum have largely been motivated by changes in the nature of employment, as job mobility demands that people know something about considerably more areas than were traditionally necessary. A little about a lot allows for the job mobility which has become so common. No matter what the final verdict may be, one thing is for sure – change will be slow, and not always for the best.

Questions 27–32   Choose the most suitable headings for sections A–F from the list below. Use each heading once only.

List of headings

i	A question of time
ii	Lack of teacher training
iii	Student success
iv	The argument for flexibility
v	Importance of teaching experience
vi	Extra-curricular pressures
vii	The benefits of a varied curriculum
viii	Imbalanced focus
ix	Overreliance on examinations
x	Quality of quantity?

27 Section A
28 Section B
29 Section C
30 Section D
31 Section E
32 Section F

Questions 33–37   Do the following statements agree with the views of the writer?

Write   **YES** if the statement agrees with the writer
NO if the statement does not agree with the writer
NOT GIVEN if there is no information about this in the passage.

33 Classes are often too short.
34 No subjects can be comprehensively learned without time to discuss and debate the facts.
35 Tests are a fair measure of ability.
36 Schools are trying to be responsible for too many aspects of a child's education.
37 Future changes in the curriculum will improve the situation.

Questions 38–40	Complete the summary below using **NO MORE THAN TWO WORDS** from the text.

Too much emphasis is placed on learning **(38)**_____. The modern school curriculum is largely a response to increased **(39)**_____ for which graduates are expected to have a much broader general knowledge. One potential solution to this could be to give individual schools **(40)**_____ regarding what is taught.

Unit 9.8   Test

ESSAY TASK

This task should take about 20 minutes.

The graphs below show three exports from South East Asia and the four sources of revenue for 1970 and 1995.

Write a report for a university lecturer describing the information shown below.

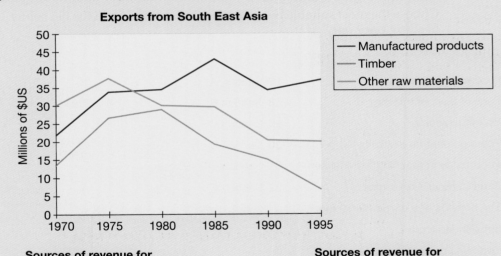

Exports from South East Asia

- Manufactured products
- Timber
- Other raw materials

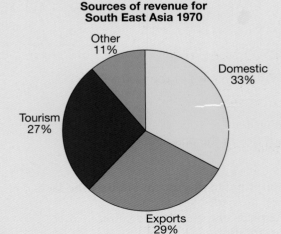

Sources of revenue for South East Asia 1970

Other 11%
Domestic 33%
Tourism 27%
Exports 29%

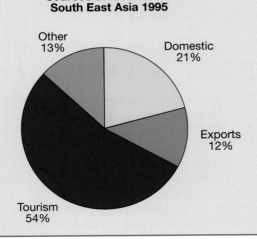

Sources of revenue for South East Asia 1995

Other 13%
Domestic 21%
Exports 12%
Tourism 54%

ESSAY TASK

This task should take about 40 minutes.

Drug addiction is becoming an increasing problem. In order to reduce this problem, anyone caught using drugs should be automatically sentenced to time in prison.

Do you agree or disagree?

(Minimum 250 words)

Unit 9.9   Test

Part One
Tell me about your hobbies.
Do you live in a house or apartment?
Talk a little about your hometown.
How often do you watch TV?
Describe your typical day.

Part Two

Describe a person who had a great influence on you.
You should say:
• who they are
• when you met
• what they were like.
You should also say why they had such an influence on you.

Part Three
Do you think it is important for young children to have a role model?
What are the advantages and disadvantages of being an only child?
How do you imagine traditional relationships changing in the future?
Why do you think celebrities become role models to so many people?
What is the importance of having friends?
How have families changed over the last 50 years?
What factors do you think are important in a good relationship?

Unit 9.10   On your marks ...

EXERCISE 1 Which do you think is the best answer for the following multiple-choice questions? Write your answer in column A.

A I think	B According to the text

1 The most important factors in reducing stress just before the test are
   A preparation and study
   B study and organisation
   C organisation and preparation
   D coffee and study.

2 What's the best strategy for the night and the morning before the exam?
   A Study and review as much as I can.
   B Eat well, relax and rest.
   C Go out for the night to relax.
   D Invite some friends over and have a few drinks.

3 On the morning of the test, what should I do?
   A Stay in bed as long as possible so I have plenty of energy.
   B Meet with friends early, so that we can discuss possible questions.
   C Avoid speaking in my native language.
   D Arrive with time to spare and take a last look at my notes.

4 What if I have trouble answering a question?
   A Go on to the next one.
   B Read the complete text slowly.
   C Choose the longest answer.
   D Just leave it blank.

5 What if I still can't understand some parts of the reading or listening?
   A Randomly guess.
   B Give up.
   C Be logical, but go with the first answer I guess.
   D Write a short note to the examiner explaining that I cannot understand the question.

6 What should I do when I have finished the reading?
   A Quietly leave.
   B Go through the three reading texts again.
   C Relax.
   D Make sure that I have transferred my answers accurately.

EXERCISE 2   Now write the answers to the multiple-choice questions in *Exercise 1* according to the article (column B). Are they different from your answers?

Exam nerves

Feeling nervous is perfectly normal just before an exam. After all, it is the culminating point of months or sometimes years of study, and you have only a few short hours to prove your abilities to an examiner. However, do not despair! There are some ways you can control your nerves.

The two most important factors in minimising exam stress are preparation and organisation. Ensure well in advance of the test that you know where you are going, how you are getting there, what room you should be going to and at what time. Check that you have the right equipment – pens, erasers, identification, a watch, etc. Some people even go so far as to lay their clothes out the night before, making sure even the smallest detail is prepared.

Another important factor for a successful exam is sleep. Going to bed slightly earlier than normal, waking up in time for a refreshing shower and a good breakfast have proven benefits. Do not stay up all night cramming as this will leave you tired, and what you have not learned by now you are unlikely to learn in one long night. Relax as much as you can.

When you arrive at the examination centre, avoid speaking either in your native language or discussing possible exam questions. This will only make you more nervous, but more importantly you should be using this time to get your brain thinking in English. It can be a good idea to find someone who is not from your country and just wish them luck. This might start a short conversation, which will help you start thinking in English.

During the exam, make sure you keep a close watch on the time and remember the planning and preparation skills you have learned in this book. A lot of students find themselves panicking, mistakenly thinking that they don't have time to follow the skills they have learned. The results for these kinds of students are always the same, and always disappointing. If the techniques were not effective, your teacher would not have taught you them!

You will almost certainly meet a question or two in the reading or the listening that you cannot understand. Remember that every question is worth one point, so do not spend too much time lingering on the most difficult and then losing points that were easier. With one hour to read the text and answer 40 questions, you have an average of one minute per question; if it is taking longer than that, put a mark in the margin beside the question and move on. When you have finished the easier questions, you can come back to the ones you found more difficult. As a rough guide, very often the first answer you guess is right, even though you may not fully understand it – trust your instincts.

Throughout the exam, keep a close watch on the time. If you finish a few minutes early, do not concern yourself with what others are doing or let your mind wander. Use the time to check that you have accurately transferred your answers and your handwriting is legible. No matter what happens, you have not completely finished the test until the examiner tells you to stop. Leaving early is only a good idea if you want to throw points away.

As a final word, just remember this. Only you know how hard you have worked to get this far: confidence in your ability is the most important psychological key to success, and nobody, not even the best linguist in the world, understands everything.

EXERCISE 3   Listen to the recording and answer the questions below. This is a review of all the question styles you have studied. You will not get so many different question types in one listening in the final test.

REVIEW   **Short-answer questions (Unit 1.10)**

Answer the following using *NO MORE THAN THREE WORDS*.

1   How did Eileen feel before the test?

REVIEW   **Multiple choice (Unit 2.1)**

Circle the correct answer A–C.

2   She felt calmer
   A when her friend got her results
   B after she had spoken to her mother
   C the night before the test.

REVIEW   **Text completion (Unit 5.10)**

Complete the sentence below in *ONE WORD*.

3   The hardest part of the listening test was _____.

REVIEW   **Maps and plans (Unit 8.10)**

Label the diagram below.

4   In which room was Eileen's speaking test?

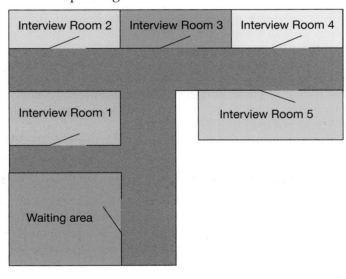

REVIEW   **Matching (Unit 6.10)**

Match a problem with a solution.

5   If you feel nervous   **A** stop and rephrase your sentence.
6   If you make a mistake   **B** stop and take a deep breath.

REVIEW   **Table completion (Unit 3.10)**

Complete the table below using *NO MORE THAN TWO WORDS*.

	The most difficult section	The most difficult question type
Writing	(7)	Writing about tables
Reading	(8)	(9)

READING & LISTENING   READING & WRITING   WRITING   WRITING   WRITING   WRITING

REVIEW   **Labelling diagrams and objects (Unit 4.10)**

Choose the correct letter A–D.

10 What does Eileen recommend just before going in to the test?

       A   B   C   D

Unit 9.11   Get set ...

EXERCISE **1**   Make a plan for the Task I essay below.

ESSAY TASK

The graph shows typical levels in enthusiasm, confidence and ability of students attending a ten-week IELTS course.

Write a report for a university lecturer describing the information shown below.

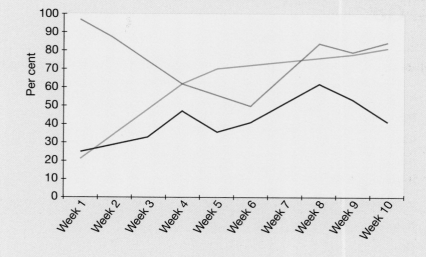

Topic words?	
Tense?	
Axes?	
About?	
Trend(s)?	

POINT OF IMPACT   You have studied how to plan, write and edit an essay, yet on the day of the test, many students panic and feel that they simply do not have time to follow the skills they have learned. In the test, remember the skills you have practised will help you. At this stage, confidence is everything!

EXERCISE **2**   Now brainstorm ideas and prepare a plan for the following Task II title.

ESSAY TASK

Attitude is as important as knowledge in a test situation.

To what extent do you agree?

Unit 9.12   ... Go

EXERCISE **1**   What do you think the following prompts are suggesting about the speaking test?

Simplicity
Pronunciation
Ease
Attitude
Knowledge
Intonation
Natural
Go

SPEAKING   SPEAKING   SPE

EXERCISE 2

Recall an event or situation that made you laugh.
You should say:
- when it was
- where it happened
- who you were with.
You should also explain why you thought it was amusing.

POINT OF IMPACT   Good luck!

Appendix A   Unit 5.4, Exercise 4 questions

a   What does RSI stand for?
b   What particular piece of office equipment has caused a rise in RSI in the workplace?
c   Name two warning signs of RSI.
d   What is the best way to avoid RSI?
e   What colour is recommended as being most suited to reducing eye strain?
f   What can be used to reduce the risk of RSI in the workplace?

Appendix B   Vocabulary sheet

Noun	Person	Verb	Passive?	Adjective	Adverb	Meaning